QSE
QUICK SMART ENGLISH

Advanced

Maurice Forget

BROOKEMEAD ENGLISH LANGUAGE TEACHING

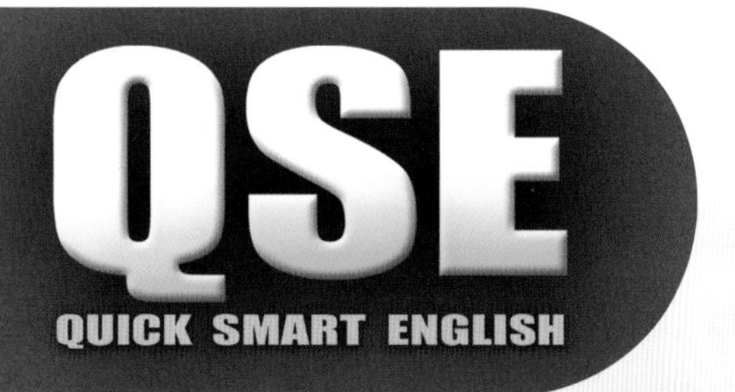

Advanced

Series editor: Duncan Prowse
Consultant: Rosemary Harris
Editor: Picot Cassidy
Glossary: Mary Rigby
Designers: Wendi Watson, John Anastasio
Research and permissions: Veena Holkar
Artists: Cedric Knight, David Lock,
Sami Myllyniemi
Recordings: John Green

QSE Advanced
Common European Framework Level B2-C1

Student's Book and Workbook
ISBN: 978-1-905248-00-1

Also available:
QSE Advanced
Student's DVD ISBN 978-1-905248-03-2
Teacher's Guide ISBN 978-1-905248-26-1
Teacher's DVD ISBN 978-1-905248-02-5
Student's Audio CD ISBN 978-1-905248-22-3
Exam Practice Audio CD ISBN 978-1-905248-23-0

Other books in the QSE Series:
QSE Pre-Intermediate (CEF A2-B1)
QSE Intermediate (CEF B1-B2)

Published by
Brookemead English Language Teaching, London
www.brookemead-elt.co.uk

Acknowledgements

Cover: top: Ed Bock/Corbis, bottom left: Stewart Cook/Rex Features, original source: Gunther von Hagens, Institut for Plastination, Heidelberg/Germany, www.bodyworlds.com, middle: Abaca Press/Empics, bm: AP Wide World Photos. **Unit 1** (p8-11): p8: © Toyota, p9: Ri chard Young/Rex Features, TEXT 1: From Newsweek, 2/23/04 © 2004 Newsweek, Inc. All rights reserved. Reprinted by permission, TEXT 2: www.advertising.about.com, p10tl, ml: licensed under Health Canada copyright, tr: www.stopesso.com, mr: © Courtesy www.adbusters.org. **Unit 2** (p12-15): p12: © Musee d'Orsay, Paris, France/Bridgeman Art Library, Giraudon/Bridgeman Art Library, p13: British Museum, London, UK/www.bridgeman.co.uk, TEXT 1: © BBC News Online (www.bbcnews.com) reproduced with kind permission. Further copying prohibited, http://newsbbc.co.uk/ 2/hi/uk_news/magazine/ 3102853.stm, TEXT 2: as previous, http://newsbbc.co.uk/2/hi/uk_news/magazine/ 3394951.htm, p14l: Stewart Cook/Rex Features, Original source: Gunther von Hagens, Institut for Plastination, Heidelberg/Germany. www.bodyworlds.com, r: www.warrug.com, p15: Action Press/Rex Features, AV: © Gunther von Hagens, Institut for Plastination, Heidelberg/Germany. www.bodyworlds.com. **Unit 3** (p16-19): p16: © AP Wide World Photos, p17t: © W.Disney/Everett/Rex Features, b: Source: The Times of India, TEXT 1: © 2004 Lee Server, p18tl: Justin Kase/Alamy, bl: BILL DAVILA/ Rex Features, tr: © Sami Myllyniemi, AV: Interviews by Kirsi Hantula. **Unit 4** (p20-23): p20: © Grea Korting, p21: Photofusion Picture Library/Alamy, TEXT 1: © Rod Liddle 2002, TEXT 2: © Observer/Denis Campbell, p22l: Thinkstock/Alamy, m: Photo by Scotch Macaskill, www.wildlife-pictures-online.com, r: Steve Bloom Images/Alamy, p23: Duncan Prowse. **Unit 5** (p24-27): p24l: Comstock Images/Alamy, m: © Steve Sands/New York Newswire/Corbis, r: © Larry Williams/CORBIS, p25t: © Tom Wagner/CORBIS SABA, b: © Phil Noble/Pool/Reuters/Corbis, TEXT 1: Copyright AFP 2005, TEXT 2: © The Economist Newspaper Limited, London (3rd July 2003), p26l: MATT BARON/BEI/REX FEATURES, m: Credit: PETA, r: © Julio Donoso/CORBIS SYGMA, AV: Courtesy of PETA: People for the Ethical Treatment of Animals. **Unit 6** (p28-31): p28 t: Rex Features, m: David Paul Morris/ Getty Images, p29t: ERIK C. PENDZICH/Rex Features, b: Glyn Kirk/Action Plus, TEXT 1: New Scientist. 19th November 2003, TEXT 2: Reprinted with permission from the Boston Herald, p30l: Peter Brooker/Rex Features, r: REUTERS/Reinhard Krause, p31l: Action Images/Brandon Malone/Livepic, r: Action Images/Richard Heathcote/Livepic. **Unit 7** (p28-31): p32: Brand X Pictures/Alamy, p33: Ernst Wrba/Alamy, TEXT 1: article by James Cox. Copyright, 2004, Tribune Media Services. Reprinted with permission, TEXT 2: Reproduced with permission from New Scientist, p34l: AP/Wide World Photos, r: The Fairtrade Foundation, p35bkgd: INSADCO photolibrary/Alamy. **Ext Read 1** (p36-37): TM& © 20th Century Fox/Everett/Rex Features, TEXT: TM and copyright © 2000 by Twentieth Century Fox Film Corporation. All rights reserved. Buffy the Vampire Slayer: Prime Evil by Diana G. Gallagher reprinted by permission of Simon and Schuster UK Ltd. **Unit 8** (p38-41): p38t: Redferns Music Picture Library/Alamy, m: Mireille Vautier/Alamy, p39: Argonne National Laboratory, TEXT 1: © Reuters 2004. All rights reserved, TEXT 2: Reproduced with permission from New Scientist, p40l: Empics, r: View to the disintegrated Larsen B Ice Shelf south of Seal Nunataks (on the right), on 13th March 2002. In background Antarctic Peninsula plateau. Photo courtesy of Pedro Skvarca, Instituto Antártico Argentino, p41: © Climate Prediction Center/NOAA, AV: Voice of America. **Unit 9** (p43-47): p43: Teresa Black/Imagestate, TEXT 1: © Dott. Andrea Antonioni, www.umbriasearch.com, p44l: Photo courtesy of Guide Dogs for the Blind, www.guidedogs.com, r: Colin McPherson/Corbis Sygma, p45: © Pic Adam Elder/Parliamentary copyright. Scottish Parliamentary Corporate Body 1999, AV: "Seeing Eye Dog: 75th Anniversary" by Beth Finke. Originally broadcast January 28, 2004. Copyright 2004, Chicago Public Radio (www.chicagopublicradio.org). **Unit 10** (p46-49): p46: Arch White/Alamy, p47t: Sarah Williams/Anti-Slavery International, b: Arthur Turner/Alamy, TEXT 1: Beth Herzfeld/Anti-Slavery International and U.N. Observer. www.antislavery.org, TEXT 2: Copyright Guardian Newspapers Ltd 2004, p48l: BananaStock/Alamy, r: John Stillwell/PA/Empics, p49t: Peter Arnold, Inc./Alamy, m, b: Robert Estall Photo Agency/Alamy. **Unit 11** (p50-53): p50l: William Campbell/Still Pictures, m: Haydar Yurtsever Ali/Abaca/EMPICS, r: Terje Pedersen/Rex Features, p51: Eduardo Di Baia/AP/Empics, TEXT 1: Copyright © 2006 by the New York Times Co. Reprinted with permission, p52l: Jose Luis Magana/Empics, r: REUTERS/Arko Datta, p53: ABACA PRESS/ABACA/Empics. **Unit 12** (p54-57): p54r: Photo courtesy Hole-In-The-Wall Education Ltd, p55: World Cyber Games. www.worldcybergames.com, TEXT 1: Reprinted by permission of The Wall Street Journal, Copyright © 2004. Dow Jones & Company, Inc. All Rights Reserved Worldwide. License number 1235890683112, TEXT 2: Copyright Guardian Newspapers Limited 2002, p56 tl: Pat Behnke/Alamy, ml: Karen Su/Corbis, mr: Photofusion Picture Library/Alamy, p57t: Joe Cavaretta/AP/Empics, b: Lucas Schifres/Corbis, AV: Source: Click Online (August 5th 2004) BBC World Ltd. **Unit 13** (p58-61): p58: www.CartoonStock.com, p59: REUTERS/Yves Herman, TEXT 1: © R. Spiezio, 60l: Brian Buckley/Alamy, r: Ace Stock Limited/Alamy, 61bl: Moviestore Collection Ltd, tr: Brave New World by Aldous Huxley, published by Vintage. Reprinted by permission of the Random House Group Ltd, AV: Extract from Outfoxed: Rupert Murdoch's War on Journalism © Carolina Productions. Footage from The O'Reilly Factor: Personal Story Segment with Jeremy M. Glick © Fox News Channel reproduced with due thanks to News Corporation Inc. **Unit 14** (p62-65): p62l: JOHN D MCHUGH / AFP / Getty Images, m: ABACA Press / Empics, r: Empics, p63t: Empics, b: Hulton Archive, TEXT 1: This article was written by young members of the Belfast Bureau of Children's Express. For further information visit: www.childrens-express.org, p64tr: Paul Doyle/Alamy, l: Moviestore Collection Ltd, p65l: Jeff Morgan/Alamy, r: Allen Ginsberg/Corbis. **Ext Read 2** (p66-67): p66 l: WorkbookInc/Photolibrary, r: Aflo Foto Agency/Alamy, TEXT: © www.BoardtheWorld.com. **Unit 15** (p68-71): p68t: Alyson Aliano / Getty Images, b: Elvele Images/Alamy, p69t: Photofusion Picture Library/Alamy, b: Matthew Fearn, TEXT 1: Reproduced courtesy The West Australian, TEXT 2: From Newsweek, 2nd August 2004 © 2004 Newsweek, Inc. All rights reserved. Reprinted by permission, p70l: Mirror Syndication International, r: Tim Hall/Getty, AV: The Nolan Show, BBC Radio Ulster. **Unit 16** (p72-75): p72l: educationphoto.co.uk/westmore, r: Index Stock/Photolibrary, p73: © Adam Rumball, Creative Director, Mad Cow Studio (a division of STE Publishers), TEXT 2: © BBC News Online (www.bbcnews.com) reproduced with kind permission. Further copying prohibited. http://news.bbc.co.uk/hi/education/2707515/stm, p74l: (c) Jacky Chapman/Photofusion, r: RS Support and Norwich School, p75l: educationphotos.co.uk/walmsley, r: REUTERS/William Philpott, AV: original story by Anne Minard, for Arizona Public Radio (KNAU) in Flagstaff. **Unit 17** (p76-79): p76l: © PHOTOTAKE Inc./Alamy, r: Greenpeace/Morgan, p77t: © REUTERS/Yuriko Nakao, b: © Christinne Muschi, TEXT 1: © New Scientist, TEXT 2: The Daily Telegraph 2002, p78t, m: Photo courtesy of NASA, p79tl: 'Microbivore' was conceived by Robert Freitas, and designed by Robert Freitas with Forrest Bishop. Artist: Forrest Bishop, tr: Iris scanner R&D at Micrarium Enterprises Ltd, bl: © NASA/The Earth Observatory. http://earthobservatory.nasa.gov/Newsroom/NewImages/images.php3?img_id=10268, br: © Leopold Gregorac, AV: With thanks for the provision of archive material to the European Space Agency - ESA. **Unit 18** (p80-83): p80l: David Turnley/Corbis, r: Marco Di Lauro/Getty Images, p81t: Crispin Hughes/Photofusion, b: Peter Titmuss/Alamy, TEXT 1: Copyright Guardian Newspapers Limited 2004. John Carvel, TEXT 2: Scotsman Publications Ltd, p82l: © PIERINO MASSENZI, r: Reuters/CORBIS, p83l: Jon Arnold Images/Alamy, r: Paul Thompson Images/Alamy, AV: © Panos London / www.interworldradio.net. Abridged from "Brazil: Computers in the Favelas" by Paula Gobbi. **Unit 19** (p85-88): p85t: Stephen Hird/Reuters, TEXT 1: © BBC News Online (www.bbcnews.com) reproduced with kind permission. Further copying prohibited. http://news.bbc.co.uk/go/ pr/fr/-/1/hi/uk_politics/ 3206554.stm, TEXT 2: www.disabilityuk.com/health/stress/str5.htm, p86l: Reuters/Corbis, r: Bill Truslow/Getty, AV: "Laughter therapist visits Australia" with Dr Madan Kataria interviewed by Geoff Thompson first broadcast 26 February 2004 on PM for ABC Radio. Reproduced by permission of the Australian Broadcasting Corporation and ABC Online. © 2004 ABC. All rights reserved. The transcript is available at: http://www.abc.net.au/pm/content/2004/s1054285.htm **Unit 20** (p88-91): p88l: Bananastock/Imagestate, r: Dynamic Graphics Group/IT Stock Free/Alamy, p89t: Courtesy www.interpunk.com, b: CP/Winnipeg Free Press (Joe Bryksa), TEXT 1: Reprinted with the permission of AlterNet.org, TEXT 2: © CTV.ca News Staff (Genevieve Beauchemin),2004, p90l: image100/Alamy, r: Everynight Images/Alamy, p91: Richard Young/Rex Features, Ex 8: 'Life For Rent' Words & Music by Dido Armstrong & Rollo Armstrong © 2003 Warner/Chappell Music Ltd. and BMG Music Publishing Ltd. All rights on behalf of itself administered by Warner/Chappell Music Ltd, London W6 8BS. Reproduced by permission. **Ext Read 3** (p92-93): p92: ImagesState/Alamy, TEXT: © Mr. Bernie H. Bates, Native cartoonist and writer for Canada's largest indigenous newspaper, The First Nations Drum.

Every effort has been made to trace and acknowledge the copyright holders of all material used in this book. The publishers apologise for any omissions and will be pleased to make necessary arrangements when this book is reprinted.

QSE Advanced

CONTENTS

Unit	Title	Subject	The *BIG* question	Reading	Language
1	**Buy now, think later**	Advertising	*Is advertising all a con?*	Marketing: Decline of TV commercials; Celebrities out of a job	Expressions used before challenging
2	**Express yourself**	The arts	*Are the arts relevant?*	Arts: Monarchy and high culture; Spoils of war	Signposting phrases: Sequencing (1)
3	**The sky's the limit!**	Ambitions	*What would you do to succeed?*	Film: Success stories: Jackie Chan, Shah Rukh Khan	Expressions for downplaying
4	**Are you looking at me?**	Bullying	*Is bullying just part of life?*	Youth culture: Satire: delinquent murders teacher; Steroid use among victims of bullying	Modifying words
5	**Frills and thrills**	Designer goods / Fashion	*Are we all fashion victims?*	Fashion: Japanese women and designer fashion; Metrosexual man	Grammar: Adjectives
6	**Playing to win**	Competitiveness	*How important is winning?*	Sport and leisure: Man versus machine; Sports and competitiveness	Grammar: The passive
7	**Profit and loss**	Economic issues	*Does economics really affect me?*	Business: Farm subsidies; Virtual reality economy	Grammar: Intransitive and transitive verbs
	Extended Reading 1	Equal opportunities		Buffy the Vampire Slayer	
8	**Into the future**	Future of the planet	*Does the Earth need rescuing?*	Environment: Gulf Stream; Viruses and epidemics	Signposting words: Arguments (1)
9	**Free to choose**	Independence	*Why do people want to be independent?*	Society: Leaving home; Regional independence movements	Signposting phrases: Arguments (2)
10	**Do I get a say?**	Individual and young people's rights	*Can't we just do what we want?*	Human rights: Slavery in Africa; Crackdown on anti-social behaviour	Intensifiers
11	**Peace around the world**	International events	*Will we ever have peace?*	International news: Chávez, Latin American revolutionary; Peaceful protest	Tentative expressions
12	**Click here!**	Using the internet	*Are we all online now?*	Cyber news: Professional computer gamers; Internet dating	Grammar: Uncountable nouns

Functions	Vocabulary	Listening Audio/Video	Presentations Speaking Strategies	Writing	CLIL (Content and Language Integrated Learning)	Pages
Contradicting	Marketing, consumers, industry	**Audio**: cigarette warning labels	Presenting company profile; Strategies: mapping the presentation	Review; Letter; Email; Information Sheet	**Public relations**: Marketing, society and advertising, government regulation	Unit 1 8-11 94
Inferring	High culture, pop culture, history	**Video**: The Body Worlds exhibition	Presenting musical styles	Biography; Proposal; Creative writing; Review	**History of music**: African-Americans, civil rights	Unit 2 12-15 95
Justifying an argument	Measures of social success	**Video**: The myth of the American Dream	Presentation on jobs; Strategies: rhetorical questions	News article; Biographical article; Email; Guide to success	**Careers**: Jobs in the future	Unit 3 16-19 96
Expressing beliefs	Forms of bullying	**Audio**: Bullying in the workplace	Presentation on psychological experiment	Letter or email; Creative writing; Email; Report	**Psychology**: Prisoner rights; Effects of power	Unit 4 20-23 97
Expressing opinions tentatively	Fashion trends	**Video**: PETA campaign against wearing fur	Presentation on consumer habits; Strategies: de-emphasising	Short story; Article; Email; Information sheet; Competition entry	**Consumer studies:** Maslow's Hierarchy of Needs; Manipulating desire	Unit 5 24-27 98
Expressing reservations	Competitiveness, sports	**Audio**: Alternative beauty contests	Presentation on sports	Creative writing; Article; Press release; Sports report	**Physiology**: Effect of extreme sport on the body	Unit 6 28-31 99
Defending a point of view	Economics, trade	**Audio**: How war affects the economy	Financial presentation; Strategies: discussing graphs	Business report; Proposal; Financial article; Email	**Business Studies**: Reading data from a graph; Comparing prices	Unit 7 32-35 100
				Summary; Creative writing		36-37
Affirming	Environment	**Audio**: *The Skeptical Environmentalist*: Bjorn Lomborg	Scientific presentation	Formal Letter; News report; Article; Story	**Meteorology**: Climate change and El Niño	Unit 8 38-41 101
Interrupting		**Audio**: Hanni, the guide dog	Presentation on government; Strategies: active and passive voices	Letter; Creative writing; Article; Story	**History**: Scottish independence	Unit 9 42-45 102
Challenging arguments and opinions	Rights	**Audio**: Tough-discipline schools for 'problem' teenagers	Presentation on rights of minorities	Official report; Email; Letter; Summary	**Law**: Rights for minority language speakers	Unit 10 46-49 103
Evaluating different viewpoints	News items	**Audio**: A tropical storm and flooding in Haiti	Presentation on drama; Strategies: the power of three	Press release; Article; Email; Summary	**Drama**: Anti-war drama	Unit 11 50-53 104
Deducing	Computers, information technology	**Video**: Languages used on the internet	Technology presentation	Personal profile; Article; Email; Creative writing; Competition entry	**Information technology**: Viruses	Unit 12 54-57 105

Unit	Title	Subject	The *BIG* question	Reading	Language
13	**What's in the news?**	The media	*Do you trust the media?*	Media: Media mogul Berlusconi; Censorship	Colloquialisms
14	**Heroes and villains**	Role models	*Do we need someone to look up to?*	Pop culture: Eminem, pop culture icon; Christopher Reeve, disability campaigner	Idiomatic expressions
	Extended Reading 2	Lifestyles		Snowboard Nirvana: A snowboarder's blog	
15	**Family matters**	Roles in the family	*What's a normal family?*	Family: New feminism; Fathers' rights	Grammar: Conditionals
16	**Let's change the subject!**	School curriculum	*Are students learning the right things?*	Education: Rewriting the history books; Making the school system fairer	Signposting words Sequencing (2)
17	**Adventures in science**	Scientific developments	*Is science making life better?*	Science and technology: Bionic suit; 'spider-goats' super web material	Expressions used to introduce assertions
18	**The company we keep**	Social issues	*Are we doing enough to help?*	National news: Hidden homeless; Waiting for medical treatment	Expressions used to contradict
19	**Stressed out!**	Stress management	*Are we seriously stressed?*	Health: Prime Minister, fitness fan; Watching fish eases stress	Language of empathy and sympathy
20	**Shock tactics**	Young people's behaviour	*Are all teenagers rebels?*	Crime: Rock group with no drugs message; Part-time jobs in the marijuana industry	Language of caution
	Extended Reading 3	Stereotypes		Not all Natives are created equal	
	Workbook 1–20				
	Teamwork Scenarios				
	Unit-by-unit Glossary				

unctions	Vocabulary	Listening Audio/Video	Presentations Speaking Strategies	Writing	CLIL (Content and Language Integrated Learning)	Pages
nplying	TV, radio, newspapers	**Video**: TV news channel documentary	Presentation on the media; Strategies: using quotes	Email; Article; Literary article; Story	**Media studies:** Media criticism; Control of free expression	Unit 13 58-61 106
oftening xpressions	Personal qualities	**Audio**: Comic book superheroes	Literary presentation	Job application; Satire; Letter; Play outline	**Literature:** Iconic writers	Unit 14 62-65 107
				Summary; Creative writing		66-67
eneralising	Family	**Audio**: Interview with a teenage mother	Presentation on family; Strategies: emphasising a point	Magazine article; Email; Letter; Story on future	**Home economics:** Running a household	Unit 15 68-71 108
sserting	School subjects	**Audio**: Teaching creationism in Arizona schools	Presentation on education	Letter; Creative writing; Diary entry; Essay	**Physical education**: Learning through experience with outdoor activities	Unit 16 72-75 109
eveloping an rgument	Science	**Video**: Space debris	Technical presentation; Strategies: using key words	Report; Article; Scientific article; Report	**Engineering**: New products and developments	Unit 17 76-79 110
ummarising nformation, deas and rguments	Social problems	**Audio**: Computer training for slum dwellers in Brazil	Presentation on cities	Report; Email; News article; Email	**Social studies**: Community development	Unit 18 80-83 111
alming	Ways of reducing stress	**Audio**: Laughter Clubs	Presentation on stress; Strategies: anticipating questions	Article; Diary; Email; Magazine article	**Biology**: Effects of stress on the body and on behaviour	Unit 19 84-87 112
liciting eedback	Types of teenage behaviour	**Audio**: Binge drinking among young British people	Presenting poetry	Official report; Letter; Email; Story	**Poetry and music:** Analysing the meaning of a song	Unit 20 88-91 113
				Summary; Creative writing		92-93
						94-113
						114-119
						120-128

Unit 1

Buy now, think later

Subject: Advertising *Function:* Contradicting
Language: Expressions used before challenging

The BIG question: IS ADVERTISING ALL A CON?

- Among the world's largest spenders on advertising are Proctor & Gamble, Unilever, L'Oreal, General Motors, Toyota, Ford, Johnson & Johnson, Nestlé, Coca-Cola and Sony. Together, they spend about $25 billion a year on advertisements.

> *If advertisers spent the same amount of money improving their products as they do on advertising, then they wouldn't have to advertise them.*
>
> ***Will Rogers***

> *Half the money I spend on advertising is wasted. The trouble is I don't know which half.*
>
> ***John Wanamaker***

? Is advertising more about creating an image than giving information?

1 WORD POWER

A There are many different types of advertising:

- billboards (US), posters (UK)
- celebrity endorsement
- classified ads
- full-page ads
- junk mail, flyers
- movie trailers
- pop-up ads
- product placement
- radio spots
- spam
- sponsorship
- TV commercials

1. Where do you see or hear each type of advertising?
2. What do you like / dislike about each type?
3. What kinds of advert have you seen for any of the companies listed in **Viewpoint**?

B Use **Language Bank 1** to contradict or challenge these sentences.

1. Even a product placement in a top action film won't convince anyone to buy that.
2. Brand names use bad English like *luv* and *kwik*.
3. Ad campaigns are only good if they're funny.

C
1. Advertisers often try to create hype for a product. Do you think the advertisers in **Viewpoint** create hype very well? Why? / Why not? Is advertising hype a con?
2. Have you ever been excited about the launch of new products, for example, a car or a film? What made it so exciting?
3. Besides companies, who else uses advertising?

SEE WORKBOOK FOR MORE ACTIVITIES.

2 READING

A In the first article find the words that match these definitions:

1. the period when most viewers are watching TV
2. to catch someone's attention unexpectedly
3. a new phrase or word that has become very popular
4. a word and / or symbol which represents a company

B Compare what the two articles say about how each kind of advertising is working.

C
1. Are people watching fewer commercials?
2. Is a subtle approach in advertising better? Why? / Why not?
3. How do you think Britney Spears or Beyoncé Knowles feel about the Pepsi decision?

3 SPEAK YOUR MIND

A Who are your favourite celebrities? Would you buy products because they advertise them?

B Give examples of celebrities or companies that have been in trouble. Do their actions change your view of the products they advertise?

C Some industry sectors are often not allowed to advertise. Give some examples. Do you agree with these restrictions? Why? / Why not?

GONE IN 30 SECONDS

Sarah Sennott, Newsweek, USA

Once the most powerful tool for marketers, the 30-second TV commercial is under siege. In the heartland of TV land, the United States, prime-time ratings are down and viewers are increasingly inattentive when they do watch.

One alternative to the 30-second spot is to blindside consumers with more quick-hit advertising. On average, a Westerner now gets more than 3,000 marketing messages each day, up from 100 messages a day in 1984. E-mail spam, text messages, Internet pop-up ads – even the dollar bill has become an advertisement. One U.S. marketer recently circulated 50,000 real $1 bills in New York and Los Angeles with stickers advertising a network mini-series. Product placement – like putting Coca-Cola cups in the hands of 'American Idol' judges – has jumped in popularity. Product placement agencies now number more than 500 in the United States, up from only a handful 20 years ago.

Advertisers are also going in the opposite direction, competing with the entertainment industry to hold consumer's attention for 30 or 60 minutes at a time. 'Branded entertainment' is the new buzzword for sponsored programs. BMW set the new industry standard in its short films, with stars like Madonna and Pierce Brosnan behind the wheel and director Ang Lee behind the camera. The ads drew more than 13 million consumers to BMW's website.

Others are following. The French water company Evian produced a platinum CD single and an award-winning music video of a song in its popular commercial, in which adults with children's voices sang Queen's 'We Will Rock You.' The Evian logo was nowhere to be seen. Instead a small cartoon figure called Water Boy bounced around the video (aired on MTV Europe and MTV Asia) to the music from Evian's commercial. Consumers got the message: Evian sales jumped 12 percent in Belgium and 4 percent in France.

COMPANIES DITCH CELEBRITY ENDORSEMENTS

Apryl Duncan, About.com Advertising Guide

From Michael Jordan to Shakira, Tiger Woods to Catherine Zeta-Jones – companies have always paid big bucks for a famous face to be associated with their products. That's about to change. Many companies are shying away from big names and dumping celebrity endorsements altogether. Powerful execs say their brand is overshadowed by the likes of high-profile celebs.

Take Pepsi, for example. The soft-drink maker canned such celebrities as Beyoncé Knowles and Britney Spears. Pepsi officials said the celebrities were too big and the Pepsi brand didn't get the promotion out of the ad campaign that the stars were getting. Instead, Pepsi's putting the spotlight on its product and replacing the 'Joy of Pepsi' campaign with the endorsement-free 'Pepsi. It's the Cola.' campaign.

Sometimes companies are quick to drop celebrity endorsers when the celebrity gets caught in a sticky situation. Kobe Bryant's endorsement deals are up in the air, while Michael Jackson's legal issues will make it practically impossible for him to gain sponsors for his tours and endorsements as well.

Companies have to make quick decisions when one of their endorsers comes under fire or their own image could be tarnished. Guilty by association in a consumer's eyes describes it best. While you'll never hear of all companies dumping their celebrity endorsers, some are finding out multi-million dollar contracts with celebrities are not a surefire way to move products ahead of their competitors.

Celebrity names: Britney, Pink and Beyoncé.

4 LISTEN

Estimated Deaths in Canada, 1996

- Murders - 510
- Alcohol - 1,900
- Car accidents - 2,900
- Suicides - 3,900
- Tobacco - 45,000

WARNING
EACH YEAR, THE EQUIVALENT OF A SMALL CITY DIES FROM TOBACCO USE

Health Canada

A Look at the photos of government health warnings on Canadian cigarette packets and answer the questions.

1. What do you think about smoking?
2. What do you think of the health warnings?
3. Decide what the following will think about this kind of health warning:
   - Tobacco companies
   - Smokers
   - Non-smokers

Check your answers after listening.

B Listen to the audio clip and make notes to answer the questions.

1. How many people in Britain develop smoking-related illnesses each year?
2. How do people feel about these labels being introduced in Britain?
3. Why does the woman think her boyfriend smokes?
4. How have the labels affected smoking rates among younger people?

C You decide: What do you think of the Canadian government health warnings? Do you think the health warnings interfere with the tobacco companies' right to sell their products? Should advertising be protected as freedom of speech?

5 TEAMWORK

Work in groups of three. Read the **Teamwork Scenario for Unit 1** and present your idea for a television advert to the class. The class asks questions and votes on the best ad idea.

6 CONTROVERSY

Work in pairs, or groups of four.

1. Discuss the content and meaning of the spoof ads. What messages do they carry?
2. Prepare a debate with another group. Use **Language Bank 1** to challenge or contradict.

Group A: You run the companies targeted in the ads. Discuss the issue of spoof ads with the ad creators. Some questions you could ask:

- What is the aim of the spoof ads?
- Is there a risk of trademark infringements?
- Will the ads damage the company's reputation?
- What will be the effect on jobs and the economy?

Group B: You are from Adbusters, which publishes a magazine challenging commercialism in society. Discuss the spoof ads with the companies targeted. Some issues you could ask questions about:

- What were the original aims of the adverts?
- Does advertising encourage mindless consumerism?
- What are the business ethics of advertising?

7 PORTFOLIO WRITING

A Choose an advert that you like or dislike. Write a short review (220-260 words) describing it and explaining why you think it is good or bad. Make sure you mention the message, the product, the company, the target group, the location and the style.

B Look at the opinions in **Viewpoint**. Write a letter or email to Will Rogers or John Wanamaker (180-220 words) explaining why you agree or disagree with his opinion.

8 PUBLIC RELATIONS in English

A Work in pairs. Each person gives a formal presentation based on the information given. Use your own knowledge and sequencing phrases from **Language Bank 2**. The other person is a reporter who asks questions about the presentation, using expressions from **Language Bank 1**.

Presentation A: You work in public relations (PR) for Nike. Give a presentation at a press conference highlighting Nike's positive corporate image. Focus mainly on positive aspects but explain how Nike is dealing with some of the negative ones.

Presentation B: You work for an organisation that monitors social responsibility in companies. Give a presentation at a press conference about the positive and negative sides of Nike's corporate image.

CASE STUDY NIKE'S CORPORATE IMAGE

POSITIVE FOR NIKE'S IMAGE		NEGATIVE FOR NIKE'S IMAGE	
Supporters	Satisfied customers; sports stars such as Tiger Woods and Michael Jordan, who promote Nike products; some governments in Asia, where Nike has products manufactured.	***Critics***	Naomi Klein (author of *No Logo*), Oxfam's NikeWatch, Adbusters, Clean Clothes Campaign.
Products and market	Sports shoes and clothing. Main market: 13 to 17-year-olds in developed countries. Marketing budget: Over US $600 million a year.	***Production***	Subcontracted to factories in developing countries with low labour costs, such as China, Vietnam, Thailand, Indonesia and India. Average monthly earning for worker in Indonesian factory: US $45.
Corporate practices	▲ Corporate Responsibility Report on the company website gives a list of subcontractors. Nike has ordered its suppliers to improve conditions. ▲ Reuse-A-Shoe: Athletic shoes are recycled into Nike Grind material for athletic surfaces and fields. Approximately 16 million pairs recycled.	***Corporate practices***	Nike (along with other clothing and shoe brands) has been accused of using sweatshop factory suppliers by moving production to countries with fewer controls on working conditions.
Workers' rights	Nike's Code of Conduct for subcontractors (1992) includes: 1. No forced labour, i.e. no prisoners. 2. No child labour, i.e. all over 16 years. 3. Minimum wage or going industry rate. 4. Maximum working hours: 60 hours a week. 5. Inspections and monitoring.	***Working conditions***	Nike's own audit of working conditions in south Asian subcontractors' factories (2003 and 2004) found 25% to 50% of them: ▲ Restricted access to drinking water and toilets during the working day. ▲ Only allowed workers one day off in seven. Some workers are punished for refusing to do overtime.

B Is it possible to change a company's image? Does pressure from protestors have an effect on companies? Are initiatives like Nike Grind and the Code of Conduct just PR? Discuss the presentations and find out what the class thinks of the company's policies and performance.

9 FURTHER DISCUSSION

Discuss in pairs. Use the words and phrases from this unit and **Language Bank 1** to develop your argument.

A Commercial TV and radio stations make money from advertising. Do advertisers have too much influence on TV and radio programmes?

B Is publicly owned TV and radio better than commercial TV and radio? Why? / Why not?

C Trends have a strong effect on getting people to buy new products. What have been recent trends in fashion, music, food, drinks or sports? Who creates trends: advertisers, companies, or ordinary people?

D What might advertising be like in the future?

10 *Your answer*: IS ADVERTISING ALL A CON?

Is advertising necessary to sell products, or would we buy things anyway? Is it necessary for the economy, or is it a waste of money that should be spent on other things? Could we do without advertising?

Express yourself

WHAT'S NEW?

Subject: The arts
Function: Inferring
Language: Signposting phrases: Sequencing (1)

The BIG question: ARE THE ARTS RELEVANT?

VIEWPOINT

- London's British Museum contains 7 million artworks and artefacts. The National Museum of Greece has 17,500.
- In his lifetime, Vincent Van Gogh (1853-90) sold only one painting and died poor. In 1990, his painting *Portrait of Dr Gachet* (left) sold for $82.5 million.

Every child is an artist. The problem is how to remain an artist once he grows up.
Pablo Picasso

? What makes Van Gogh's art more popular now than in his lifetime?

1 WORD POWER

A There are many ways to express yourself creatively:

- photography
- rock music
- painting
- classical music
- pottery
- rug weaving
- drawing
- modern dance
- writing
- sculpture
- architecture
- musicals

1 Which of these art forms do you think are high culture and which popular culture? Why?
2 Which are you most interested in?
3 Who creates, sells and buys these art forms?

B Find the person connected with each word.

1 vulgar → vulgarian
2 patronage ...
3 performance ...
4 monarchy ...
5 composition ...
6 collection ...

C Use **Language Bank 2** to infer how each person in **B** might feel about the arts.

SEE WORKBOOK FOR MORE ACTIVITIES.

2 READING

A Skim through the first article to find three arguments to suggest that the British Queen is not interested in the arts.

B In both articles, how has history affected the debate today? How are today's values different from those of other times?

C 1 Why do you think the critics are so harsh in their criticism of the Queen?
2 Why do you think the British government does not want to return the Parthenon Marbles?

3 SPEAK YOUR MIND

A What does it take to be a successful artist: natural talent, marketing skills, luck, hard work, help from others, choosing shocking subjects, or something else?

B What do you think of modern art? How is it different from traditional art? Should art try to give an important message?

C Why are opera, ballet and classical music not as popular as pop, hip hop or rock music? Will there ever be opera on MTV?

D Should art and artefacts like the Parthenon Marbles be sent back to the countries they were taken from? Should things taken in war always be returned?

WHY THE QUEEN IS NO CULTURE VULTURE

Jonathan Duffy, BBC News, UK

She's not a fan of classical music, has bought only 20 paintings during her reign and is an avid reader of the Racing Post. When it comes to the arts, the Queen, it seems, is not a huge fan.

The Queen may be patron of such distinguished institutions as the Royal Shakespeare Company and the London Symphony Orchestra, but culture, at least in the traditional sense, is not one of her greatest loves. When the Queen takes her seat at the Royal Albert Hall for a concert to celebrate the 50th anniversary of her coronation, it will be only the second time she has been to the Proms in her reign, the first time being in 1994. One might also include the Prom at the Palace, staged as part of the Golden Jubilee celebrations. But the fact that, two nights later, she also sat through performances by the likes of Atomic Kitten, Emma Bunton and Ozzy Osbourne, only muddies the picture of what Ma'am likes and dislikes.

Norman Lebrecht, music critic of London's Evening Standard, is unambiguous about Her Majesty's attitude to classical music.

"She doesn't like it at all," says Lebrecht. "Even in those orchestras of which she is patron, she would become patron on the condition that she would never have to attend, or at least not more than once every couple of years."

Whether it is an aversion or, as some believe, mere indifference, it marks her out from many of her forebears on the throne, who passionately supported new compositions and composers. Henry VIII's love of music was legendary, and he was known to be handy with lute, harpsichord, harp and recorder. It's not only music where the Queen's cultural credentials have been questioned. Last year it was revealed that in her 50 years on the throne, she has purchased just 20 new works of art for the prestigious Royal Collection. The collection comprises 7,000 paintings. At times, critics have painted her attitude to high art as a neglect of her potential powers of patronage.

"The Queen is a vulgarian. She could be the most important patron of the arts. Instead she collects glass animals," said the writer and critic Germaine Greer some years ago. And writing in the Sunday Times last year, critic Waldemar Januszczak, said she would "be remembered as a monarch with next to no aesthetic sense. You have succeeded in adopting the tastes and textures of a Blackpool landlady."

But the picture is more complicated, says classical music writer Andrew Stewart. The Queen's reign has been a missed opportunity for those who believe it's the monarch's role to push the cultural boundaries. "But those with more traditional tastes in classical music will perhaps be pleased that she has not taken this opportunity," he says. "Now, the majority of people's exposure to music is through pop or rock," says Stewart. So, would we rather the monarch commissioned an album from Robbie Williams?

ELGIN MARBLES CAMPAIGN LAUNCHED

BBC News, UK

The Elgin Marbles were taken from Greece two hundred years ago.

A campaign to return the Elgin marbles to Greece has been launched. Run by umbrella organisation Marbles Reunited, it is based on research suggesting three out of every four British people want them returned. The group wants them put alongside the other surviving Parthenon sculptures in a museum specially built for the Athens Olympics. British ambassador to the Ottoman Empire, Lord Elgin, took them from the Greek capital's Parthenon in 1801. The seventh Earl of Elgin, Thomas Bruce, then sold the marbles to the British Museum in 1816.

The British government has repeatedly refused Greek government requests to return them. And the British Museum insists the marbles, which depict gods, men and monsters, are seen more in an international context in London than they would be in Athens. Director Neil MacGregor said: "The British Museum is the best possible place for the Parthenon sculptures to be on display. The Parthenon marbles have been central to the museum's collections, and to its purpose, for almost 200 years." He added, "The British Museum is a truly universal museum of humanity, accessible to five million visitors from around the world every year entirely free of entry charge. Only here can the worldwide significance of the sculptures be fully grasped."

4 WATCH AND LISTEN

A Look at this photo of a real person from the Body Worlds exhibition and answer:
1 In your culture, what are the attitudes to death and human bodies?
2 Do you think the Body Worlds exhibition is art, science or something else? Why?
3 What is your reaction to the photo?
4 Do you think this exhibition is educational? Should children see it? Why / Why not?

B Before you watch, decide what reasons you think Gunther von Hagens will give for creating the exhibition?
- Money
- Art
- Education
- The Renaissance

Check your answers after watching.

C Watch the video clip. When it pauses, decide what the people are thinking about the exhibition.

D Watch the video clip and answer the questions
1 What idea is suggested by the exhibition?
2 How can this exhibition help people?
3 Who inspired von Hagens to do this?
4 What did Andreas Vesalius do for the first time?

E You decide: Would you be interested in seeing the Body Worlds exhibition? Why / Why not? Should human bodies be used in this way? What connections are there between the arts and science? How can artists and scientists learn from each other?

5 TEAMWORK

Work in groups of three. Read the **Teamwork Scenario for Unit 2**. Present your art manifesto to the class, which votes on the most successful manifesto.

6 CONTROVERSY

Work in groups of four. Prepare a debate with another group. Use expressions from **Language Bank 2**.

In Afghanistan, rug weaving is a traditional form of artistic expression. Since the 1980s, weavers have also used images of war, including guns and tanks. Recently, rugs have included images of the World Trade Centre attacks in September 2001.

Group A: You want to import and sell Afghan rugs, including some with war images. Some points you could mention:
- Art and freedom of speech
- Traditions, low incomes and difficulty of life in Afghanistan
- Discrimination against other cultures

Group B: You are from a group of families of World Trade Centre victims. You want to ban the import of the rugs. Some points you may wish to mention:
- Is it art?
- Possible links between Afghanistan and 9/11

7 PORTFOLIO WRITING

A Choose an artist, writer or actor and write a short biography about them (220-260 words). Use the library, magazines or the internet to help you. Remember to mention any sources you use.

B Write a proposal (180-220 words) on behalf of the Greek government to the British prime minister to try and get the Elgin Marbles returned to Greece.

8 HISTORY OF MUSIC *in English*

A Work in groups of three. Read the timeline of African-American music. Each person gives a short presentation on one or more aspects (for example: the 1970s or rap music). Use your own knowledge and sequencing phrases from **Language Bank 2**.

B Other students ask questions and discuss which of the styles is high culture or popular culture.

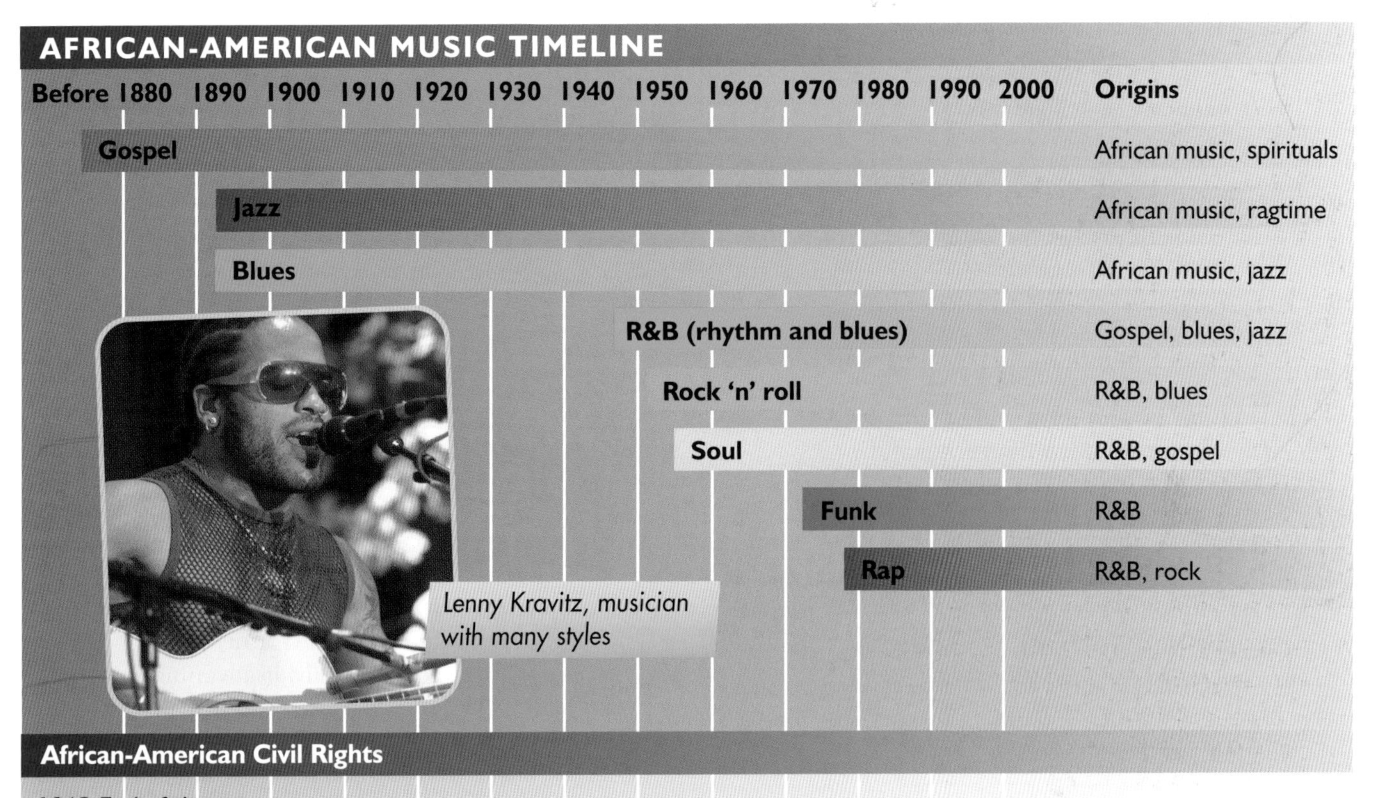

Lenny Kravitz, musician with many styles

1863 End of slavery.

Booker T. Washington (1856–1910): First black person to dine at the White House.

1909 NAACP formed by W.E.B. DuBois (1868–1963) to demand civil rights for black Americans.

1964 Civil Rights Act ended segregation.

1968 Martin Luther King shot.

1970s Integration movement.

9 FURTHER DISCUSSION

Discuss in pairs. Use the words and phrases from this unit and **Language Bank 2**, taking turns to develop and justify your ideas and arguments.

A Do traditional arts differ from one country to another? If so, how?

B Leonardo da Vinci was considered a Renaissance man for his interest in many subjects. Are there any Renaissance men or women today?

C How has technology affected the arts? Analyse some examples to show the effect.

D Some political groups and religious groups believe their tax money should not be spent on controversial art. Could this be a form of censorship?

10 *Your answer:* ARE THE ARTS RELEVANT?

If traditional supporters of the arts such as the Queen of Britain no longer seem interested, why should we support the arts? Is public funding of the arts a waste of money?

Unit 3 The sky's the limit!

WHAT'S NEW?

Subject: Ambition
Function: Justifying an argument
Language: Expressions for downplaying

The BIG question: WHAT WOULD YOU DO TO SUCCEED?

People in the USA who will be poor all their lives

African-Americans	79%
White Americans	24%

People in the USA who will be affluent all their lives

African-Americans	4%
White Americans	33%

The dictionary is the only place where success comes before work. **Unknown**

? How do people from disadvantaged backgrounds become successful?

1 WORD POWER

A Different people measure success in different ways:

- career
- possessions (luxury car, home)
- family and friends
- power
- happiness
- respect
- admiration
- fame
- status
- leisure time
- wealth

1 How important are each of these to you? To your family and friends?
2 What are some other measures of success?
3 Describe a successful person. In which ways is he or she successful?

B Match up the collocations:

1 floundering	a determination
2 celebrity	b lifestyle
3 meteoric	c personality
4 charismatic	d gesture
5 token	e rise
6 grim	f career

C Using the collocations in **B** and **Language Bank 3** develop at least three short dialogues about careers. Person A justifies an argument using each collocation and Person B downplays the argument. Example:
A *It's a well-known fact that...*
B *I wouldn't go so far as to say that...*

SEE WORKBOOK FOR MORE ACTIVITIES.

2 READING

A Read the articles. Which statements refer to Jackie Chan, Shah Rukh Khan, both or neither?
1 He grew up economically disadvantaged. ....
2 His movies have all been box-office hits. ....
3 He triumphed over adversity. ....
4 He places a strong emphasis on family life. ....
5 He nearly abandoned acting altogether. ....

B 1 How do you think Jackie Chan feels about his childhood?
2 How do you think each actor's childhood shaped their personalities?

C 1 What does it take to become a movie star?
2 Musical films are popular in India; action films are popular in China. Is there a cultural explanation for why certain movies are more popular in some countries?

3 SPEAK YOUR MIND

A What did you dream of becoming when you were a child? What do you think of those dreams today?

B What would you like to be doing in ten years? In twenty years? What will it take to reach your goals?

C Why do you think it is important for Jackie Chan and Shah Rukh Khan to make it in America?

D Some careers are very secure and some are very risky. Give some examples. What are the benefits and drawbacks of each?

CHAN THE MAN: THE EARLY YEARS

Lee Server, Gallery, USA

The man whose face is as familiar to the Chinese as Mao Zedong's, and who has been called the most successful actor in history, began life nearly sold off by his parents for $26. According to Bey Logan, author of *Hong Kong Action Movies*, "At the time Jackie Chan was born, his father was so poor he seriously considered an offer to sell his baby to one of the doctors. In fact, Chan wasn't sold until his seventh birthday. It was then that his mother was paid a token sum by Sifu Yu Chan Yuan to enroll her boy in his Peking Opera Academy."

In Hong Kong's Peking Opera Academy, contingents of Hong Kong children were consigned to ten years of rigorous training in the performing arts. Students followed grinding regimes of gymnastics and martial arts fighting, non-stop, year after year, put through their paces by disciplinarian Masters.

"It was bad," Chan told Logan. "If I tell you how bad it was maybe you won't believe me. If you didn't train hard enough, you were beaten. At night we all slept under one blanket. That blanket! The dog had slept on it!"

Chan was made part of a troupe of boy stage performers known as the Seven Little Fortunes. Even as Chan trained for it, the elaborate Peking Opera was dying out as a popular form of entertainment and the burgeoning Hong Kong film industry was becoming a much more likely source of employment for the fearless Academy graduates. Chan actually made his first appearance in a motion picture at the age of eight in 1962.

It was the early '70s when Chan went out on his own looking for work in the movie business. He began in cheap action pictures, doing stunt work. Although he managed to get steady supporting roles, Chan's career had been floundering; he was ready to give up the film business and join his parents in Australia, where he hoped to start a new life. Then Hong Kong producer Lo Wei, signed him to do a sequel to a Bruce Lee hit, calling it *New Fist of Fury*. Chan's brief moment in the limelight

Jackie Chan

seemed about to fade when he was given the lead in *Snake in the Eagle's Shadow*. Sensing that this was perhaps his last chance for success, Chan was determined to avoid doing another grim Bruce Lee imitation in favor of something closer to his own fun-loving persona. After so many years of Lee's ferocity and the deadpan pieties of the historical kung fu actioners, Chan's slapstick martial arts innovation and the warm lovable character he brought to the screen made *Snake in the Eagle's Shadow* a smashing success.

THE SHAH OF BOLLYWOOD

Martin Smith

Diminutive Shah Rukh Khan is the reigning King of Bollywood. Born on November 2, 1965, to a middle-class Muslim family in New Delhi, Shah Rukh Khan's rise to fame has been characterised by breaking down many traditional barriers in the Indian film industry.

After studying at the National School of Drama in Delhi, he underwent a two-year stint on Indian television before breaking into film. As many Indian TV actors will confirm, joining the celluloid elite is no idle feat. India's film industry has long been dominated by acting-family dynasties.

Coupled with his religious background, few would have expected his meteoric rise. Yet, in his

From Bollywood to Hollywood?

first twelve years, he made close to fifty films. While some of these have been flops, Shah Rukh's films have largely been profitable – a unique quality in Indian film. Among his best performances is the remake of the classic *Devdas* about a heartbroken man who turns to alcohol.

While he's the chain-smoking, wisecracking, charismatic performer in public, this superstar is a consummate family man in private. Forgoing the typical Mumbai celebrity lifestyle, he prefers spending his free time with his wife, Gauri, and their two children, insisting that his life is very 'middle class-ish'. His middle class lifestyle affords him probably more than most, with luxury homes, BMWs and his own production company.

After successfully showing *Devdas* at Cannes, it now seems Shah Rukh has his sights set on Hollywood. Given his ability to break down barriers, don't bet against him.

4 WATCH AND LISTEN

Homeless in the USA

Successful talk show host, Oprah Winfrey

A Look at the photos and answer the questions.
1 Do you think people have a better life in the US?
2 What is the American Dream? Is it a universal dream?
3 Why do people emigrate to Western countries?

B Watch the video and choose the answer (A, B, C) which fits best according to what you hear.
1 What is the girl's idea of the American Dream?
A She can become a Music Television host.
B She can become famous like Angelina Jolie.
C She can play music for large crowds.
2 What is the woman's reaction to the statistics on ethnicity and poverty?
A People can blame themselves for being poor.
B Education would solve many problems.
C The root of the problem is large families.
3 Which was described as **not** making a successful person?
A Having enough money for food and housing.
B Having a lot of playthings like cars.
C Having a goal and working towards it.

C You decide: Is the American Dream myth or reality? Why / Why not? Are people individually responsible for their own success and failure?

5 TEAMWORK

Work in groups of three. Read the **Teamwork Scenario** and create a problem tree to share with another group.

6 CONTROVERSY

Work in groups of four. Prepare a debate with another group. Use expressions from **Language Bank 3**.

Most developed countries have some kind of welfare system. It aims to keep the poorest from starving and being homeless. Some groups argue that welfare simply encourages people to be lazy.

Group A: You are conservative politicians and business leaders. You favour reducing welfare benefits and forcing people on welfare to work. Some points you could mention:
- Higher taxpayers should decide how taxes are spent.
- Work ethic versus laziness
- Bad start for children on welfare
- Encourages immigration

Group B: You represent single mothers, police and anti-poverty organisations. You favour keeping welfare benefits. Some points you could mention:
- Impact on crime rates if welfare removed
- Reasons why long-term unemployment exists
- Impact on children and recent immigrants
- Compassion for people with disadvantages

7 PORTFOLIO WRITING

A Imagine you are your country's leader. Write a newspaper article (220-260 words) to say why you would make a good leader and what you would do.

B Write an article (220-260 words) for a company magazine about a very successful person who has just retired from the company. Mention his / her backgound, career and family.

8 CAREERS *in English*

Ten jobs that will be in demand in the next few decades

Bioinformatician: uses computers to predict which drugs work best on which diseases.

Adventure travel guide: guides people on extreme travel adventures.

Home-care nurse: helps elderly people at home.

Fuel-cell engineer: develops hydrogen fuel cells for vehicles.

Forensic accountant: discovers where companies have used bad accounting practices.

Lawyer: argues the finer points of copyright and patent laws.

Data miner: creates software to find information about people on the internet.

Odd-job person: does many different jobs, like mowing lawns and cleaning houses.

Wireless engineer: designs wireless phones, equipment and network.

AI (Artificial Intelligence) programmer: develops software so machines can respond more like humans.

Source: www.mycoolcareer.com

A Work in groups of two or three. One student is a career consultant; choose up to five jobs and give a one minute presentation on them. Explain the jobs and how someone might go into that career.

B The other(s) are university students, who respond by asking questions and discussing with the career consultant for about 30 seconds why these jobs will be in demand in the future and whether they could also be out of date one day. Use your own knowledge of the subject area and phrases from **Language Bank 3**.

9 FURTHER DISCUSSION

Discuss in pairs. Use the words and phrases from this unit and **Language Bank 3**, taking turns to develop and justify your ideas and arguments.

A What are the advantages and disadvantages of being famous? Does fame or success change people?

B Where do we get ambition from? Is it biological drive, social pressure or something else? Is the ambition to survive very different from the ambition to succeed?

C Some highly ambitious people are willing to break rules to succeed. What do you think of this?

D Some people reject the rat race. What reasons could they have? Do you think you could live outside society?

E Do all groups in your society have the same opportunities in life? Why / Why not? How do racism, sexism and other discrimination prevent people from fulfilling their ambitions?

10 *Your answer*: WHAT WOULD YOU DO TO SUCCEED?

Would you break rules to succeed? Why / Why not? Successful entrepreneurs risk losing family (long hours away), friends (asking them too many favours) and fortune (bankruptcy). Would you risk it all for success?

Are you looking at me?

WHAT'S NEW?

Subject: Bullying
Function: Expressing beliefs
Language: Modifying words

The BIG question: IS BULLYING JUST PART OF LIFE?

- In the UK in 2002, 51% of primary school students and 28% of secondary school students were bullied.

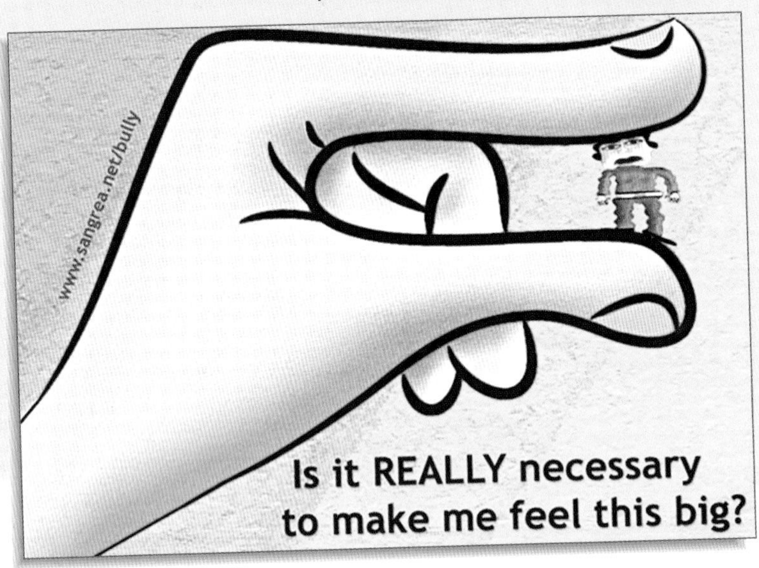

The measure of a society is found in how they treat their weakest and most helpless citizens.
Jimmy Carter

? How well does this poster make people understand what a victim of bullying feels like?

1 WORD POWER

A Bullies can come in many forms, for example:

- older brothers and sisters
- popular students
- bosses
- colleagues
- powerful countries
- players in sports
- abusive parents
- police, soldiers
- racists
- politicians

1 How could these people act as bullies or intimidate people?
2 Describe a bully you know about. Why do you think they became a bully?

B Match the words from the articles opposite with the correct antonym:

1 factual	a exclude
2 famous	b transgression
3 conformity	c notorious
4 comfort	d negate
5 support	e distress
6 admit	f anecdotal

C Write six sentences about bullies in **A**. Use the words in **B** and **Language Bank 4** for expressing beliefs.
Example: *I am convinced that transgressions by powerful countries happen all the time.*

D 1 What can people do if they are being picked on?
2 Why might feelings of insecurity turn someone into a bully?

SEE WORKBOOK FOR MORE ACTIVITIES.

2 READING

A Find the words in the first article from these definitions:
1 to remove someone's head
2 consequence of an action
3 say that you strongly disapprove
4 done quickly without thinking much

B 1 How can you tell that the first article is satirical?
2 Compare the feelings of Darren's mother with those of the parents in the second article.

C 1 Is the first article in good taste? If not, why not?
2 According to the second article, why do young people take steroids?
3 Is such an extreme reaction to bullying justified?

3 SPEAK YOUR MIND

A How common is bullying? What kinds of bullying have you heard about?

B Is bullying something that only happens in school? Do you think bullying gets worse or decreases as people get older?

C The use of technology (mobile phone text messages, email and the internet) to bully people is on the increase. How and why do you think this happens?

D Does teasing naturally lead to physical violence?

E Do you think society takes bullying seriously enough?

is satirical column was written after two British pupils were
:cluded from school for making 44 obscene and threatening
ıonecalls to a teacher, and then allowed to go back to school.

LEAVE THE POOR PSYCHOPATH ALONE

Rod Liddle, The Guardian, UK

We should not be too hasty in judging the case of Darren Bennett, the young man who was peremptorily excluded from school last week and then, just as suddenly, reinstated by his local education authority. Things are never quite as simple as they might at first seem.

Darren, you may remember, decapitated his mathematics tutor, Mr McCreevey, with a kitchen knife and mounted his head on a 40-foot pole outside the staff room of the Daniel Ortega Technology College in Cheam, Surrey. Smeared with the blood of his victim, he then cavorted naked around the pole, whooping and hollering and, at one stage, invoking the Antichrist.

It is beside the point as to whether the Antichrist actually turned up, as some have alleged. More relevant is whether it was right for the school's headmaster to condemn Bennett – without consultation or psychiatric reports – to an immediate and humiliating detention, followed by an indefinite exclusion, with all its multifarious, antisocial repercussions. (Not to mention the educational repercussions on Bennett, who was studying towards a career in human resources.)

Yes, we might argue, Bennett's behaviour was intemperate and tasteless. It undoubtedly caused distress to the family and colleagues of the unfortunate Mr McCreevey. It also discomforted the student body, which was unable to decide whether to remonstrate with Bennett or join in the cavorting.

But we might agree with the findings of the local education authority committee that pondered the case. The headmaster's decision to exclude was, it ruled, 'inappropriate and regrettably precipitous'. The committee was swayed by one piece of irrefutable logic: Bennett's rage was directed solely at his mathematics teacher. That teacher was now, sadly, dead. Therefore the direct threat to his person was negated. Darren should be readmitted to the school. However, Mr McCreevey's head should be taken down from the pole.

And then, more facts began to emerge. With dignity and some moral force, Bennett's mother appeared on GMTV to plead her son's case. It transpired that he had suffered the attentions of this teacher on several occasions, for various unsubstantiated transgressions – truancy, possession of Class A drugs. In other words, there was a history of bullying. Things were not quite what they seemed.

DRUG WARNING AS BULLIED CHILDREN TURN TO STEROIDS

Denis Campbell, The Observer, UK

No peace in the playground

Victims of bullying as young as 11 are using muscle-building steroid drugs to build up their bodies in a desperate attempt to scare off their tormentors. Children have turned to steroids, which are notorious because of their widespread misuse by elite sportspeople, in the hope that enlarging their physiques will make them too big to be pushed around. The worrying trend has been revealed by UK Sport, the government-funded sports agency, which has been receiving calls from worried parents in different parts of Britain, shocked to find these muscle-boosting substances in their child's possession.

"Parents of secondary school children as young as 11, almost always boys, have rung us and said their child is either taking steroids or contemplating taking them," said Michele Verroken, UK Sport's head of anti-doping. "The commonest reason these children have cited for doing so is being bullied, but others want to bulk up to achieve 'a better body' or get onto the school team."

"Although steroids are used mainly by bodybuilders, there is now anecdotal evidence that some young people are taking them and that's a worrying concern," added Verroken. "School pupils have got them from the same people who push the drugs around the school gates."

Drug expert Professor Vivian James, of the University of London, said information about steroid use by under-18s in Britain was sketchy. But surveys abroad showed that up to 11 per cent of teenagers in America admitted having taken them.

4 LISTEN

A Before you listen, look at the photo and answer:
1 What would your perfect workplace be like?
2 What kind of jobs have you had? What were your employers like? What were working conditions like?
3 What jobs do you think have the greatest amount of stress? Why?

B Before you listen, decide what experts on workplace bullying would say about:
- what kinds of behaviour are bullying
- who are the bullies
- how to solve the problem

Check your answers after listening.

C Listen to the audio clip. Choose the answer (A, B or C) which fits best with what you hear.
1 What did Gemma feel about bullying in the office?
 A She felt traumatised.
 B She felt that she had a mental problem.
 C She told people to shut up in meetings.
2 In Martin's opinion, the main cause of bullying is:
 A Rudeness and disrespect in the workplace.
 B Competition and rapid change.
 C Company policy about bullying in the workplace.

D At the end of the audio clip, try to imagine what Roger might say.

E You decide: What action would you take if you were bullied at work? What rights do employees have? How seriously do companies take workplace bullying?

5 TEAMWORK

Work in pairs. Read the Teamwork **Scenario for Unit 4** and talk about stereotypes. What role do physical characteristics (height, weight, skin colour) play in bullying?

6 CONTROVERSY

Survival of the fittest?

Work in groups of four. Prepare a discussion with another group. Use expressions from **Language Bank 4**.

In the late 19th and early 20th centuries some scientists thought that Charles Darwin's theory of evolution (1859) could be used to justify the idea of survival of the fittest for humans. They thought that only the strongest people should have children. This led eventually to the Nazi theory of the master race. Views have changed, but some people still think that successful individuals should not feel concerned if they do better in life than other people.

Group A: You argue that survival of the fittest is the natural order of things. Some points you could mention and questions you could ask:
- There are elites in both human and animal worlds.
- Humans are naturally selfish. Why can't we accept it?
- Isn't human society based on competition – in careers, sports, exams, beauty and capitalism?

Group B: You argue that the idea of survival of the fittest is just an excuse for bullying. Some points you may wish to mention and questions you could ask:
- A civilised society helps people who are less able.
- Don't humans generally want to be kind?
- What about the evil extreme – Hitler's persecution of the Jews, Romanies and others?
- What about democracy and equality?

7 PORTFOLIO WRITING

A Write an email (180-220 words) to the local education authority, expressing your feelings about Darren Bennett and their decision to reinstate him.

B Creative writing: Write a short story (220-260 words) about a superhero who protects students from bullies.

8 PSYCHOLOGY *in English*

A Work in groups of three. Using the information below, each prepare a one minute presentation about the Stanford Prison experiment. The first student represents the prisoner's point of view; and the second represents the guard's point of view. The third person talks about the psychological aspects of the situation.

B After the presentations, ask the presenters questions from the point of view you represented. Discuss what kind of bullying and intimidation you think goes on in prisons and the reasons for it.

STANFORD PRISON EXPERIMENT

1 THE IDEA

In 1971, an experiment was set up at Stanford University, in California, USA. Volunteers, taking roles as prisoners or guards, were filmed 24 hours a day.

2 AIMS

- To simulate the physical and mental environment of prisons
- To study the mental and behavioural changes in prisoners

3 GUARDS

- Dressed in prison guard uniforms, with mirrored sunglasses, armed with sticks
- Had complete power over prisoners, with minimal supervision by observers

4 PRISONERS

- Wore loose smocks and were in chains
- Locked in cells and called only by number

5 METHODS OF CONTROL

- Privilege cell for model prisoners
- Using informants among prisoners
- Rebel leaders isolated mentally and physically
- Later, guards were more sadistic when bored and when they thought no one was watching.

6 PRISONER REACTIONS

- Rioted on Day 2
- Confused and aggressive
- Crying, not able to think straight
- Desperate and hopeless

7 POWER CORRUPTS

- Punishments began with push-ups and exercise.
- Later, guards stopped food and toilet privileges.
- Prisoners had to clean toilets with bare hands.
- Prisoners put in solitary confinement

8 THE RESULT

- The experiment was stopped on Day 6 when psychologists realised how violent guards had become.
- Experiment became a model for understanding prison life and the relationship between the powerful and the powerless.

9 FURTHER DISCUSSION

In pairs, use the words and phrases from this unit and **Language Bank 4** and take turns to develop and justify your ideas and arguments.

A Do you think the victims of bullying are more likely to take out their anger and pain on other people?

B How common is bullying in sport? Which sports involve some physical or mental intimidation?

C Do you think most people could get involved in bullying?

D How important is being popular at school? Is it related to bullying?

E Why do some larger countries use their economic, political or military advantage to bully smaller countries?

10 *Your answer*: IS BULLYING JUST PART OF LIFE?

Are victims of bullying just people who like to complain? How much responsibility do we have for allowing bullying to happen? What lessons can we learn from bullies and victims? Will we ever stop all bullying? Why / Why not?

Frills and thrills

WHAT'S NEW?

Subject: Designer goods / Fashion
Function: Expressing opinions tentatively
Language: Adjectives

The BIG question: ARE WE ALL FASHION VICTIMS?

- Imelda Marcos, wife of the former Philippines dictator, owned over 3,000 pairs of designer shoes.

Style is knowing who you are, what you want to say, and not giving a damn.
Gore Vidal

The really great thing about my shop is that there's not one dead animal in it.
Stella McCartney

? Contrast the two fashion styles in the photos. Which style do you prefer and why?

1 WORD POWER

A Use the vivid adjectives and the tentative expressions in **Language Bank 5** to comment on the photos in **Viewpoint**. Example: *I might be wrong in saying this, but I think the skirt is very tasteful.*

B Which of these adjectives have positive and negative meanings? Why?

- trendy
- materialistic
- retro / vintage
- authentic
- urban
- minimalist
- suave
- straight, gay

C 1 Most fashion houses create a new range of clothing for each season. Is this necessary?
2 What does it mean that fashion tends to be cyclical? Can you give examples?
3 Many companies like Marlboro and Caterpillar use clothing for brandstretching, so their brand is seen in more places. What do you think of this?

SEE WORKBOOK FOR MORE ACTIVITIES.

2 READING

A Match these headlines to the paragraphs a-f in the first article.
1 Shopping sprint
2 Japanese groupthink
3 Stand out from the crowd
4 Designer mania
5 Dedicated shopper
6 Recycled fashion

B Imagine you are Erina Kobayashi's friend. Use reported speech to explain what she told you about her shopping experience.

C 1 Why are young people so interested in designer fashion?
2 What cultural changes have lead to the emergence of the metrosexual man?

3 SPEAK YOUR MIND

A What is the point of fashion? Are you fashion-conscious?

B What makes designer goods different from ordinary goods? What do you like / dislike about designer goods?

C Would you want to be a designer? What kind of training or skills does it take?

D Why is good grooming seen as a female pursuit? Do you agree?

JAPANESE GIRLS GO CRAZY FOR FOREIGN DESIGNER GOODS

Francoise Kadri, Things Asian

a Erina Kobayashi has been waiting since the previous night for a Tokyo warehouse packed with nearly new designer goods to open. The 23-year-old Japanese clerk already owns six or seven Vuitton handbags but is so determined to buy another she camped out overnight in a cardboard box to ensure she was first in line.

b The flood of young women to this sale, organised a few weeks before end of the year festivities, demonstrates their insurmountable passion for foreign-brand handbags, wallets and other luxury goods.

c At 9:30 am the doors of the warehouse open and the race begins. A surge of young women, rush inside and gather as many trendy handbags as they can out of a huge mountain of Vuitton, Chanel, Coach or Guccis.

This warehouse event is organised twice a year by a group of 70 pawnshop owners in Tokyo to sell the authentic goods they have bought at a quarter or even a third of the original price.

d "We have lots of Vuitton or Chanel bags pawned by young women because they have received too many of the same version as presents or they have gone out of fashion," Sasao Makoto, an official from the sale, said. Erina is the perfect target customer for big fashion labels: she is single, lives with her parents and earns 170,000 yen per month. She uses half of it to fund her taste for expensive accessories.

e These women want to be different from other girls, according to Toshi Marks, author of the book *Japanese Women Who Do Not Have Confidence Buy Brand Goods*.

f "But how can you be different, so the only way is to buy foreign brand goods," said Marks, who is also a professor of multi-cultural studies at Shumei University. For her, Japan's lust for luxury goods stems from the education system which does not teach people to think for themselves.

A NEW MALE MARKET EMERGES

The Economist, UK

James Bond always gets the girl. His suave image is attractive to advertisers, which is why Ford renewed the spy's association with Aston Martin with a product placement for him to drive one of its British-built sports cars in *Die Another Day*. But Bond is no Beckham. When David Beckham ties back his hair or wraps himself in a sarong, he sends a powerful message to a new kind of male, according to Marian Salzman of Euro RSCG Worldwide, a leading advertising agency. This new target market is 'metrosexual', a term coined a few years ago to identify straight urban men who enjoy such things as shopping and using beauty products.

Mr Beckham, says Ms Salzman, is a classic metrosexual. Ms Salzman has tested the market and concludes that 30-35% of young men in America have metrosexual tendencies: tell-tale signs include buying skin-care cream and fragrances. Also popular is having non-leg body hair removed. Celebrities such as Mr Beckham make it all right for straight men to do such odd things.

If Ms Salzman is right, then much advertising for men's grooming products could be way off the mark, as it uses images of a hot, sweaty hulk rolling deodorant under his hairy armpits. This matters: the grooming market for young males in North America was worth around $8 billion last year, and is growing fast.

David Beckham, the image of metrosexual man

4 WATCH AND LISTEN 5

A Look at the photos and answer:
1 Why do people wear fur?
2 Do you or would you wear fur or other animal products such as leather? Why / Why not?
3 What do you think the pictures show?
4 What rights do animals have?

B Watch the video and choose the answer (A, B, C) which fits best according to what you hear.
1 Who started the 'I'd rather go naked than wear fur' campaign?
A An activist in Florida
B PETA's director
C The Go-Gos
2 How did the campaign affect fur sales?
A Sales increased by 20 per cent.
B Manufacturers had decreased to 201.
C Over 500 garment makers closed.
3 PETA received over 10,000 donated fur coats. What have they **not** done with the garments?
A They sent them to Afghan refugees.
B They turned them into beds for wildlife.
C They sold them to homeless people.

C At the end of the video, decide how you would respond if you were the homeless woman.

D You decide: For PETA supporters, wearing a fur coat, eating a hamburger, testing drugs on animals and keeping animals in zoos is cruelty to animals. What do you think of PETA's strong views and their campaign?

5 TEAMWORK

Work in groups of three. Choose an ordinary object from home, school or work and see if you can use it differently or re-design it. See the **Teamwork Scenario for Unit 5**. Tell the class about your ideas and discuss which idea works best.

6 CONTROVERSY

Work in groups of three. Prepare a three-minute conversation with another group.

Haute couture is the best in fashion design. Talk about the merits of *haute couture* and who buys it. Try to use the adjectives in **Language Bank 5** to help you.

Group A: You are designers and customers. Some questions you may wish to ask:
- Isn't a unique product worth paying a lot for?
- How else can you buy clothes that are tailor-made?
- Shouldn't rich people be free to spend their own money as they want to?

Group B: You are from a very poor country. Some points you could mention and questions to ask:
- Isn't it wrong to spend so much on one garment when other people in the world face starvation?
- Do you really need *haute couture*, or just want it?

7 PORTFOLIO WRITING

A Imagine you won a €10,000 shopping spree. Describe what would happen, where you would go and what you would buy (220-260 words).

B You write a magazine advice column. You have had emails and texts from some macho men who worry that their friends might be metrosexual. What advice would you give them (220-260 words)?

8 CONSUMER STUDIES *in English*

A Work in pairs. Abraham Maslow's Hierarchy of Needs explains what are the basic and higher needs of humans. One person prepares a short presentation explaining the hierarchy of needs. The other student prepares a short presentation on how it affects consumers. Use examples.

B After the presentations, discuss any similarities and differences between the presentations and how the hierarchy can be used to explain the desire for fashion and designer goods.

Abraham Maslow's Hierarchy of Needs: Each need has to be fulfilled before a person can move up to the next level.

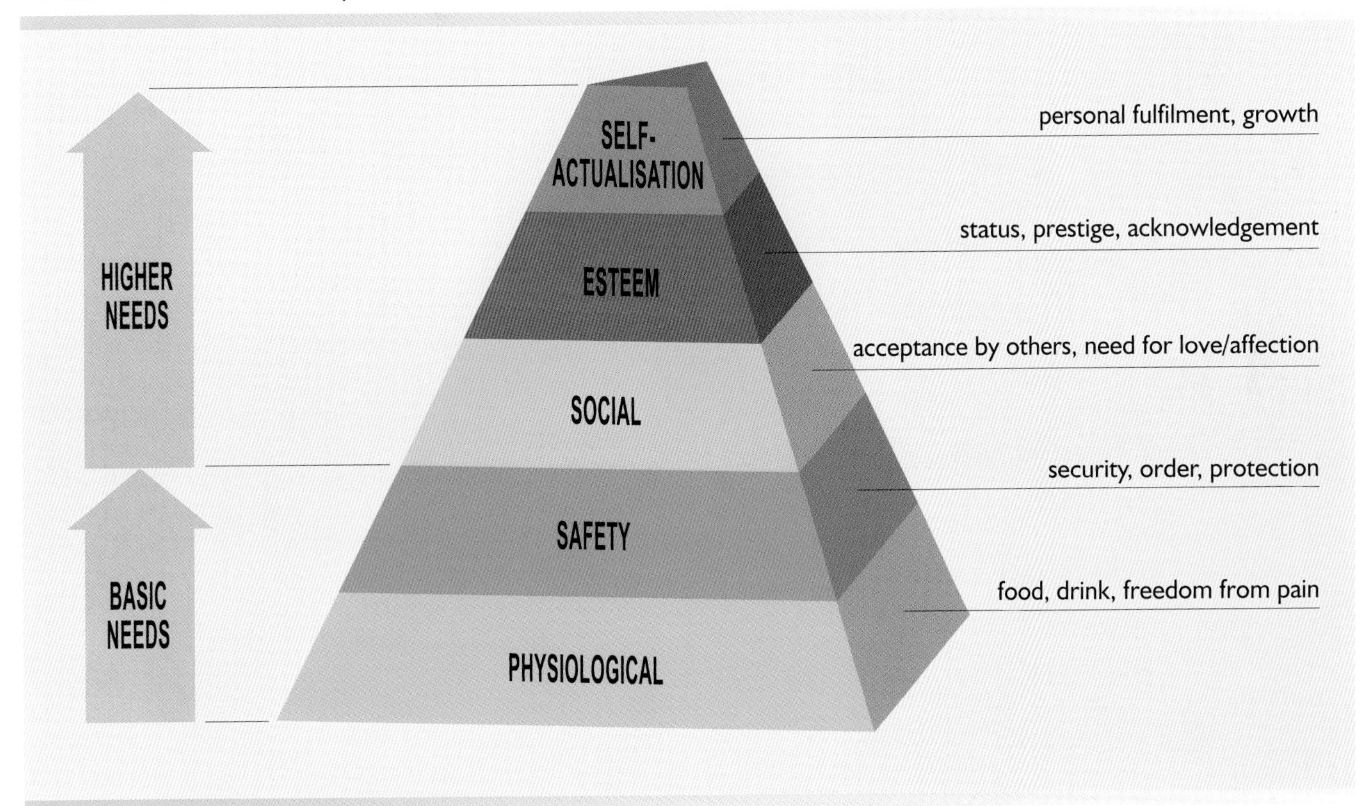

9 FURTHER DISCUSSION

Discuss in pairs. Use the words and phrases from this unit and **Language Bank 5**, taking turns to justify and develop your ideas and arguments.

A Something well designed must look good and be functional. What other things must designers think about when they design clothes, furniture and household items?

B Many critics argue that today's MTV music culture is too obsessed with 'bling' (flashy, expensive jewellery, cars and designer goods). What effect might this have on young people?

C Design is often taught at art schools. Why do you think design is taught alongside art? Is there a connection between art and design?

D Why do you think designer goods are so expensive? What affects the price of the product? Are designer goods worth the price?

E What do designer goods say about their owners? Do designer goods improve a person's status?

10 *Your answer*: ARE WE ALL FASHION VICTIMS?

Are we too materialistic? What are the positive and negative aspects of our consumer culture? Do you think it is possible to break out of the fashion cycle?

Playing to win

WHAT'S NEW?

Subject: Competitiveness
Function: Expressing reservations
Language: The passive

The BIG question: HOW IMPORTANT IS WINNING?

VIEWPOINT

- The US film Academy Awards, the Oscars, are watched by about a billion people around the world every year.

> *Winning isn't everything – it's the only thing.*
> ***Vince Lombardi***

> *The world is divided into people who do things – and people who get the credit.*
> ***Dwight Morrow***

? Should all activities in life be competitive, even eating hotdogs?

1 WORD POWER

A 1 Match the words and their antonyms.

1 defeat	a insecurity
2 boast	b team spirit
3 bad loser	c underdog
4 fit	d victory
5 confidence	e honesty
6 cheating	f injured
7 favourite	g good sport
8 rivalry	h be modest

2 Which of these words should apply to competitors? Why?

B Use **Language Bank 6** to express reservations about these sentences.

1 There will be a landslide victory in the election.
2 The Czechs will win hands down in ice hockey.
3 Estonia is odds on to win the next song festival.
4 It was a walkover for our team; the score was 5-0.
5 New Zealand will come first in the race.

C 1 What is competition for?
2 Do you or others feel pressure always to come out on top? Why?
3 Is taking part in sports more important than winning?

SEE WORKBOOK FOR MORE ACTIVITIES.

2 READING

A Four sentences have been removed from the article on the opposite page. Choose from the sentences (A)-(E) the one which fits each gap (1)-(4). There is one extra sentence which you do not need to use.

B 1 Using the passive **(Language Bank 6)** and the words in brackets to give information about:
a) The 4 x 100 relay (US team)
b) Kasparov's victory (long-term strategy)
c) Why things were difficult in 2000 in Sydney (boastful behaviour)
d) Closed games (humans, long-term strategy)

2 In the second article is Lloy Ball supporting good sportmanship or not?
3 Why should the US Olympic committee care about the behaviour of US athletes?
4 What would you do if you were competing against the US team?

C 1 Are computers smarter than humans? Why do we need to prove humans are better?
2 Based on their actions, what can we assume about Amy Van Dyken's and Maurice Green's personalities?

3 SPEAK YOUR MIND

A Are all sports competitive? Which other activities are people competitive about?

B Who or what is your favourite professional sportsperson or team? Why are fans are so passionate about their teams?

C Are intellectual games like chess as competitive as sports? What do Kasparov's matches against Deep Blue and X3D Fritz tell us about the human mind and our limitations?

D Do you follow the Olympics? What are they for? Are the Olympics just for wealthy countries?

(A) If that's what you need to win, then you should do it.
(B) "The stakes were high for both sides in terms of pride."
(C) You need to have the right strategy to win.
(D) The human chess legend famously lost to the program Deep Blue in 1997.
(E) "This is going to be tough."

Garry Kasparov wears virtual reality goggles while playing X3D.

MAN VERSUS MACHINE CHESS MATCH DRAWN

Celeste Biever, New Scientist, UK

World number one Garry Kasparov tied his final game with the chess program X3D Fritz, meaning the exciting and sometimes emotional tournament ended in a draw. Experts say that although computers keep getting faster and smarter, humans seem to be keeping up.

"Machines are getting better, but we humans are also learning," said Kasparov after the fourth and final game on Tuesday. "Today, I know much more about computers than six years ago." (1) ......

After a tied first game, followed by a win each for Kasparov and Fritz, the match score was 2-2. Kasparov's victory was achieved via long-term strategy, while Fritz's win stemmed from its ability to ruthlessly capitalise on human blunders. Experts described the final game as a display of 'perfect chess' from both teams. "Kasparov adopted the right match strategy. He wanted to guarantee above all that he didn't lose," says Jonathan Schaeffer, of the computer science games group at the University of Alberta, Canada. (2) ....

Tuesday's game was the shortest of the tournament, concluding in less than two hours and just 27 moves. It was evenly balanced from the beginning. Playing white, Fritz kept the game open, a situation that typically favours the computer. Open games involve more possibilities per move and so enable computers to exploit their advantage in performing 'brute force' calculations. This contrasted sharply with Sunday's game, which Kasparov won by keeping it closed. In closed games the human has the advantage, as there is more opportunity to implement a long-term strategy, which computers cannot spot. The result fails to close the human versus machine debate. "Until programs can formulate long-term plans, they will still lose games like game three," says Schaeffer. "But I personally expect computers to push ahead eventually." John Fernandez, consultant to X3D Fritz, is not so sure. "Man and machine will keep pulling each other up," he says. "It is still an open question."

USOC: BE GOOD SPORTS

Stephen Harris, Boston Herald, USA

Among the final tasks for the 538 members of the United States Olympic Team before the start of the 2004 Summer Games: a lesson in etiquette.

"We're not the favorite kid in the world as a country," Olympic Committee president Bill Martin said earlier this summer. "This is going to be a tough Games for us as a country, not only as individual athletes, administrators, coaches. (3) ......

To encourage athletes not to make it any tougher by exhibiting boorish or boastful behavior, the U.S. Olympic Committee prepared a video showing many high points of good sportsmanship by American Olympians and two infamous low points: the garish boasting and flagwaving by the U.S. 4 x 100 relay team after its victory at the 2000 Sydney Games, and swimmer Amy Van Dyken's spitting into a competitor's lane just before the start of the 50- meter freestyle at Atlanta in 1996.

The rawest display of flaunting was delivered by the Sydney relay team of Maurice Green, Jon Drummond, Bernard Williams and Brian Lewis.

"I think we tend to rub everyone the wrong way no matter how hard we try not to, whether it's the Ryder Cup or the track athletes after the winning the Olympics," volleyball veteran Lloy Ball said. "That's just the way we are. We're confident people, and that's just the way we demonstrate it.

"Would I recommend to young athletes that they take it easy a little bit? Yeah. But some athletes need that edge, that overconfidence, to win. (4) ......

Victorious sprinter Maurice Greene

4 LISTEN 6

A Look at the photos and answer:
1. How would you define beauty? How important is it?
2. Are there beauty contests in your country? What do you think of them?

B Before you listen, decide how the following might relate to beauty pageants.
- Relationships
- Plastic surgery
- American values

Check your answers after listening.

C Listen to the audio clip. When it pauses, decide how you would reply to the comment.

D Listen to the audio clip and complete these sentences (maximum three words).
1. The Miss America pageant was originally a way to keep tourists (a) .... after Labor Day.
2. In the late 1950s, one Miss USA contestant was actually (b) .... with (c) ....
3. Although contestants must follow many strict rules, there is no rule against (d) ....
4. Newer beauty contests try to promote (e) .... of different people.

E You decide: Are beauty contests sexist or empowering to women? Should beauty contests be used to promote acceptance of different groups: large-sized women, AIDS, homosexuality? What do you think of child beauty contests?

5 TEAMWORK

Imagine you are TV producers. Read the **Teamwork Scenario** and present an idea for a new television reality show. The class can decide on the best line-up.

6 CONTROVERSY

Work in groups of four. Prepare a debate with another group. Use expressions from **Language Bank 6**.

A federal law in the US says that there should be equal government funding for school-based men's and women's sports. Discuss whether women are as competitive as men in sports.

Group A

You feel that the government should not make schools and universities give equal funding to men's and women's sports. Some points you may wish to mention:
- The law forces equal participation, even in sports where one sex may not be very interested.
- Means cutting existing men's sports more than expanding women's sports
- Men are physically stronger and better at most sports.
- Some people think women should not be taking part in something that's really for men.

Group B

You think that the government should make schools to fund women's and men's sports equally. Some points you may wish to mention:
- There are higher drop-out rates and criminal activity among male university athletes.
- Sexism still exists, so women need more help.
- There is now a larger audience for some women's sports (for example, tennis, skating).
- 1970: women made up 5% of US high school athletes; 2001: women were 40%

7 PORTFOLIO WRITING

A Creative writing: Imagine you are an athlete at the Olympic Games. Write about the experience to your family (220-260 words).

B Write a newspaper announcement (180-220 words) seeking contestants for a new beauty contest for men and women over 65.

8 PHYSIOLOGY *in English*

A For many people the triathlon is the ultimate test of human endurance, but there is a race that is ten times harder – the decatriathlon. Work in pairs. Student A is an athlete giving a one minute presentation about competing in the decatriathlon and why you do this kind of event. Remember to mention some of the problems. Student B is a doctor asking about the effects of the decatriathlon on the body. Try to use the passive from **Language Bank 6** and your own knowledge.

B After the presentations, ask questions using the tentative expressions in **Language Bank 6** and discuss why people want to be ultra-athletes.

ABOUT THE DECATRIATHLON	
The competition:	Ten triathalons held back to back: a 24-mile (38-km) swim, a 1,120-mile (1800-km) cycle ride and a 262-mile (422-km) run.
Competitors:	The athletes are called ultra-athletes.
Fastest time:	Just over eight days.
Competition locations:	Various places, including Mexico, Hawaii and South Africa.
Problems for ultra-athletes	***Weight loss:*** Athletes can burn off more than 5 lbs (2.5 kg) a day. ***Dehydration from excessive sweating:*** If the body overheats: fever, heat exhaustion, sunstroke. Can damage kidneys and other organs. ***Skin damage:*** – Accidents while running and cycling – Friction burns and blisters from constant rubbing ***Ligaments / Tendons / Muscles*** Sprains (often Achilles tendon); tears, and pain and swelling ***Extreme fatigue / Sleep deprivation:*** – Can cause mental / emotional problems or dizziness and fainting. – During the competition competitors sleep about an hour a day.

9 FURTHER DISCUSSION

Discuss in pairs. Use the words and phrases from this unit and **Language Bank 6** taking turns to develop and justify your ideas and arguments.

A Can intellectual or creative works really compete against each other, for example in film festivals, Nobel prizes or art awards?

B Which is more valued in your society: intellect or sporting ability?

C What role do sporting events have in international relations? Does nationalism in sport improve relations or make them worse?

D Why keep national or world records? Would you like to have a world record? Which one?

10 *Your answer:* HOW IMPORTANT IS WINNING?

How competitive are you? Are you competitive in everything you do? Why / Why not?

Profit and loss

WHAT'S NEW?

Subject: Economic issues
Function: Defending a point of view
Language: Transitive / intransitive verbs

The BIG question: DOES ECONOMICS REALLY AFFECT ME?

VIEWPOINT

Saying we're in a slow recovery, not a recession, is like saying we don't have any unemployed – we just have a lot of people who are really, really late for work.
Jay Leno

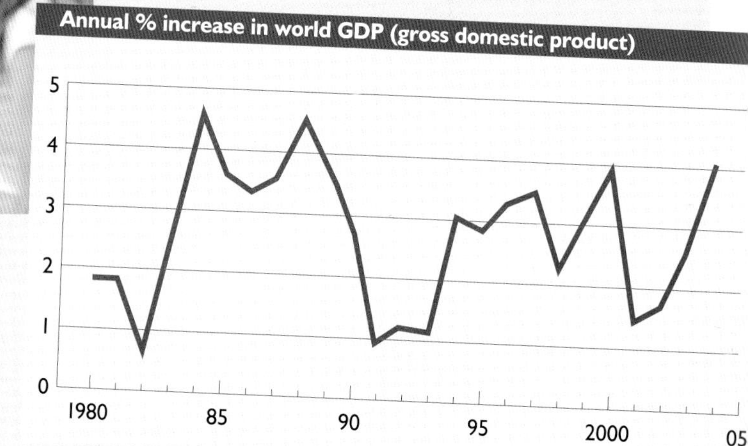

- US consumer spending accounts for 70% of the American economy and 20% of the world economy.

? What could happen if consumers decide to save their money instead of spending it

1 WORD POWER

A Use the intransitive verbs in **Language Bank 7** to describe the graph above showing economic growth.

B Defend or reject these statements using the graph and phrases from **Language Bank 7**.
1. The internet bubble burst in 2000 and affected the economy badly.
2. We had a recession from 1988 to 1991.
3. Commodities would have sold better in 1991 than 1984.
4. Unemployment rates would have been highest in 2006.
5. We see steady growth from 1990 to 1998.

C
1. Which products are the most important exports from your country? Where are they sold?
2. Which are the five biggest companies you know about? Do they operate internationally?
3. Is capitalism always a good thing? How have you personally gained or lost from it?
4. Is it ethical to encourage consumers to keep spending on credit when they may already be in debt?

SEE WORKBOOK FOR MORE ACTIVITIES.

2 READING

A Read the first article and rank these areas by the amount of subsidies their farmers receive, starting with the biggest.
- European Union
- New Zealand
- Switzerland
- United States

B The main idea of the second article is that:
1 ...online game players have invented a new country.
2 ...the players have invented a new type of money.
3 ...the online game works like the real world economy.
4 ...players can make real money playing the game.

C
1. Compare how farmers in developing and developed countries might feel about farm subsidies.
2. What are virtual economies? Do you think they will continue to grow in the future? Why?
3. What can Norrath tell us about how a country's economy works?

3 SPEAK YOUR MIND

A How closely do you follow economic issues? How is the economy doing today?

B How do world events affect the economy? Give examples.

C What do taxes pay for? Do you think taxes are too high?

D How important are the internet and the computer industry to the economy? Is it more important than farming in developed countries? In developing countries?

FARM SUBSIDIES KEY AS WTO WORKS ON TRADE PLAN

James Cox, USA Today, USA

Government subsidies to rich-country farmers make up 32% of their income on average and 18% for American farmers. The 147-nation World Trade Organization is pushing to produce the outline for a global trade accord. Developing countries led by Brazil and India are demanding an end to export subsidies and want cuts in other farm supports by the United States, European Union, Japan and others. The U.S. and EU say they are willing to scrap export subsidies and consider cuts to other farm payments if poorer countries open their markets to farm imports. "You've got to get an agreement if you're going to get anything else," says Bill Reinsch, president of the National Foreign Trade Council, a group of 300 U.S. multinationals.

A closely watched survey of farm supports, released by the Organization for Economic Cooperation and Development, says New Zealand and Australian farmers get the least amount of their income from payments. Japanese, South Korean, Swiss and Norwegians count on subsidies for most of their income, the OECD says.

EU farmers get 37% of their income from payments. But a greater portion of the EU payments goes to subsidise exports of European goods to Africa and other developing countries.

Reinsch says it's time for developing countries "to make some meaningful concessions of their own to close a deal. It's so easy to say, 'We're poor, give us everything,' which they've been doing successfully for a long time."

A fair deal for farmers in developing countries

Cuts in support for American farmers could be targeted at sugar, citrus, dairy, rice and cotton producers, which benefit from a variety of federal programs that shield them from imports or make their exports more competitive. Across the board, though, the negotiations could ultimately put an end to the use of export credits backed by the federal government. Other countries contend the cheap financing terms offered by the credits are an export subsidy.

Big U.S. farm operations stand the most to gain and lose from a WTO accord. The Agriculture Department said that 3% of American farms produce 62% of the country's agricultural goods. Since 1995, 2.8 million individuals and farm corporations have collected subsidies. But 71% of the money went to just 10% of recipients, says the Environmental Working Group, a non-profit research and watchdog group.

VIRTUAL WORLD GROWS REAL ECONOMY

Will Knight, New Scientist, UK

A computer game played by thousands of enthusiasts over the internet has spawned an economy with a per-capita income comparable to that of a small country, according to new research by a US economist. The online fantasy game EverQuest lets players create and control characters within a fantasy world called Norrath. Characters gain skills and possessions that they can then trade with other players using the game's currency of 'platinum pieces'. However, many EverQuest players have found this process too complicated and have instead opted to sell their assets for real money through trading websites such as eBay.

Edward Castronova, of the economics department at California State University at Fullerton, studied thousands of EverQuest transactions performed through eBay to determine the real-world economic value generated by the inhabitants of Norrath.

Castronova discovered that Norrath's gross national product per capita is $2,266. If Norrath was a country, it would be the 77th most wealthy in the world, just behind Russia.

Castronova also found that Norrath's virtual currency is more valuable in the US than the yen. And his research shows that EverQuest players earn an average of $3.42 for every hour spent playing the game.

"It's a robust, free-market economy filled with wealthy, hardworking people," Castronova told the online news service CNet. "If you get a bunch of people together and they have things they can produce and opportunities to exchange them, you've got the makings of an economic system."

Castronova says that EverQuest's economy can be studied like any normal economy because of the social importance attached to the game by its players.

4 LISTEN 7

A Look at the photo and answer:

1. Imagine what this soldier is doing and why.
2. Do you think, from looking at the photograph, that war is good for the economy? Do companies benefit from war?
3. How much should be spent on defence, compared to education or health?
4. Should all countries be allowed to have armies?

B Decide whether Carla (C), Steve (S) or Neither (N) has said each statement.

1. Before WWI, wars were financed by printing more cash causing high inflation.
2. President Roosevelt followed the ideas of Keynes to help end the Great Depression.
3. Car manufacturing such as in the Tennessee Valley project started the economy roaring.
4. Britain had high inflation during the Korean War.

C

1. In what ways were John Maynard Keynes' ideas like jumpstarting a car?
2. How did the death of so many men in the world wars affect the role of women?
3. What were the economic effects of the Iraq war?

D You decide: Is war ever good for the economy? What are the positive and negative economic effects of wars? Have many wars have been fought over money and resources? Give examples.

5 TEAMWORK

Works in groups of three. Read the **Teamwork Scenario** and make some suggestions about what to do about pensions. The class decides which are the two best ideas.

6 CONTROVERSY

Work in groups of three. Prepare a discussion with another group. Use **Language Bank 7** to defend your point of view about the advantages and disadvantages of the increasing range of Fairtrade products, for example: coffee, tea, fruit, chocolate, sugar, wine, vegetables.

Group A: You are a group of Fairtrade representatives and co-operative farmers from developing countries. You want restaurants in Britain to promote and buy more Fairtrade products. Some questions you could ask.

- Shouldn't we help farmers in developing countries?
- If the quality is the same, does it matter who made it?
- Haven't EU & US farm subsidies hurt world commodity prices?
- Can British farmers produce Fairtrade products like bananas, coffee or tea?

Group B: You are a group of British politicians and farmers who want restaurants to keep buying British products. Some questions you could ask.

- Doesn't Britain already give lots of overseas aid?
- Doesn't transporting goods from developing countries affect the environment?
- Can't local farmers produce more, and more cheaply?
- Won't local agricultural jobs be lost?

7 PORTFOLIO WRITING

A Write a report (180-220 words) for international investors about your town or local area and its economy. Describe the area, the main exports and examples of successful local companies.

B Imagine you work for a Fairtrade Foundation. Write a proposal (220-260 words) to a large company to persuade them to buy your products.

8 BUSINESS STUDIES *in English*

A Work in pairs. You work for a small low-cost airline set up in 2004. To be profitable, the company needs oil prices to stay within a certain range. The head of the airline has asked for a formal presentation about oil prices and how they have affected company profits.
- One student talks about oil prices from 2004 to 2007.
- The other student discusses prices since 2007.

Try to use your own knowledge and phrases from **Language Bank 7.**

B With your partner discuss what you think will happen to the price of oil in the future and how this could affect the airline and its ticket prices.

Budget Air: Oil price and profitability

Price per barrel	Profit per quarter
Less than $30	$1.5 million
$30 to $44	$1 million
$45 to $59	$0.5 million
$60 to $74	No profit (break even)
$75 to $89	$0.5 million loss
$90 to $104	$1.0 million loss
$105 to $119	$1.5 million loss

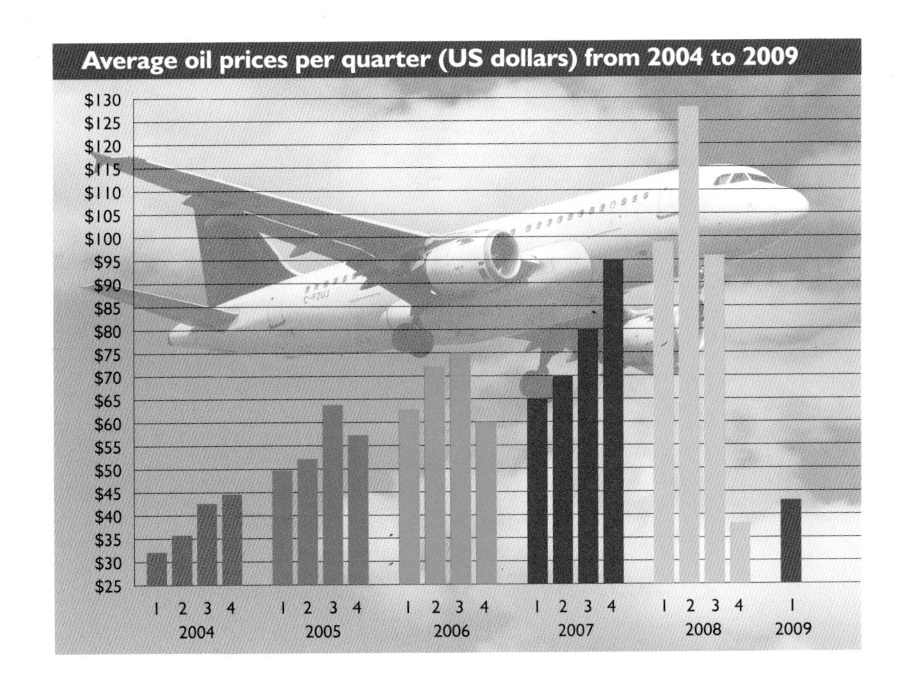

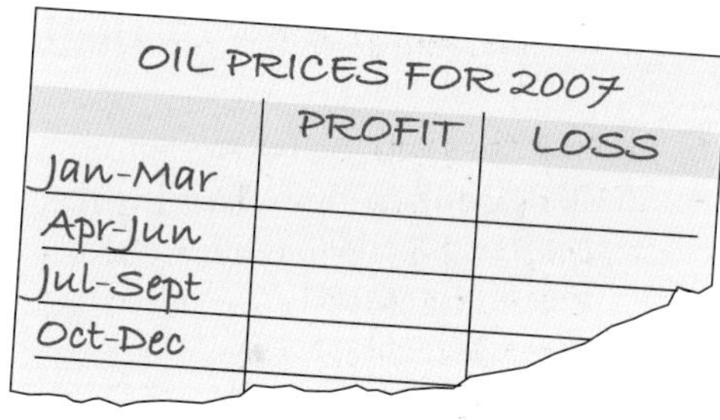

OIL PRICES FOR 2007

	PROFIT	LOSS
Jan-Mar		
Apr-Jun		
Jul-Sept		
Oct-Dec		

9 FURTHER DISCUSSION

Discuss in pairs. Use the words and phrases from this unit and **Language Bank 7** taking turns to develop and justify your argument.

A How are unemployed people treated? What is the unemployment rate? Why do economists watch the unemployment rate closely? What affects employment?

B Companies often move to countries with cheaper labour and lower taxes. What are the advantages and disadvantages of this? Which countries seem to be attracting the most business today?

C What is the black economy? What kinds of goods are sold? Where do they come from? Who are the winners and losers in the black economy?

D Have there been privatisations in your country (for example, water or electricity)? Do businesses operate more efficiently than governments?

10 *Your answer*: DOES ECONOMICS REALLY AFFECT ME?

Do economic issues really affect your life? If so, how? If not, why not? How can you help the economy in your country to grow? What difference can you make?

Buffy the Vampire Slayer

Diana G. Gallagher

This American English reading extract comes from a novel based on the US television show, *Buffy the Vampire Slayer.*

1 READING

A Scan through the extract to find the connection to:

287 jelly butterflies car

B Now carefully read through the extract and answer:

1 Why is Joyce Summers giving Buffy so much to eat?
2 Why is no one walking on the streets?
3 Why does Buffy go to see Big Jack? What happens?

C Answer from your own experience.

1 What vampire myths does the reader need to know already to understand this story?
2 Why do you think this vampire story is set in California, USA?

2 IDIOMS

A Match these meanings with the idioms underlined in the text:

1 to be buried
2 to learn to accept a difficult emotional situation
3 when very little effort is needed to get someone / something
4 to face someone / something with the same strength or abilities
5 to rest for a short while

B Complete the text using the idioms from 2A. Change the verb tense where necessary.

1 Six hours of studying? You should .... and come to play snooker with us.
2 They had trouble .... the death of their grandmother.
3 The zebra was .... for the lions, as it stood alone in the tall grass.
4 Oscar Wilde, Jim Morrison and Edith Piaf .... in the same cemetery in Paris.
5 The chess champion had .... in the latest supercomputer.

"Did you have enough?" Joyce set her fork down and wiped a dot of cheese fondue off her chin with a paper napkin.

"Stuffed." Buffy's smile gave no hint that she knew what was really going on in her mom's mind. Joyce Summers just couldn't deal with being that transparent, not when she was trying to accomplish exactly the opposite of what her well-meaning actions implied.

Buffy was anything but convinced that Joyce had finally <u>come to terms with</u> being the mother of the Vampire Slayer and didn't worry every time her daughter left the house after dark. Nor did paper plates at the kitchen counter disguise the statement made by Caesar salad, boiled shrimp, and chunks of French bread dipped in cheese fondue. For the fourteenth time in two weeks, Buffy felt like she had just been served her last meal. Like her mother couldn't stand the idea that she might <u>meet her match</u> on peanut butter and jelly.

"You're sure?" Joyce slid off her stool and reached for a paper plate piled with shrimp husks.

"One hundred percent." Buffy set her silverware aside and stacked her plates as her mom started to clear.

"You've been awfully quiet tonight." Joyce flipped open the trash container, dumped the shrimp peels, and hesitated before she remembered the plate was disposable, too.

"It's hard to talk in the middle of a feeding frenzy."

"Everything all right at school?"

"Lunch was a bust today, but other than that, school's fine." A guarded truth, but Buffy didn't see any reason to add to Joyce's unspoken list of major woes.

"Are you cool with finishing up here, Mom?" Buffy placed the heel of the bread loaf back into the bag and rolled it closed. "I really should get moving."

"I think I can manage throwing away the rest of the dishes." Joyce grinned, her expression casually questioning. "Any chance you can <u>take a break</u> tonight? I rented this great old movie –"

"I would, but I've got a date with a headstone." She pulled two stakes out of the junk drawer and shoved them into her back pockets.

"Anyone we knew?" Joyce asked cautiously. Although she wasn't happy that her daughter was the world's chosen exterminator of the undead, being clued into the Slayer routine and jargon gave her a sense of belonging that helped her cope.

Buffy shook her head, "Not unless you've got a tattoo, you didn't tell me about."

"Uh...no." A mischievous smile erased a fleeting frown of dismayed resignation. "Although, I've been thinking about getting one of those little butterflies," Joyce teased, paused. "On my ankle."

"Beats a skull and crossbones where no one can see it." Joyce scowled playfully and threw a wadded napkin.

Laughing, Buffy ducked and grabbed her black leather jacket as she headed out the door.

No one else walked the dark streets, which wasn't unusual in
outhern California where driving down the block to get a gallon
milk was standard procedure. In Sunnydale, avoiding the
dewalks wasn't a matter of eccentric convenience. Too many
eople never returned from walking the dog.

Big Jack Perkins had been closing up Tom's Tattoo Emporium
hen he had been attacked. Now she had to stand watch over
s grave to finish the job, which would be so much easier if
amp victims were laid to rest on top of the ground where the
un could cremate the remains. No muss, no fuss. But ritual
urial was another concession to Sunnydale denial syndrome the
esidents wouldn't give up, not even if the town's undertakers,
ho thrived on the booming business of death, agreed.

Buffy darted into the woods that flanked the old Shady Hill
emetery, a shortcut that would shave a few minutes off her
me. She was running late and didn't want to lose the element
f surprise when Big Jack's two hundred and eighty-seven
ounds of hungry demon broke ground.

Yanking a stake from her pocket, Buffy jogged quietly down
deer trail toward the cemetery fence. Muscles taut, her senses
uned to every nuance of sound and movement, she was in
rime Slayer mode. If she flinched, she wouldn't have depleted
hysical prowess as an excuse.

As Buffy jumped to the top of the crumbling stone wall that
eparated Shady Hill from the forest, her senses jumped to full
ampire alert. In the glow of a street lamp on the far side of the
raveyard, a disgusted man walked away from his broken-down
ar. Halfway between the street and her position, Big Jack
lawed his way out of the dirt and lumbered to his feet. She was
n the ground and running a split second after the newbie vamp
potted easy pedestrian prey and sprang toward his first kill.

"Hey mister!" Buffy yelled without slackening stride, her
take gripped in a steady hand. "Run!"

The stranded motorist looked up and froze.

"Get out of here! Now!" Calculating the distance as she
losed in on the new vamp, Buffy leaped and threw her arms
round a thick leg. The massive undead man staggered and
umbled to the ground.

Coming to his senses, the motorist took off running down
he street.

Buffy was instantly on her feet, her instincts and reflexes
unctioning without flaw as Big Jack grunted and rolled over.
'Hi! Sorry I'm late."

Beady yellow eyes glowered under the hard ridges of the
ampire's countenance, the ferocity of the demon undiminished
y puffy cheeks, his bared fangs no less lethal though set
midst crooked, rotting teeth. With surprising alacrity given
is bulk, Jack regained his footing and lunged.

Buffy stood her ground, driving the stake through layers of
at into the heart as he barreled into her. Unbalanced by the
nomentum of his charging weight, she fell backward. He
lisintegrated before she hit the ground.

"Well, I handled that nicely." Buffy stood up, brushed
ampire ash off her arms and clothes, then fisted her stake and
tarted after the fleeing motorist. On foot in this isolated part
of town, the frightened man was still easy pickings.

3 UP IN ARMS

Find ten verbs and phrasal verbs in the extract that relate to movements of the arms and hands.

4 PORTFOLIO WRITING

A Summarise the story (180-200 words) from the point of view of ONE of these characters: Joyce, Big Jack Perkins or the stranded motorist.

B Write an ending (210-250 words) to the extract about what happens to the motorist after he runs away.

5 INTERACTIVE TASK

Work in pairs. A chooses one of the comments below to start and B asks questions to find out more about the situation, then discusses it with A. You should both use all the Language Banks you have covered so far and eliciting responses (Language Bank 20). Switch roles when you have talked about the first comment for four minutes.

> I really think I ought to talk to a friend of mine who likes to watch violent action films all the time. Recently he seems to be behaving a lot more aggressively.

> It's all very well to see all these tough women characters in films, but real life's not like that. We can't all be superwomen.

Into the future

WHAT'S NEW?

Subject: Future of the planet *Function:* Affirming
Language: Signposting words: Arguments (1)

The BIG question: DOES THE EARTH NEED RESCUING?

VIEWPOINT

- There have been five great mass extinctions in the Earth's history. The last one wiped out the dinosaurs 65 million years ago.
- The world teenage population is 1.2 billion, the largest in history, and 90 per cent live in the developing world. About half the world's population is under 25.

Now there is one outstandingly important fact regarding Spaceship Earth, and that is that no instruction book came with it.
R. Buckminster Fuller

? Are there too many people in the world?

? Are we wasting the world's precious resources?

1 WORD POWER

A Which of these threats to life on Earth do humans have some control over? Use the signposting words and phrases in **Language Bank 8** to support your beliefs.

- an asteroid
- nuclear war
- overpopulation
- global warming
- pollution
- thinning of the ozone layer
- shortage of fresh water
- infectious diseases
- volcanic activity
- loss of biodiversity

B Some pessimists believe that politicians are not willing to do anything about the situations we could control. Use **Language Bank 8** for the problems you agree with the pessimists about.

C 1 How important are green issues in your country? Why?
2 Some radical environmentalists believe the Earth is more important than humans. Do you agree?

SEE WORKBOOK FOR MORE ACTIVITIES.

2 READING

A Read both articles and choose the best answer below.

1 The collapse of the Gulf Stream is:
a) seen by EU politicians as a US problem.
b) a naturally occurring geological event.
c) causing a collapse of fish stocks.

2 One important finding of the IGBP book is that
a) the negative effects will appear suddenly.
b) global warming is only caused by humans.
c) 5,000 scientists agree on the need for change.

3 Before the events of 2001, the author believes that Western governments had been too:
a) complacent. b) lazy. c) bureaucratic.

B Should we experiment with viruses and bacteria? Do the benefits outweigh the drawbacks?

3 SPEAK YOUR MIND

A Explain global warming in your own words.

B The Kyoto Protocol (1997) is meant to reduce carbon dioxide output to 1990 levels. Why would countries be for or against it?

C The Amazon rainforest is mainly in Brazil. About 28 square miles (76 sq. km) of it are cut down every day. Should the rest of the world tell Brazil how to manage the rainforest?

D Some virologists predict a super-flu pandemic will happen soon. What would help or slow down its spread?

NORTH AMERICA, EUROPE MAY COOL IN WARMER WORLD

Alister Doyle, Reuters

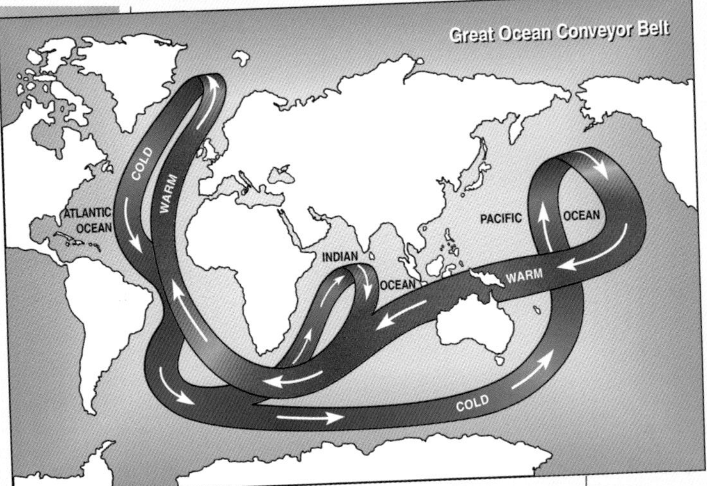

Warm and cold water currents in the world's oceans

Parts of Europe and North America could get drastically colder if warming Atlantic ocean currents are halted by a surprise side-effect of global warming, scientists said on Wednesday. The possible shutdown of the Gulf Stream is one of several catastrophic changes – ranging from collapses of fish stocks to more frequent forest fires – that could be triggered by human activities, they said in a book launched in Sweden.

"In the worst case it (the Gulf Stream) could shut down... it might even happen this century," said Stefan Rahmstorf of the Potsdam Institute for Climate Impact Research in Germany. "This would trigger a regional cooling, but not an Ice Age."

Climate models indicated a surge of fresh water into the North Atlantic from a melting of northern glaciers caused by global warming could stop the current that sweeps warm waters from the Gulf of Mexico toward Europe.

"The Eastern coast of Canada and the United States would also be affected. This is sometimes wrongly perceived as a European problem by American politicians," he told Reuters.

He said the Gulf Stream had collapsed about twenty times in the past 100,000 years, most recently at the tail of the last Ice Age about 8,000 years ago after an abrupt melting of icecaps. If the Gulf Stream stopped, average temperatures might fall by 5-10 Celsius (10-20 °F) in Scandinavia or by 3-4 °C in Germany. By contrast, global warming, widely blamed on emissions of gases like carbon dioxide from cars and factories, is expected to raise global average temperatures by 1.4-5.8 °C by 2100. Rahmstorf's study was included in a new book, *Global Change and the Earth System: A Planet Under Pressure*, which looks at the impact of the surge in the human population to six billion people, ranging from stripped forests to rising temperatures.

"A major finding is that change will not be progressive. There will be abrupt changes and tipping points," said Will Steffen, executive director of the International Geosphere-Biosphere Program, which issued the book based on work by 5,000 scientists.

"Never before have we seen the range of change or the rate of change at the same time," he told Reuters. "You can get to a point where forests are too hot and too dry and sudden fires rip through them," he said, referring to blazes last year in nations from Australia to France. "Global warming may make these events more frequent."

OPEN TO ATTACK

Rachel Novak, New Scientist, UK

Natural or manmade, infectious diseases showed they still have us at their mercy. The fear of infectious disease has largely faded in the wealthy West over the past century, thanks to sanitation, antibiotics and the like. But it re-emerged with a vengeance in 2001 when some humans switched allegiance and began working on the side of the killers.

Weapons-grade anthrax sent through the mail in the US has killed five people so far. Although the perpetrator's identity remains a mystery, the FBI suspects a rogue scientist. And it's not just rogue scientists that have been giving infectious agents a helping hand – far from it. New Scientist revealed that Australian scientists had accidentally created a killer mousepox virus, unwittingly providing a blueprint for the ultimate bioweapon.

Then there were the agricultural epidemics. A particularly virulent strain of foot and mouth disease hit Britain after rampaging through Asia and the Middle East. It probably arrived in contaminated meat products, and got into the swill fed to pigs. Four million animals were slaughtered, and around £3 billion lost in trade, tourism and in eradicating the disease.

The events of 2001 are forcing governments to change their attitude towards epidemics – be they natural or deliberate, animal or human. And for the first time since genetic engineering became routine in the 1970s, molecular biologists are talking seriously about the need to police their patch.

4 LISTEN

Polar icecap melting in the Antarctic Peninsula
Photo Pedro Skvarca

Shortage of clean water in Africa

A Look at the photos and answer the questions.
1 Do you believe Earth has a problem with global warming? Why / Why not?
2 Should developed countries help developing countries to deal with environmental problems?
3 Which is the more important world issue: global warming or clean drinking water?

B Listen to the audio clip about a sceptical environmentalist and complete the sentences.

Bjorn Lomborg is a Danish professor and former (1) ...... activist. After reading about Julian Simon, an (2) ...... , he asked his students to help him check Simon's statistics. To his surprise, Lomborg found his own ideas were (3) .... Today, his favourite target is the (4) ...... on global warming. Lomborg claims that it would cost up to (5) ...... billion per year compared to the $50 billion spent on aid. He suggests that this money could be better spent giving everyone on Earth clean water and (6) .... Professor Klaus Heinberg suggests Lomborg manipulates statistics to make weird (7) .... Heinberg compares Lomborg's idea to European children giving up (8) ...... to pay for the cost of fighting disease in Africa.

C At the end of the audio clip, think of what arguments Bjorn Lomborg might use to answer Klaus Heinberg.

D You decide: Do you agree things are getting better with the environment? Should the world spend more on providing drinking water than on the Kyoto Protocol? If Lomborg says that all sides in the debate have ulterior motives, do you believe his own motives?

5 TEAMWORK

Work in groups of three. Read the **Teamwork Scenario for Unit 8** and make a five-point action plan to deal with the situation. The class decides on the best plans.

6 CONTROVERSY

Work in groups of four. Prepare a debate with another group. The UN Food and Agriculture Organisation (FAO) estimates that over 70 per cent of the world's fish species are fished close to sustainable limits or overexploited. One per cent of the international fishing fleet, factory trawlers, catches about 50 to 60 per cent of the global catch.

Group A: You are international fishermen who want to keep fishing at the same levels as now. Some points you could mention:

- For many people, fish is the main source of protein (15-20 per cent).
- Thirty million people work in fishing-industry jobs worldwide; 95 per cent live in developing countries.
- Efficient factory trawlers are just applying modern industrial methods to ocean food production.

Group B: You are ocean conservationists who want lower worldwide fishing quotas. Some points you could mention:

- Some reasons for fish stock decline: pollution and overfishing
- From 1950 to 1994, the annual ocean fish catch has increased by over 400 per cent.
- Coral reef diversity represents 25 per cent of ocean species. Overfishing may kill them off.

7 PORTFOLIO WRITING

A Write a letter or email (180-220 words) to the European Union demanding an end to government subsidies that promote overfishing.

B Choose a potential natural disaster or an environmental catastrophe and write a report (220-260 words) on how people can prepare for this.

8 METEOROLOGY *in English*

A Meteorologists are beginning to understand more about the Earth's weather patterns, including the way that warm (El Niño) and cold (La Niña) episodes alternate in the Pacific Ocean. Some climatologists believe there may be a link between more El Niño episodes and global warming.

Work in pairs. You are meteorologists giving a one minute presentation on El Niño. Student A explains what El Niño is, the most recent El Niño episodes and how information is gathered, using information from the box and the SST map. Student B talks about the effects of El Niño on the climate in different parts of the world, using the box and the world map.

B After the presentations, ask questions and discuss any climate changes you have noticed where you live.

El Niño

Scientific definition
More than three months of surface sea temperature (SST) of 0.5 °C warmer than normal across equatorial Pacific Ocean. El Niño moves west to east near the Equator.

Information-gathering methods
- Using satellites and supercomputers
- Measuring SST

Recent episodes of El Niño
1991-92, 92-93, 94-95, 97-98, 2002-03
El Niños (since 1950): 31% of the time.
Worst El Niños: 1982-83, 1997-98

Some effects of El Niño
- Changing weather patterns
- Storms more intense
- Changes in hurricane routes
- Dry regions: more forest fires, droughts
- Wet regions: floods, landslides

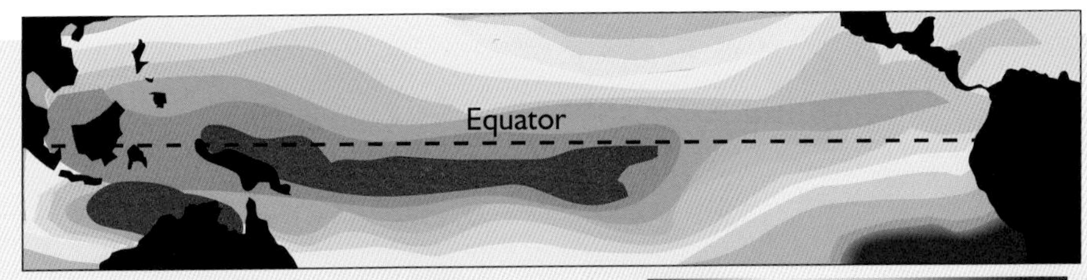

Sea surface temperature (SST)
32°C 30°C 28°C 26°C 24°C 22°C 20°C

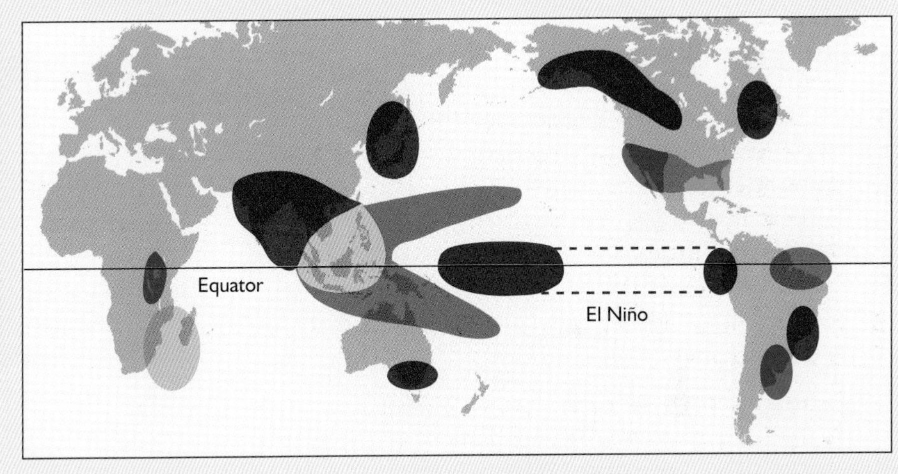

Effects of El Niño around the world December 1997 to February 1998
Wet | Wet and cool | Wet and warm | Warm | Dry | Dry and warm

9 FURTHER DISCUSSION

Discuss in pairs. Use the words and phrases from this unit and **Language Bank 8** taking turns to develop and justify your ideas and arguments.

A In the 18th century, Thomas Malthus predicted that the human population would eventually exceed food production. Are we running out of food and water?

B Will technology solve all our environmental problems? Why / Why not?

C Some religious believers feel that we should not worry about the Earth's environment – it is just part of a divine plan. What do you think?

D Name some films with plots about the end of the world. Are they just science fiction and fantasy?

10 *Your answer:* DOES THE EARTH NEED RESCUING?

What will happen to the world? Are humans part of the problem or part of the solution? What can we do to make the world a better place?

Free to choose

WHAT'S NEW!

Topic: Independence *Function:* Interrupting
Language: Signposting phrases: Arguments (2)

The BIG question: WHY DO PEOPLE WANT TO BE INDEPENDENT?

VIEWPOINT

The percentage of 30-year-old men still living with their parents

- Some of the newly independent members of the UN are: East Timor (2002), Serbia and Montenegro (2000), Tuvalu (2000), Tonga (1999), Andorra (1993) and Eritrea (1993).

> *Human beings are the only creatures on Earth that allow their children to come back home.*
> ***Bill Cosby***

? What does being independent mean to you? Is it the same for a person as for a country?

1 WORD POWER

A Use the definition to complete the words about aspects of independence. Which of these apply to countries, to people, or to both?
Example:
elect<u>ion</u>: *n.* when people vote for a government.

govern.... :	*n.* system by which a country is governed
decentral.... :	*v.* to break up a concentration of government authority (or industry, population) and distribute it more widely
legit.... :	*adj.* lawful, within the law
nation.... :	*n.* love for one's own country
free.... :	*n.* state of being free
emancip.... :	v. to be freed from a social or legal restraint
individual.... :	*n.* person who thinks and acts independently

B Use the signposting phrases in **Language Bank 9** to create an argument about independence of at least 150 words. Also use at least four words from above.

C
1. At what age do most young people move out of their parents' house in your country?
2. What are the advantages of living on your own or with your parents?
3. Did your country have to struggle for independence? Why / Why not?

SEE WORKBOOK FOR MORE ACTIVITIES.

2 READING

A Read the articles in pairs. Take turns interrupting each other using phrases from **Language Bank 9**. Wait for the breathing pause, usually at punctuation marks, such as commas and full stops.

B What do the pronouns in italics below refer to in the first article?
1. (Paragraph 1) Just why is *it* that Italian 'children' leave home so late in life?
2. (Paragraph 2) *It* is up to their families to support them, ...
3. (Paragraph 3) One 35-year-old teacher of my acquaintance was quite frank about *it*.
4. (Paragraph 4) ...until he found a job that suited *him*!
5. (Paragraph 5) ...as *they* themselves have probably been all their lives.

C Compare independence for people and for countries, using examples from both articles.

D
1. How is the *mammoni* situation similar to or different from your situation?
2. Imagine your country was not independent. How different would your life or community be?

3 SPEAK YOUR MIND

A When people you know leave home, do they live on their own, share a place with flatmates or get married?

B Is it important for children to be independent from their parents? How strong are family ties?

C What effect have independence movements had on your country or nearby countries?

MUMMY'S BOYS (AND GIRLS)

Andrea Antonioni, Italy Magazine

They are quite a talking point in Italy at the moment, these so-called *mammoni*. Just why is it that Italian 'children' leave home so late in life? Many stay with their parents until well into their thirties. Some never leave the family nest at all.

One reason is the Italian education system. It may seem incredible to those of you who finished your degree at the age of 21, but most Italian students don't graduate until their late twenties. It is up to their families to support them financially, as the few scholarships granted are given to those from large families with lots of brothers and sisters who are also students.

Another reason is the *bella figura*, which is still such an important part of Italian life. Roughly translated, this means to create a good impression on others. In order to achieve *la bella figura* it is quite normal for Italian youngsters to be given a brand new car at the age of 18, plus a mobile phone, and of course there will be no lack of parental handouts for new clothes, shoes, sunglasses and all those other essentials. Naturally this means there is no contribution to the housekeeping, even if the child is earning. One 35-year-old teacher of my acquaintance was quite frank about it. "My parents pay the bills and in exchange I'm there for them if they need me. I'm not unusual."

It can go further than having your meals cooked and laundry done for nothing. Children can sue parents who won't pay for their upkeep. In a recent court case a 29-year-old man with a law degree, but still doing a specialisation course and refusing jobs that weren't up to his expectations, was granted the right to receive 1,500 a month from his parents until he found a job that suited him!

Other 'late nest leavers' find managing a family of their own much too difficult. Italian men can't easily come to terms with girlfriends who work and haven't got time to deal with gas rings in the kitchen. Meanwhile the girls go to university, are emancipated, and are told by their mothers to be careful not to end up as slaves of their male chauvinist companions, as they themselves have probably been all their lives.

SURPRISING CEASEFIRE

Oman Tribune, Oman

Spaniards are surely elated and hopeful with the ETA's announcement of a permanent ceasefire in its war against the government in Madrid for Basque independence. But this joy will be tempered by the reality that this extremist organisation is not very reliable and trustworthy. In the past it has declared ceasefires on many occasions. But they were all temporary as the ETA found one reason or another to violate them.

The last time, in 1998, its announcement of a truce led to secret talks with the Spanish government. But the discussions proved futile and the ETA lost no time in going back to its violent ways.

A major cause of the lack or any progress towards the resolution of the Basque problem is the Spanish government's total rejection of the ETA's demand for independence. This is understandable, as some other regions, yearning to get rid of Madrid's rule, are bound to step up pressure once the Basques are allowed to snap links with Spain. Madrid, however, has shown some inclination to redress some of the grievances of the Basque population of two million. In recent years, they have been given a great degree of autonomy. Even the Basque language has been given official status. But this has not satisfied the ETA, which has so far shown no proclivity to make compromises and has fought for more than 40 years, ruthlessly raining death and destruction all over Spain. As a result, it has lost sympathy among most Spaniards who view the ETA rebels as cold-blooded terrorists. Lacking any credibility, any attack anywhere in Spain is viewed as the handiwork of the ETA even though they were not behind it. Many Basques too deplore the ETA's violent methods and view its battle for independence as futile.

Looking to the future with the Guggenheim Museum, in Bilbao, the largest city in the Basque region

For a permanent peace to grow from the permanent truce, the ETA must also make compromises in a manner that other violent organisations in other countries have done. The IRA in Northern Ireland may be taken as an example.

4 LISTEN

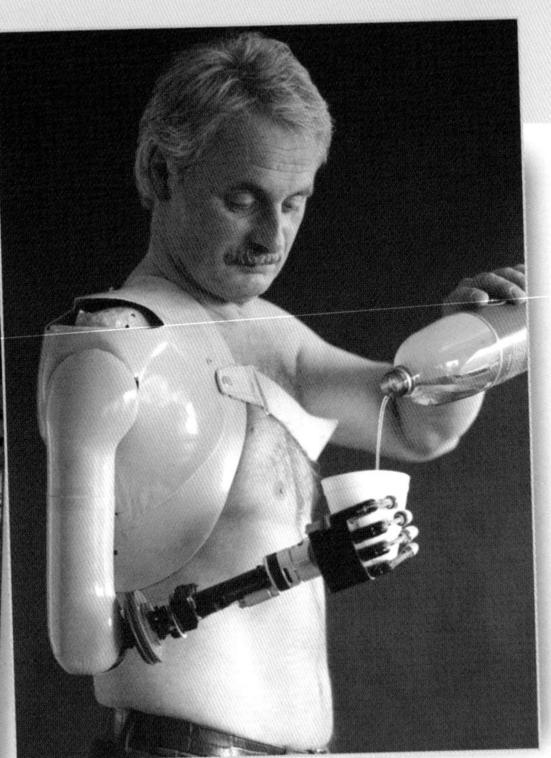

A Look at the photos and answer:
1. What kinds of physical disabilities are there?
2. How would these affect someone's life and independence?
3. How can obstacles to independent living be overcome?

B Before you listen, decide what a seeing-eye / guide dog is able to do:
- Understand street lights
- Identify dangers
- Act as a guard dog
- Lead someone down the street

Check your answers after listening.

C Listen to the audio clip and answer the questions.
1. What breed of dog is Hanni?
2. Explain how Beth Finke gets across the street with her guide dog.
3. What does Beth Finke mean by waiting for 'the cycle'?
4. How does Beth talk to her dog? What tone of voice does she use? And to the listeners to the programme?

D At the end of the clip, decide what Beth Finke would say about how important Hanni is for her.

E You decide: How are people with physical disabilities treated? How accessible are public transport, workplaces, shops and other buildings for them? What can be done to improve the lives of the physically disabled?

5 TEAMWORK

Work in threes. Read the **Teamwork Scenario for Unit 9** and make a list of useful items to equip an apartment and work out a budget with a friend of yours.

6 CONTROVERSY

Work in groups of four. Prepare a debate with another group. Use expressions from **Language Bank 9**.

Humans often seem to have two competing instincts: the drive to be part of a group and the drive to be different from the group. An extreme philosophy of not being part of the group is anarchism. Anarchists believe that we should have no government at all.

Group A: You are a group of anarchists, arguing for an end to government. Some questions you could ask:
- Don't humans instinctively want independence?
- Humans are basically good. Why do we need government or police?
- People don't need money. Can't they barter / exchange goods and services?

Group B: You don't agree with anarchism. The government may have its faults, but it is far better than no government at all. Some questions you could ask:
- Don't humans instinctively seek acceptance in a group?
- Wouldn't society collapse into chaos without government or police?
- Don't large, specialised organisations produce more goods and services than informal, unstructured ones?

7 PORTFOLIO WRITING

A Imagine you come from a country that has recently become independent. Write a letter (180-210 words) to a friend about your feelings on your country's independence day.

B Creative writing: Write a diary entry (220-250 words) for a student who has just spent their first week in university accommodation. It is their first time living away from home.

8 HISTORY *in English*

A Work in pairs. The United Kingdom is made up of England, Wales, Scotland and Northern Ireland. Since 1997, Scotland and Wales have their own parliaments. One student gives a formal presentation on decentralisation, using the example of Scottish devolution (self-government). The other student's presentation covers the British, or central government, perspective.

B Afterwards discuss the presentations from the point of view you represented.

Scottish Independence

Until 1707, Scotland was independent from England. Since devolution, it has its own parliament and more control over some areas of government.

Scotland's ultra-modern Parliament building in Edinburgh

The Scottish Parliament now has responsibility for:
agriculture, industry, education, health, culture, the environment, transport and roads, housing, tourism, social services, economic development and sports.

The UK government keeps control over:
defence and foreign policy, taxation policy, immigration, trade, energy, employment, social security, constitutional matters, gambling and some aspects of transport and industry.

Key dates

1603 Scottish king became King of England and Scotland.

1707 Act of Union: officially united Scotland to England. Scottish parliament closed.

1889 British Parliament voted against having a Scottish Parliament.

1910–1940s Several Scottish nationalist groups created, including the Scottish Nationalist Party.

1950 The Stone of Destiny, traditionally used for the ceremony of crowning Scotland's Kings, stolen from Westminster Abbey; officially returned to Scotland in 1996.

1970s North Sea oil discovered off Scotland, but the money goes direct to the UK government. This spurs Scottish nationalism.

1979 Scotland voted against devolution.

1997 Scotland voted for devolution.

1998 The Scottish Parliament opened, with a First Minister and 129 MSPs (Member of the Scottish Parliament).

9 FURTHER DISCUSSION

Discuss in pairs. Use the words and phrases from in this unit and **Language Bank 9** taking turns to develop and justify your ideas and arguments.

A How does money affect personal independence? Can people be independent if they get help from parents or the government?

B If children move far away from their parents how does it affect family relationships?

C When Americans dumped British tea into Boston harbour in 1773, they were protesting against unfair taxes, but the English considered it terrorism. What is the difference between freedom fighters and terrorists?

10 *Your answer*: WHY DO PEOPLE WANT TO BE INDEPENDENT?

Do people just not like being told what to do? Why does it matter whether we leave home? Does it matter whether we have our own place or our own land?

Do I get a say?

WHAT'S NEW!

Topic: Individual and young people's rights
Function: Challenging arguments and opinions
Language: Intensifiers

The BIG question: CAN'T WE JUST DO WHAT WE WANT?

- People who believe 'it's necessary to believe in God to be moral and have good values':
  Indonesia 99%
  Brazil 80%
  USA 58%
  Canada 30%
  Russia 26%
  France 13%

- US teenagers who feel adults are trying to restrict their freedom too much: 70%

> *The right to be heard does not include the right to be taken seriously.*
> ***Hubert Humphrey***

? Do you feel restricted in your life? What are the restrictions?

1 WORD POWER

A Which rights are affected in these legal cases? Match the legal cases with the correct rights.

Legal case:	**Right to...**
1 person wrongly shot and killed by police	a privacy
2 person detained for a year without being charged	b life
3 woman refused a promotion due to her gender	c assembly
4 group arrested for picketing an embassy	d equality
5 political refugee arrested going into another country	e hold political office
6 immigrant not allowed to be a candidate in an election	f asylum
7 hiker arrested for crossing private property	g own property
8 paparazzo arrested for spying on a celebrity	h fair trial
9 drug dealer's house is taken away away on arrest	i free movement

B Imagine you were the lawyer representing the person or people in each case in A. Use the challenging phrases in **Language Bank 10** to object to evidence in the cases.

C 1 Which rights could you live without? Which could you not live without? Use intensifiers from **Language Bank 10** to explain your answer.

2 Do you think these rights should be universal for all people, all ages and all countries? Why / Why not?

SEE WORKBOOK FOR MORE ACTIVITIES.

2 READING

A Four sentences have been removed from the articles on the opposite page. Choose from the sentences (A)-(E) the one which fits each gap (1)-(4). There is one extra sentence which you do not need to use.

B Imagine you are a journalist who interviewed Assibit. Use reported speech to explain to television viewers what she told you about her experience as a slave and her escape.

C 1 Slavery is a taboo subject in Niger. Why do you think it is taboo?

2 What percentage of yobs do you think are there among young people?

3 What are the connections and differences between the two stories?

3 SPEAK YOUR MIND

A Are rights worth fighting for? Give examples.

B Why is it important for people to be able to say what they think? Should there be limits on free speech?

C Should people be allowed to live wherever they want? How easy or difficult is it for immigrants to do this?

D Do you know of any countries where there used to be slaves? What would life as a slave be like?

E Would the British public accept the Anti-Social Behaviour Act if it targeted senior citizens, women or ethnic groups?

(A) Some race groups said it could also target ethnic minorities whose cultures traditionally involve street-corner gatherings.
(B) Now I can go to bed when I want, no one insults me.
(C) It also gives police-style powers to private security guards for the first time, if they are officially credited.
(D) Children can be taken away without cause and their parents never know what happened to them.
(E) In many cases, families are not even allowed to stay together.

SLAVERY IN NIGER – BATTLING AGAINST THE ODDS

Assibit was a slave in Niger for 50 years. She was born a slave, her mother was a slave, as were her husband and children. She had to work all day from early in the morning, preparing food for the master and his family, milking camels and doing all household chores, including moving their tent. This is heavy work, the tent alone can be made up of around 200 goat skins and has to be moved four times a day to ensure that the master and his family are always shaded from the strong sun.

On 28 June 2004, she escaped, walking 30 kilometres to freedom. "We were never paid, I was only given one tenth of the camel milk and leftovers. I have never known happiness until this month of freedom. (1) ...... Now that I am free, I can live as I please."

Slavery has a long history in Niger. People today are born into a slave class and are forced to work without pay throughout their lives. They are used as herders, agricultural labourers and as domestic servants; everything that a household needs to have done is done by slaves, the master and his family do no labour, they do not even lift a cup.

Regardless of their age, slaves are under a master's total control. They are not allowed to make any decisions for themselves, whether it is deciding when to eat and sleep or whom they marry. (2) ...... The children of slaves are removed from their mothers when they are as young as two years old, and are given to other masters.

Despite its prevalence, the true scale of slavery in Niger only became clear last year, following joint research that Anti-Slavery International carried out with the local organisation Timidria. In conducting the first national survey of this abuse, over 11,000 people were interviewed, most of whom were identified as slaves. The research establishes that at least 43,000 people are in slavery across the country.

Slavery is illegal in Niger, and officially it is claimed that there are no slaves.

POLICE POWERS EXTENDED IN YOB CRACKDOWN

Matthew Tempest and agencies, The Guardian, UK

The police were given new powers to break up groups of two or more teenagers, as part of the government's crackdown on antisocial behaviour. But the children will not need to have committed any offence to be moved on by officers, if the area has been designated an anti-social 'hotspot' by the local council.

Will ASBOs help control yobbish behaviour?

The Home Secretary launched the powers at a press conference in west London, as the first powers under the Anti-Social Behaviour Act. (3) ...... At first this will allow them to stop cyclists riding on the pavement, although later both security guards and the new community support officers will get further powers under the same act.

Less controversially, police officers will be able to close down crack houses within 48 hours, and keep them shut for up to six months. The introduction of controversial new police powers allows the police to disperse groups of people who have gathered in an area designated an anti-social hotspot by the local council. In fact, the measure narrows the number who may be dispersed from 20, under the 1986 Public Order Act, to two.

This aspect of the Act was objected to by children's charities and some lawyers, who said it would victimise youngsters who had committed no crime. (4) ...... The host of new powers were designed to target yobs, nuisance neighbours, vandals and drug dealers who make life a misery for law-abiding residents

Peace around the world

Subject: International events
Function: Evaluating different viewpoints
Language: Tentative expressions

The BIG question: WILL WE EVER HAVE PEACE?

VIEWPOINT

Some recent winners of the Nobel Peace Prize:

Ecologist Wangari Maathai (Kenya) for her work on reversing African deforestation

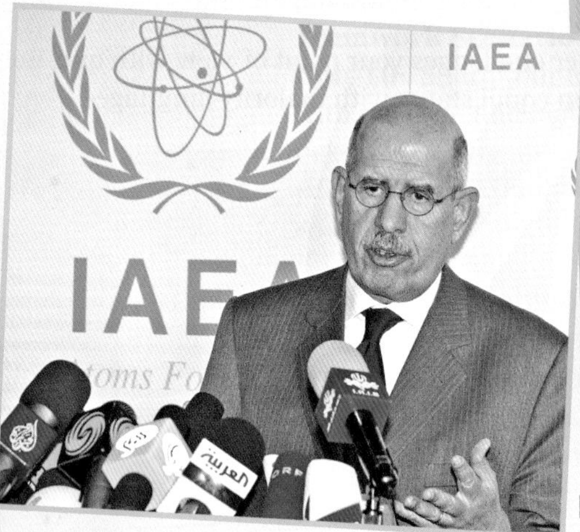

The International Atomic Energy Agency, headed by Mohamed El Baradei (Egypt), is the UN agency working to ensure nuclear energy is not used for military purposes.

Lawyer and human rights activist Shirin Ebadin (Iran) for defending the rights of women and children in Iran

The chief distinction of a diplomat is that he can say no in such a way that it sounds like yes.
Lester B. Pearson

? Compare each of these people's contribution to world peace. Who do you think does the most important work and why?

1 WORD POWER

A Give the adjectives, then match the collocations.

1 nature	natural	a	envoy
2 diplomacy	...	b	uprising
3 population	...	c	disaster
4 terror	...	d	corruption
5 region	...	e	protest
6 finance	...	f	crisis
7 politics	...	g	conflict
8 peace	...	h	attack

B 1 What news stories would these collocations appear in? Give examples.
2 Choose three collocations in A and write three dialogues about them (50-100 words) between an optimist and a pessimist. Use two or more expressions from **Language Bank 11** in each dialogue.

C 1 Is it possible to be a strong leader and a pacifist? Why? / Why not?
2 Think of a recent conflict. What attempts to resolve it have there been?

SEE WORKBOOK FOR MORE ACTIVITIES.

2 READING

A Who supports or opposes President Chavez? Give reasons why.
Example: *Many Brazilians would support him because he has helped the samba parades.*

B Who are the Mothers of the Plaza de Mayo? What are their political / social beliefs?

C 1 Do you think the US might invade a Latin American country (again)? Why / Why not?
2 What can people do for reconciliation after violence or war?

3 SPEAK YOUR MIND

A What have been the important world events of the last year? Do you think the world got better or worse?

B Should the UN be involved in peace-making? Why / Why not?

C Do you think citizens' protests in the streets can change governments and resolve conflicts?

D Make two lists of government actions you think make a government good or bad. What makes it act this way? Who benefits from these actions?

(A) Some race groups said it could also target ethnic minorities whose cultures traditionally involve street-corner gatherings.
(B) Now I can go to bed when I want, no one insults me.
(C) It also gives police-style powers to private security guards for the first time, if they are officially credited.
(D) Children can be taken away without cause and their parents never know what happened to them.
(E) In many cases, families are not even allowed to stay together.

SLAVERY IN NIGER – BATTLING AGAINST THE ODDS

Assibit was a slave in Niger for 50 years. She was born a slave, her mother was a slave, as were her husband and children. She had to work all day from early in the morning, preparing food for the master and his family, milking camels and doing all household chores, including moving their tent. This is heavy work, the tent alone can be made up of around 200 goat skins and has to be moved four times a day to ensure that the master and his family are always shaded from the strong sun.

On 28 June 2004, she escaped, walking 30 kilometres to freedom. "We were never paid, I was only given one tenth of the camel milk and leftovers. I have never known happiness until this month of freedom. (1) ...... Now that I am free, I can live as I please."

Slavery has a long history in Niger. People today are born into a slave class and are forced to work without pay throughout their lives. They are used as herders, agricultural labourers and as domestic servants; everything that a household needs to have done is done by slaves, the master and his family do no labour, they do not even lift a cup.

Regardless of their age, slaves are under a master's total control. They are not allowed to make any decisions for themselves, whether it is deciding when to eat and sleep or whom they marry. (2) ...... The children of slaves are removed from their mothers when they are as young as two years old, and are given to other masters.

Despite its prevalence, the true scale of slavery in Niger only became clear last year, following joint research that Anti-Slavery International carried out with the local organisation Timidria. In conducting the first national survey of this abuse, over 11,000 people were interviewed, most of whom were identified as slaves. The research establishes that at least 43,000 people are in slavery across the country.

Slavery is illegal in Niger, and officially it is claimed that there are no slaves.

POLICE POWERS EXTENDED IN YOB CRACKDOWN

Matthew Tempest and agencies, The Guardian, UK

The police were given new powers to break up groups of two or more teenagers, as part of the government's crackdown on antisocial behaviour. But the children will not need to have committed any offence to be moved on by officers, if the area has been designated an anti-social 'hotspot' by the local council.

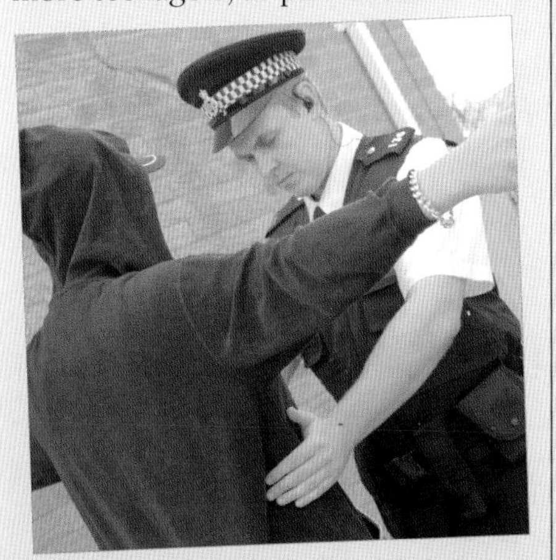

Will ASBOs help control yobbish behaviour?

The Home Secretary launched the powers at a press conference in west London, as the first powers under the Anti-Social Behaviour Act. (3) ...... At first this will allow them to stop cyclists riding on the pavement, although later both security guards and the new community support officers will get further powers under the same act.

Less controversially, police officers will be able to close down crack houses within 48 hours, and keep them shut for up to six months. The introduction of controversial new police powers allows the police to disperse groups of people who have gathered in an area designated an anti-social hotspot by the local council. In fact, the measure narrows the number who may be dispersed from 20, under the 1986 Public Order Act, to two.

This aspect of the Act was objected to by children's charities and some lawyers, who said it would victimise youngsters who had committed no crime. (4) ...... The host of new powers were designed to target yobs, nuisance neighbours, vandals and drug dealers who make life a misery for law-abiding residents

 4 LISTEN 

A Look at the photos and answer:
1. What is the worst thing you've heard about a teenager doing?
2. What kind of punishment did they receive? Was this fair?
3. How should parents and schools deal with troubled teenagers?
4. What rights do teenagers have in these situations?

B Listen to the audio and choose the answer (A, B, C) which fits best according to what you hear.
1. How are students often delivered to the school?
   - A Police officers transport students in the night.
   - B They are handcuffed in their homes.
   - C They fly out of Miami.
2. How much did this cost?
   - A $14,000 per year
   - B $40,000 per course
   - C $40,000 per year
3. Why were some students sent there?
   - A Smoking marijuana
   - B Drinking alcohol
   - C Fighting with their parents

C At the end, decide how David and Peter will respond to Mary's question.

D You decide: What do you think it would be like to be in Tranquillity Bay? Should any teenagers be sent there? Does behaviour modification work? Do you think parents have or should have the right to send their child there?

5 TEAMWORK

Work in groups of three. People in your country have found a new way of choosing politicians. Read the **Teamwork Scenario for Unit 10** . Share your ideas with the class and make tickets for a lottery of the people you have chosen. Who will be your country's leader?

6 CONTROVERSY

Work in groups of four. Prepare a discussion with another group. Use expressions from **Language Bank 10**.

It is now legal in the Netherlands and Belgium for very ill patients to seek euthanasia under very strict conditions. Should people have the right to choose when they die? Your government has set up a committee to investigate the possibility of legalising euthanasia.

Group A

You are a group of concerned citizens. You do not want your government to allow euthanasia. Some points you may wish to mention and questions to ask:
- Isn't compassionate murder still murder?
- Is it a slippery slope? Will euthanasia be just for sick people? Will it be used wrongly?
- Won't some people use it to commit suicide?
- In many religions taking human life is a sin.

Group B

You are a group representing doctors, terminally ill patients and their families. You want to convince your government to allow euthanasia. Some points you may wish to mention and questions to ask:
- Isn't it more humane to allow someone to die if they are in a lot of pain?
- It's a last resort for very ill patients.
- Euthanasia should only be used when a person agrees.
- Don't most religions believe in compassion for others?

7 PORTFOLIO WRITING

A Write a report (220-260 words) for your government on the rights of women. Explain any differences between men's and women's rights and how this has changed over the years.

B Imagine you have been sent to a behaviour modification camp. Write a letter or email (180-220 words) to a friend about your experience.

8 LAW in English

A Work in pairs. In Canada there is an English-speaking majority and a French-speaking minority, but in the Canadian province of Quebec there is a majority of French speakers. One student makes a formal presentation from the point of view of a French speaker from Quebec talking about minority language rights in Canada. The other student talks about how an English speaker living in Quebec views minority language rights in Canada.

B After the presentation, your partner challenges your point of view with questions. Discuss whether minority languages should be given equal status with majority languages.

Canada is officially bilingual (English and French).

- English speakers 59.3%, French speakers 23.1%, other languages 17.6%
- All federal agencies must provide services in English and French. All the provinces are officially English-speaking except Quebec (officially French-speaking) and New Brunswick (officially bilingual). Bilingual services vary greatly between local and provincial governments.

Quebec

Quebec is officially French speaking.

- French speakers 82%, English speakers 8%, other languages 10%
- Relations between Quebec and the rest of Canada have been difficult since the 1960s, as some people want Quebec to be independent from Canada.
- In a 1995 referendum 50.6% of Quebeckers voted in favour of staying in Canada.

Language Laws

- 1969: Canada becomes officially bilingual.
- 1977: Quebec passes the Charter of the French Language, banning English commercial signs on the outside of buildings and limiting children's attendance at English schools. The ban is rejected by Canada's Supreme Court (1988).
- 1982: Canada's Charter of Rights and Freedoms makes bilingualism part of Canada's constitution.
- 1993: Quebec allows English signs on the outside of buildings, if the lettering is half the size of the French.

9 FURTHER DISCUSSION

Discuss in pairs. Use the words and phrases from this unit and **Language Bank 10** to develop and justify your ideas and arguments.

A Which of these should be guaranteed as individual rights: abortion, alcohol use, drug use, employment, freedom of religion, gun ownership, having children, healthcare, marriage, pension, sexuality, welfare?

B Do political power, wealth and social status affect individual rights? If so, how?

C After school shootings, many US schools use metal detectors, security guards and drug testing. Do you think these measures improve security and students' lives?

10 *Your answer*: CAN'T WE JUST DO WHAT WE WANT?

Should everyone have complete freedom? Where are the limits? Who should set these limits?

Peace around the world

Subject: International events
Function: Evaluating different viewpoints
Language: Tentative expressions

The BIG question: WILL WE EVER HAVE PEACE?

VIEWPOINT

Some recent winners of the Nobel Peace Prize:

Ecologist Wangari Maathai (Kenya) for her work on reversing African deforestation

The International Atomic Energy Agency, headed by Mohamed El Baradei (Egypt), is the UN agency working to ensure nuclear energy is not used for military purposes.

Lawyer and human rights activist Shirin Ebadin (Iran) for defending the rights of women and children in Iran

The chief distinction of a diplomat is that he can say no in such a way that it sounds like yes.
Lester B. Pearson

? Compare each of these people's contribution to world peace. Who do you think does the most important work and why?

1 WORD POWER

A Give the adjectives, then match the collocations.

1 nature	natural →	a envoy
2 diplomacy	...	b uprising
3 population	...	c disaster
4 terror	...	d corruption
5 region	...	e protest
6 finance	...	f crisis
7 politics	...	g conflict
8 peace	...	h attack

B 1 What news stories would these collocations appear in? Give examples.
2 Choose three collocations in A and write three dialogues about them (50-100 words) between an optimist and a pessimist. Use two or more expressions from **Language Bank 11** in each dialogue.

C 1 Is it possible to be a strong leader and a pacifist? Why? / Why not?
2 Think of a recent conflict. What attempts to resolve it have there been?

SEE WORKBOOK FOR MORE ACTIVITIES.

2 READING

A Who supports or opposes President Chavez? Give reasons why.
Example: *Many Brazilians would support him because he has helped the samba parades.*

B Who are the Mothers of the Plaza de Mayo? What are their political / social beliefs?

C 1 Do you think the US might invade a Latin American country (again)? Why / Why not?
2 What can people do for reconciliation after violence or war?

3 SPEAK YOUR MIND

A What have been the important world events of the last year? Do you think the world got better or worse?

B Should the UN be involved in peace-making? Why / Why not?

C Do you think citizens' protests in the streets can change governments and resolve conflicts?

D Make two lists of government actions you think make a government good or bad. What makes it act this way? Who benefits from these actions?

CHÁVEZ, SEEKING FOREIGN ALLIES, SPENDS BILLIONS

Juan Forero, New York Times, USA

President Hugo Chávez is spending billions of dollars of his country's oil windfall on pet projects abroad, aimed at setting up his leftist government as a political counterpoint to the conservative Bush administration in the region. With Venezuela's oil revenues rising 32 percent last year, Mr. Chávez has been subsidizing samba parades in Brazil, eye surgery for poor Mexicans and even heating fuel for poor families from Maine to the Bronx to Philadelphia. By some estimates, the spending now surpasses the nearly $2 billion Washington allocates annually to pay for development programs and the drug war in western South America.

The new spending has given more power to a leader who has been provocatively building a bulwark against what he has called American imperialistic aims in Latin America. Mr. Chávez frequently derides Mr. Bush and his top aides. (...) He has called Mr. Bush a 'donkey', a 'drunkard' and a 'coward', daring him to invade the country.

But with the biggest oil reserves outside the Middle East, Mr. Chávez is more than an irritant. He is fast rising as the next Fidel Castro, a hero to the masses who is intent on opposing every move the United States makes, but with an important advantage.

"He's managed to do what Fidel Castro never could," said Stephen Johnson, a scholar at the conservative Heritage Foundation. "Castro never had an independent source of income the way Chávez does. Chávez is filling a void that Castro left for him, leading nonaligned nations." (...)

Antonio Ledezma, an opposition leader and one of the president's more determined foes, said the policy's aim was to build 'a political platform with an international reach'. Mr. Chávez celebrates the spending as revolutionary largesse, intended to further his dream of unifying Latin America in a way Simón Bolívar could only dream of.

With the price of Venezuelan crude rising fivefold since Mr. Chávez was first elected in 1998, the spending has not hurt international reserves or Venezuela's credit worthiness. Oil analysts say the sustainability of that situation depends on the flow of revenues, the price of oil and the amount of crude Venezuela's oil industry is able to produce. (...) While the president enjoys the support of a majority of Venezuelans, polls by Greenberg Quinlan Rosner Research, a Washington polling company that has worked for Venezuela's opposition movement, show that fewer than 30 percent of Venezuelans believe the country should spend its oil revenue abroad (...) .

HOPE ENDS 29-YEAR MARCH OF MOTHERS OF THE PLAZA DE MAYO

Regina M. Anavy, San Francisco Chronicle, USA

One month ago, a historic event took place in Buenos Aires when the Mothers of the Plaza de Mayo staged their 1,500th, and last, demonstration.

The Mothers began their protests during the Dirty War in Argentina, waged from 1976 to 1983, when the military government abducted, tortured and killed left-wing militants, stole babies born to pregnant prisoners, and obliterated any records that would help the families find the bodies or reclaim their grandchildren. During this period, the word 'disappeared' entered the lexicon. It referred to the kidnapped people who were never heard from again.

On April 30, 1977, fourteen women went to the Plaza de Mayo, across from the Pink House, the presidential palace, walking around

the pyramid in the center. They identified themselves by wearing white head scarves, symbolizing the diapers of their children. Their nonviolent witness gained them prestige abroad and earned them international awards. They became an inspiration for others who suffered similar situations under repressive governments. They also became victims of harassment. Three of the founding members eventually 'disappeared' too.

So why was last month's major demonstration their last? One of the mothers, Hebe de Bonafini, in an interview with La Nacion, put it this way: "We no longer have an enemy in the Pink House. This government has good intentions. Kirchner is a friend of the family."

She was referring to Nestor Kirchner, a Peronist with leftist leanings, who became president of Argentina in 2003. Shortly after taking office, Kirchner suspended the laws of immunity for former military leaders and announced that he would not oppose extradition for those who had escaped justice by fleeing the country. The Mothers say about 30,000 disappearances remain unresolved. The military claims 9,000. A government commission has put the number closer to 11,000.

4 LISTEN

A Look at the photos and answer:
1. What kind of natural disasters can occur?
2. Have any of these happened in your country?
3. Are people prepared for disasters in your country?
4. What do you know about Haiti?

B Before you listen, decide which of these will be mentioned as possible problems in Haiti:
- Disease
- Forest fires
- Poverty
- Drought

Check your answers after listening.

C Listen to the audio clip and complete these sentences (maximum three words):
1. Weather satellites measured the rainfall in the mountains to be .... in one day.
2. US AID reports that .... million trees are cut down every year.
3. Different countries have offered to export .... to Haiti for future housing and heating.

D You decide: Who or what is to blame for the deaths in Haiti? What role has armed conflict had on Haiti and other developing countries in times of crisis? Do you think things will get better in Haiti? What can individuals and different countries do to help Haiti's problems?

5 TEAMWORK

Work in groups of three. Imagine you are members of the newly-formed World Peace Institute. Read the **Teamwork Scenario** and come up with some ideas about resolving conflicts. The class decides which are the two best ideas for conflict resolution.

6 CONTROVERSY

Work in groups of four. Prepare a debate against another group. Use expressions from **Language Bank 11**.

The United States and the European Union seem to be at odds on many subjects (such as trade, farming, Iraq, terrorism). A debate is being arranged between politicians from the US and the EU. The opinions from both sides range from seeing the EU and the US as strong rivals to wanting more cooperation.

Group A

You are pessimists who think the EU and US will eventually become bitter rivals. Some points you may wish to mention:
- No more common enemy (Communist countries, such as the Soviet Union) to unite them
- US is increasingly religious; EU, increasingly secular
- Many Europeans against the war in Iraq (and resolving conflict by force)
- EU supports environment initiatives like the Kyoto Protocol; US against
- Most EU countries promote social equality and welfare; US prefers free-market capitalism.

Group B

You are optimists who think the EU and US will become closer allies. Some points you may wish to mention:
- Shared history
- Democratic traditions
- Close economic ties
- Cooperation in many areas (for example: security, environmental protection, peace-keeping missions)
- US and Britain share a language
- Both face economic and political competition from China and India.

7 PORTFOLIO WRITING

A Write a press release (180-220 words) for the last demonstration by the Mothers of the Playa de Mayo.

B Choose an international event from the past year and write an article (220-260 words) for a local youth newspaper about it.

8 DRAMA *in English*

A Work in pairs. You each give a formal presentation about how drama can make people think about about war and its effects. The first student talks about the origins of anti-war drama in Western theatre. The second student presents anti-war theatre after 1950.

B After the presentations, improvise a mini-scenario for a play to oppose war and promote peace. You can use songs.

Origins of Anti-War Drama

GREEK DRAMA
The Trojan Women – Euripides (415 BC) About the defeat of Troy and enslavement of its women by Athens.
Lysistrata – Aristophanes (410 BC) Comedy about Greek women who withhold sex from their husbands to stop them fighting in a war.

WILLIAM SHAKESPEARE (1564-1616)
Experts disagree whether Shakespeare was pro- or anti-war. He often glorifies war, but also shows war's many unpleasant aspects. Plays often performed as anti-war pieces: *Henry V, Troilus and Cressida,* and *Coriolanus.*

AGAINST WORLD WAR I
Journey's End – R C Sheriff (UK,1929) About life and death among British soldiers in the trenches.

AGAINST WORLD WAR II
All My Sons – Arthur Miller (US, 1945) About a family who discover their father was a secret war-time profiteer.

Post-1950 Anti-War Theatre

AGAINST THE WAR IN VIETNAM
US (US, 1966): Play critical of US involvement in Vietnam, instrumental in keeping Britain out of the Vietnam War.
Hair (US, 1968): Broadway musical about the hippie (anti-war) generation.
Street theatre: Various groups. It has since become a major part of anti-war demonstrations.

AGAINST THE WAR IN IRAQ
The Madness of George Dubya (UK, 2003): When a US general decides to drop nuclear bombs on the Middle East, President Bush and Prime Minister Blair struggle to recall the planes.
Veronique of the Mounties (USA, 2003): San Francisco Mime Troupe play about a US presidential candidate going to war with Canada to win the election.
Lysistrata Project – (US, 2003): 1,029 readings of the Greek play across the US.

"The [Vietnam] draft is white people sending black people to make war on yellow people to defend the land they stole from red people."
From the stage show *Hair*

9 FURTHER DISCUSSION

Discuss in pairs. Use the phrases from this unit and **Language Bank 11**, taking turns to develop and justify your ideas and arguments.

A What conflicts has your country been involved in since 1940? How have these conflicts changed your country?

B How are civilians and nature affected by war?

C How has technology changed the nature of war and the search for peace? Give examples.

D What are 'rogue states'? What threat do they pose? Should anything be done about them?

10 *Your answer:* WILL WE EVER HAVE PEACE?

Will we ever have universal peace? Do you think people really care?

Click here!

WHAT'S NEW?

Subject: Using the internet
Function: Uncountable nouns
Language: Deducing

The BIG question: ARE WE ALL ONLINE NOW?

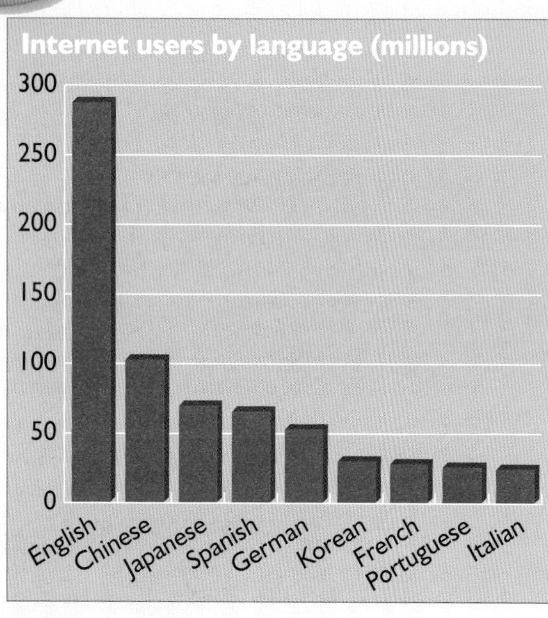

- Cost of computer viruses to businesses in 2003: £55 billion

> *Give a man a fish and you feed him for a day. Teach him to use the Net and he won't bother you for weeks.*
> ***Anonymous***

? Can anyone learn to use the internet?

? Do you need to speak English to surf the net?

1 WORD POWER

A 1 Have you used the internet for any of these?

- Downloading music, videos or software
- Looking up information with a search engine
- Talking to people in a chat room
- Sending emails
- Buying something online
- Accessing your bank account
- Using internet phones or webcams

2 Use the **Language Bank 12** uncountable nouns or other uncountables to describe how the internet has changed the world.
Example: *I think there is much more information available for people.*

3 What language do you use to surf the net?

B Make a deduction about these statements using **Language Bank 12**.

1 Hackers have shut down the website again.
2 We googled him and found over 300 pages about his life.
3 A broadband connection is much faster when you are surfing the internet.

C 1 How have emails, chat rooms and texting changed the way people communicate?
2 What is netiquette?

SEE WORKBOOK FOR MORE ACTIVITIES.

2 READING

A Read the first article. Which statement(s) refer to Lim Yo-Hwan?

1 He's a keen basketball player.
2 He practises 10 hours every night.
3 He is sponsored by Samsung Electronics.
4 He is up to eight times faster than a casual player.

B Explain how each person feels about the other person / thing.

1 Andy → Katrina
2 Katrina → Andy
3 Katrina's grandmother → Andy
4 Katrina's grandmother → Venus

C 1 Do you see video games as a career option?
2 What would be difficult to understand about Katrina and Andy's relationship?

3 SPEAK YOUR MIND

A Why do people use the internet? What do you like or dislike about it?

B Should we be worried that a lot of people don't have access to the internet or computers?

C Do you play any video games? What do you like about them? Is it better to play against a person or a computer?

D Why is internet dating becoming so popular? Where else do people go to meet someone?

DON'T TELL THE KIDS: COMPUTER GAMES CAN MAKE YOU RICH

Mei Fong, The Wall Street Journal, USA

At age 24, Lim Yo-Hwan plays computer games all day, makes a six-figure income doing it and has thousands of adoring fans. Computer games have become a spectator sport here, and Mr. Lim is a star. In a packed Seoul television studio recently, Mr. Lim stood combat-ready in a military-style white tunic with epaulettes, his spiky hairdo set off by shiny silver headphones.

Tapping frantically at a keyboard, Mr. Lim built a virtual empire and launched a daring attack on enemy forces in an imaginary electronic galaxy – and was defeated – all within five minutes. Broadcast on cable TV, his moves were also displayed on screen before 300 fans in the studio, who cheered, cried and smacked noisemakers to show support.

To be a winner Lim Yo-Hwan trains 10 hours a day.

As electronic games attract big-dollar deals with sports leagues, Hollywood and advertisers, more gamers are starting to face off in professional venues. The payoffs are particularly rich here in Korea, where there's enough commercial and cultural support for a community of pros to earn a living and maybe even get rich. Three Korean cable TV channels broadcast matches 24 hours a day. Live matches take place every week here in Seoul, and draw as many customers as movies. This gaming mecca is even drawing young men from all over the world, who are lured by prospects of fame and fortune.

Last year, Mr. Lim made about $300,000 from player fees and commercials. Another top earner, Hung Jin-Ho, whose fingers are insured for $60,000, recently signed a three-year deal with telecom provider KTF Co. that will pay him $480,000 altogether.

Computer games began taking off in Korea five years ago when the government rolled out a nationwide high-speed internet system. Instead of buying expensive consoles or handheld games, which weren't widely available here then, teens began facing off on the internet. Companies ranging from Samsung Electronics to Coca-Cola Co. started sponsoring tournaments.

Like most serious gamers, Mr. Lim plays through much of the night and sleeps most of the day. He used to play basketball but stopped about two years ago for fear of hurting his fingers, which have to move fast to win tournaments. A measure programers use to gauge ability is APM, or actions per minute. APM is the average number of maneuvers a player can execute in 60 seconds. Most casual players have an APM of between 50 and 70. Mr. Lim has been known to hit 400 APM at some games, or 6.66 moves per second.

A FEW EMAILS AND SHE KNEW HE WAS THE ONE

Dee O'Connell, The Observer, UK

Katrina, 26, was just about to give up on internet dating when Venus intervened. Venus is the matchmaking program on match.com, the website she started using after her last relationship broke up. On the very day Katrina thought, "This is silly. I'm not doing this any more," Venus sent her Andy's profile and suggested she take a look.

After a few emails, she realised her search was over. "I knew he could be the one. He made me laugh and I could see a sensitive side." When he sent her a story he'd written, she lost her heart completely and arranged to meet him.

Cockfosters tube station in north London isn't the most obvious place for love to blossom, but Andy, 31, had to come down from Nottingham to meet her and it was the nearest landmark they could think of to the M50. He brought flowers, which Katrina thought was a very good start and, contrary to what her mother thought of his photo, he didn't look like a convict. Lunch led to a walk in the park, which was followed by coffee before they went to the pub. Katrina remembers thinking, "It's getting late. Why is he still here?" Andy, of course, was still there because he had fallen for her, too.

They haven't told Katrina's Cypriot grandmother how they met because she wouldn't understand, but everyone else has been very positive about it. Andy proposed during a weekend in Vienna, after hiding the ring in a pair of shoes – the only place Katrina wouldn't look. Katrina says, "We nearly didn't find each other. But once we did, the site became redundant."

4 WATCH AND LISTEN 12

A Look at the photographs and answer:

1. Is the internet Anglocentric?
2. Can you find everything you need on the net in your language?
3. Which foreign language websites do you like? Why?
4. Do online translation programmes help when you are surfing the Net?

B Before you watch, decide what will be said about:

- Non-English speakers and the internet
- Chinese feelings about using Chinese characters
- Problems with using Chinese characters
- The future of the Chinese language online

Check your answers after listening.

C Watch the video clip. When it pauses, try to answer Paul Twomey's question.

D Watch the video clip and answer the questions.

1. How is Kuala Lumpur like the internet?
2. How many variations of Chinese characters are there?
3. Why might using Chinese characters be a problem for business?
4. How many broadband users are there worldwide?

E You decide: Should we use more than one kind of script for email and web addresses? Will there be more than one internet in the future?

5 TEAMWORK

Work in pairs. See the **Teamwork Scenario**. You are website designers creating a website. Share your ideas with the class. The class can vote on the two websites they think would be the most interesting and the most popular.

6 CONTROVERSY

Work in groups of four. Prepare a debate with another group. Use expressions from **Language Bank 12**.

Gambling has become a major internet business with people betting on everything from horseracing to card games like poker. As problems increase, people are calling for an end to online gambling.

Group A: You are a group representing the gambling industry. Here are some questions you could ask:

- No one is forced to gamble. Isn't it an individual choice?
- Doesn't gambling provide a lot of jobs?
- Can't most online gambling sites be filtered out with parental control software?
- Shouldn't companies be allowed to operate anywhere they want?

Group B: You are against the gambling industry. Here are some questions you could ask:

- Isn't gambling a dangerous addiction like alcoholism?
- Is online gambling made even more addictive when it is presented like a video game?
- Is it really possible to make sure that no one who is under-age can place bets in online casinos?
- Doesn't the government lose a lot of tax income when these companies operate from tax-havens?

7 PORTFOLIO WRITING

A Imagine a friend has decided to join an internet dating service. Help your friend write a personal profile (220-250 words) for the net. Include a description of the ideal match.

B Write an article (220-250 words) for an e-magazine with predictions for the future of the internet. How do you think it will develop?

8 INFORMATION TECHNOLOGY *in English*

A Work in pairs. You are computer consultants. Give a formal presentation about either hacking or viruses.

B After the presentations, ask questions and discuss how secure the internet is. Can hackers or viruses ever be stopped completely?

Hacking techniques

- *Guessing / Hacking* into passwords to access a computer network.
- *Social engineering*: Pretending to be someone else to obtain sensitive information, such as bank details.
- *Dumpster diving*: Looking through rubbish for old computer disks and documents.

Famous hackers

1982: Ian Murphy changed telephone company computer clocks to get cheap telephone calls.
1995: Kevin Mitnick stole 20,000 credit card numbers. After four years in prison, Mitnick became a computer-security consultant.

Kevin Mitnick

Viruses or malicious codes

- *Macro virus*: Found in applications like MS Word and Excel; spreads by opening a computer file.
- *Worm*: Creates copies of itself, uses email to spread.
- *Trojan horse*: Disguised as another programme, like a game download. It can let a hacker into your computer.
- *Spyware*: Not a virus, but sends information about you to another user. It can slow down and crash your computer.

Famous viruses

- *MyDoom:* Highest rate of replication ever (infected one in 12 emails worldwide).
- *Big-F:* Sent huge numbers of emails, shutting down mail servers.
- *Bugbear-D:* Recorded keystrokes like passwords or credit card numbers; later accessed by the virus writer.

9 FURTHER DISCUSSION

Discuss in pairs. Use the words and phrases from this unit and **Language Bank 12**, taking turns to develop and justify your ideas and arguments.

A What are your favourite websites? What do you like about them?

B Is the internet a safe or dangerous place? How can parents protect children and teenagers using the internet? What are the advantages and disadvantages of anonymity online?

C New mobile phones are becoming more like computers, with internet access and other features. What are the advantages and disadvantages of this?

D Government and corporate websites have been hacked into for political reasons. What could happen if important sites are accessed illegally?

10 *Your answer*: ARE WE ALL ONLINE NOW?

Can the world function without the internet any more? Could people manage without emails? Will the internet be even more important in future?

Unit 13 What's in the news?

WHAT'S NEW?

Subject: Media *Function:* Implying
Language: Colloquialisms

The BIG question: DO YOU TRUST THE MEDIA?

VIEWPOINT

? What should the media be for? Finding out the truth or entertaining people?

> *You should always believe all you read in the newspapers, as this makes them more interesting.*
> *Rose Macauley*

1 WORD POWER

A Complete the newspaper headlines with the correct preposition.

about for from
at with of in

1. Arrested .... stealing police car
2. Pensioner bought shares .... risky deal .... best friend
3. What's wrong .... the Prime Minister?
4. Cost of living too expensive? Tired .... being poor?
5. Politicians sensitive .... electoral fraud
6. Do men do their fair share .... home?

B
1. Make these headlines more sensational using colloquialisms from **Language Bank 13** to replace the underlined words.
2. What could you imply about the content of each story? Use **Language Bank 13** to help you answer.

C
1. Are human interest stories real news?
2. Besides news, what does the media offer us?
3. Is all news biased?

SEE WORKBOOK FOR MORE ACTIVITIES.

2 READING

A Scan through **Italy Trails in Press Freedom** to find out what Silvio Berlusconi owns.

B Compare and contrast the situation for an editor for a TV news programme on a channel owned by Berlusconi and the editor of the paper in Chile. Which editor has more freedom to choose news items?

C
1. What do you think Silvio Berlusconi's views of the media are?
2. Who should choose news stories: journalists and editors or the public? What advantages or disadvantages would there be?

3 SPEAK YOUR MIND

A Where do you get your news from? Why does knowing about current events matter?

B What do you like and dislike about television? What are your favourite TV programmes and channels?

C What would it like to be a journalist or a foreign correspondent? Would you like either of these jobs?

D Why is the media an important part of democracy? Why would politicians want to influence the media?

ITALY TRAILS IN PRESS FREEDOM

Roberto Spiezio, Oh My News

Invited to give a speech at the U.N. General Assembly in 2003, former Prime Minister Silvio Berlusconi spoke in front of very few people. TG1, the main Italian public TV journal, edited the TV camera angles so that the assembly looked crowded, with people enthusiastically applauding the prime minister. In the relative silence of other TV journals, only a satirical evening show would find out the truth – the ovations were for the U.N. Secretary General Kofi Annan's speech, and TG1's editing distorted the facts.

This problem hasn't passed by unnoticed. Freedom House has released a report about the freedom of the press in the world. It emerges that out of the 194 countries subjected to the research, 54 are 'partly free,' (40 percent of world population), 73 'free' (17 percent), and 67 are 'not free' (43 percent). For the third year in a row, Italy has been placed among the 'partly free' countries.

Freedom House, points the finger at the anomalous concentration of the mass media in the hands of one person: "Freedom of speech and the press is constitutionally guaranteed. However, media freedom remains constrained by the continued concentration of media power in the hands of Prime Minister Silvio Berlusconi, who, through his private media holdings and political power over the state television networks, controls 90 percent of the country's broadcast media."

Silvio Berlusconi

Berlusconi owns Mediaset, the main private TV company in Italy, and as prime minister he has de facto controlled the national public Rai TV network by installing several people who are loyal to him both as chief editors of the broadcasts and in the management committee.

Add the total control of his channels' broadcasts, especially the show-like 'news' program TG4, and you'll get an idea of how extended his control is over public opinion.

His media empire is not only televisual. Through Fininvest, a holding company controlled by Berlusconi's family, he also controls a large share of the publishing and newspaper market, with *Mondadori*, Italy's largest book and magazine publishing group, and *Il Giornale*, a leading national newspaper, just to name a few.

Some commentators believe the center-left coalition led by Romano Prodi managed to win recent elections by a razor's edge thanks to Italian voters abroad who, because of better media diversity in their respective countries of residence, could get a more complete and truthful picture of the Italian social and political situation and therefore voted for the 'right' side.

Now, many electors are waiting for things to change. We'll see if the new government will be able to satisfy these high and legitimate expectations.

PAY-PER-CLICK JOURNALISM

Techdirt.com

As the news rooms continue to try to adjust to a world in which the internet exists (yeah, it's taking them quite a while to come to terms with this), there's an interesting experiment happening down in Chile. The publisher of the paper set up a system where everyone in the news room gets real time stats about what stories readers on the newspapers' website are clicking on, and those clicks drive what news stories will appear in the next day's print edition. In other words, the website acts as market research for what stories people want to read in their newspapers... and apparently, the paper is doing quite well because of the change.

While some decry the lowest common denominator of journalism this brings out, the publisher claims he's just showing people what they want, rather than trying to lecture them about what they should be reading about. What's even more interesting, however, is how it appears to be impacting the journalists. They constantly monitor stories to see who gets the most clicks – and the publisher is going to offer salaries based on how many clicks they get. In other words, it's pay-per-click journalism, which (of course) is going to promote more sensationalistic stories. It also makes you wonder how long it will take before we get stories of journalistic click fraud, where a journalist hires one of these click fraud services to repeatedly click on his or her articles, just to make them seem more 'popular'.

4 WATCH AND LISTEN

A Look at the photos of 9/11 in New York and answer:

1. How would you expect a news interviewer to treat a person who had just lost relatives or friends in a terrible disaster?
2. How would you expect a news interviewer to treat an interviewee with political views that he / she did not agree with?

B Watch the video clip from *Outfoxed*, a documentary film about Fox News, a 24-hour US TV news channel, and read our review of it:

TV REVIEW

***Outfoxed* – do you agree?**

We found the documentary extract very dramatic television. The body language of the participants was sometimes even more significant than the actual dialogue. Jeremy Glick kept his hands clasped tightly together while Bill O'Reilly used his hands to point and gesticulate. We don't think that O'Reilly was really interested in what Glick had to say, and he was more concerned to communicate to his viewers that Glick's view was unpatriotic. Glick kept his cool under pressure from a professional broadcaster. Fox News' slogan is 'Fair and balanced'. In this case we don't agree.

1. Do you think we have criticised Fox News fairly?
2. If not, what was your understanding of what was being said and what was happening in the clip?
3. Do you think the documentary presented the evidence fairly?
4. If not, explain why.

C You decide: Do you think that news is generally reported with or without bias? Give some examples.

5 TEAMWORK

Works in groups of three. Read the **Teamwork Scenario**. When you have come up with your stories, discuss: Should newspapers be used to report fiction? Does this change your view of newspapers?

6 CONTROVERSY

Work in groups of four. Prepare a debate with another group. Use expressions from **Language Bank 13**.

Government intelligence agencies have at times recruited journalists as spies. Although repeatedly asked by journalist organisations to stop this, some agencies refuse.

Group A

You are from an intelligence agency. Some points you may wish to use:

- Journalists can get into places that most others cannot.
- National security is the most important issue; not all stories should be told.
- It is sometimes in a country's interest to change the news.
- The government should be able to ask all of its citizens for help.

Group B

You are journalists. Some points you may wish to use:

- Journalists' lives are put in danger.
- Journalistic integrity is the most important issue; all important stories should be told.
- Politicians should not use the press for their own aims.
- Good-quality journalism requires a lack of bias, even when writing about your own country.

7 PORTFOLIO WRITING

A Write an email (180-220 words) to the editor of the newspaper in Chile giving your views about pay-per-click journalism.

B Choose an article from a magazine or newspaper. Write 220-250 words about why you thought the article was good or bad.

8 MEDIA STUDIES in English

A When people argue about a lack of media freedom, they often refer to novels about future dystopias, where life is rigidly controlled. Work in pairs. Each student gives a formal presentation on one of these novels. Try to give examples of how the writer's predictions have become real. After each presentation, the other student asks the presenter a question.

B Discuss how a free press could change the way people see these societies.

Brave New World (1932) by Aldous Huxley

Dystopia: In a single world state people are placed in a caste-system culture – from the smart leader Alphas down to the low intelligence worker Epsilons. Babies are mass-produced, and children programmed to be happy with life. There is no war, poverty, disease or pain, and people are kept happy by mindless entertainment, sports, sex and drugs. There is very little resistance.

Main characters and plot: Bernard Marx is an Alpha man, who is discontented. He takes a friend Lenina to a special wild reserve where life is not like the technological world in London. They meet John, son of a lost Beta woman. John falls in love with Lenina and comes to London. Disturbed by this new society and Lenina's rejection, John commits suicide. Marx is exiled.

Ideas from the novel used as criticism in the media:

- **No public awareness:** People are programmed so they don't care about the truth.
- **Disinformation:** Only a few leaders ever know the whole truth.
- **Ignore history:** History is wrong and should not be taught.

VINTAGE FUTURE CLASSICS EDITION WITH READING GUIDE

ALDOUS HUXLEY
BRAVE NEW WORLD

Fahrenheit 451 (1953) by Ray Bradbury

Dystopia: In a futuristic USA, books are banned because special interest groups resented what was in books, and less literate people resented not knowing much. Strong desire to make everyone in society the same, and technology is used to do this. TV and radio are the only media allowed. Secret resistance by some booklovers.

Main characters and plot: Guy Montag is a fireman whose job is to burn books. A young girl, Clarisse, shows him how empty his life is. After Guy decides to fight the system, his wife Mildred tells the police. Chased by firemen and a giant robot dog, he joins the resistance.

Ideas from the novel used as criticism in the media:

- **Book censorship:** Banning one book leads to more bans (slippery slope argument).
- **Against political correctness (PC):** Blocking non-PC ideas is a form of censorship.
- **Television better than literature:** 'Dumbing down' of culture.

9 FURTHER DISCUSSION

Discuss in pairs. Use the words and phrases from this unit and **Language Bank 13** to develop and justify your argument.

A Could you live without the news?

B How has technology changed the way we get news and information? What are the media of the future?

C Do you think today's news focuses too much on entertainment and gossip?

D A *New York Times* journalist, Jayeson Blair, lost his job for making up stories. Why would a journalist want to create fake stories? Do you think other journalists may have done the same?

10 *Your answer*: DO YOU TRUST THE MEDIA?

Should we believe what we are told? By everyone? Should we believe what the media tells us? How does the media earn our trust?

Heroes and villains

WHAT'S NEW?

Subject: Role models
Function: Softening expressions
Language: Idiomatic expressions

The BIG question: DO WE NEED SOMEONE TO LOOK UP TO?

VIEWPOINT

Let every man be respected as an individual and no man idolised.
Albert Einstein

? What is the point of having role models?

Christina Aguilera

Kofi Annan

Tanni Grey-Thomson

1 WORD POWER

A Which of these adjectives would you use to describe a role model? Can you find other adjectives?

- intelligent
- courageous
- compassionate
- self-confident
- talented
- generous
- attractive
- caring
- determined
- athletic

B 1 Why are the people in the photos in **Viewpoint** role models? For whom? Use the softening expressions from **Language Bank 14** to help you answer.
2 What kind of values do they suggest?

C 1 Do we use the word 'hero' too easily now? What is a heroic act?
2 How important are role models in child development?
3 Is it the job of teachers to be mentors who guide and advise their students?

SEE WORKBOOK FOR MORE ACTIVITIES.

2 READING

A Four sentences have been removed from the articles on the opposite page. Choose from the sentences (A)-(E) the one which fits each gap (1)-(4). There is one extra sentence which you do not need to use.

B 1 Do the three Belfast teenagers share the same ideas about role models? Explain your answer.
2 What is ironic about Christopher Reeve's famous film role and what happened in real life?

C 1 Do pop stars expect and want to be role models?
2 Compare Eminem and Christopher Reeve as role models for young people.

3 SPEAK YOUR MIND

A Who are your role models? How much do you really know about them?

B Who are better role models: parents or pop stars? Have you modelled yourself on your parents?

C What kind of messages do your favourite music stars send in their music and actions?

D Why are anti-establishment role models so popular?

E Is there is a lack of positive role models for some groups?

(A) "He is the Superman of music and a role model for all young people."
(B) "He has been our champion."
(C) He has something to say and he doesn't care who gets annoyed.
(D) But what do young people here think about him and other contemporary icons?
(E) "He became a real-life Superman."

Eminem – Is He A Poet Or Bigot?

Children's Express, Belfast Telegraph, UK

Foul-mouthed pop star Eminem is poet and icon to many of Ulster's young people it emerged today. But for many others he is a gutter dwelling bigot that deserves no air play.

Various groups are up in arms because they say the music of the Brit award winner – the biggest selling male artist in the world at the minute – is anti-women and anti-gay. Eminem – real name Marshall Mathers – has sparked outrage because of his non-compromising quick-fire lyrics. His songs include a vicious attack on his own mother, whom he calls 'a drug-addicted slut'.

(1)...... And do they want to embrace them as role models?

Drew Mikhael, 17, from Belfast, believes pop stars should not be role models for young people. "Look at the girl bands today with their perfect hair, skin and push-up bras. They send out an image, which us foolish guys are attracted to. It also influences good-looking 15-year-olds to have breast implants.

"Boy bands also have a large influence on the guys as well. Deep down we want to be as attractive to the ladies. So out we go and try to look like 'Mr. Popstar of the month'. Then there's Marilyn Manson, the US performer who provides fans with a conglomeration of hard rock, heavy metal and punk music. I don't think young people are looking to Manson as a role model but instead are buying into the anti-establishment image he offers."

Mairead Duffy, 16, from Belfast, said: "I love Eminem because his music is right in your face.

(2) ...... He doesn't offend me and I don't think he's trying to offend anyone, he's just saying it how it is." Lisa Skinner, also 16, from Belfast thinks young people should be more choosy about who they decide to model themselves on. "Pop stars don't have to be role models because we have so many other role models around us, like parents, boyfriends, girlfriends or teachers. Personally, I think parents are the best role models. They can help you, comfort you, influence you, look after you and most of all they will always be there for you, no matter what."

Reeve Was Real-Life 'Superman'

China Daily, People's Republic of China

Although he will always be remembered for portraying Superman, the greatest role of actor Christopher Reeve's life was as a champion of sufferers of spinal cord injuries and an advocate of stem cell research.

Unlike the man of steel, he wasn't faster than a speeding bullet, more powerful than a locomotive and he couldn't leap tall buildings in a single bound. But the courage and determination Reeve displayed in trying to overcome his paralysis from a 1995 horse-riding accident far surpassed any of the feats of the comic book hero.

(3)...... His heroism, his courage was extraordinary," Colin Blakemore, the chief executive of Britain's Medical Research Council said. "Like many people who suffer some terrible injury, Christopher Reeve was reinvented by that experience and brought the kind of energy and enthusiasm that made him successful as a film star to an entirely different issue, with huge effect."

Reeve, 52, died on October 10, 2004, of heart failure after having treatment for an infected pressure wound without realizing his dream of walking again.

(4)...... If you think of spinal injuries you automatically conjure up a picture of Christopher Reeve," said Paul Smith, executive director of the Spinal Injuries Association in England.

LISTEN 14

A Look at the photos and answer:
1. Name five superheroes as quickly as you can.
2. What do they have in common?
3. Which comic book or cartoon character could you identify most with? Why?

B Before you listen, decide what the experts will say about these comic book characters as role models:
- Spider-man
- Wonder Woman
- Superman

Check your answers after listening.

C Listen to the audio clip. When it pauses, try to guess how Dr. Joanne Sykes will answer the presenter's question.

D Listen to the audio clip and answer the questions.
1. When was the golden age of comics?
2. What family connection did Jim have with the world of comics?
3. What values did the early superheroes have?
4. What are the two types of female superheroes?

E You decide: Are superheroes good role models? Why? / Why not? Do you think their values reflect society's values?

5 TEAMWORK

Work in pairs. A group of concerned parents is looking for role models for teenagers. Read the **Teamwork Scenario**. Discuss your role models with the class.

6 CONTROVERSY

Work in groups of four. Prepare a debate with another group. Use expressions from **Language Bank 14**. Some people say the fashion industry creates bad role models by always showing pictures of very thin models. This makes teenagers worry about not being thin enough, and some may even develop eating disorders like anorexia nervosa (being dangerously thin) or bulimia (eating too much and vomiting afterwards).

Group A: You are writers from women's and men's fashion magazines. Here are some questions you could ask:
- Not all models are thin. Don't some also come in larger sizes?
- Can't people be strong and choose not to buy the magazines or the clothes?
- Why target the fashion industry? Shouldn't this be dealt with by families and society?
- What about the teenagers in remote areas with no TV who have still developed anorexia?

Group B: You are a group of parents and doctors. Here are some questions you could ask:
- In a survey of 500 female models 75 per cent were underweight and 25 per cent could be considered anorexic. Isn't that proof?
- Magazines digitally change images to make models look thinner. Is that being responsible?
- What about the many teenagers with eating disorders who say the media was an influence?
- The average starting age is 16 for anorexia and mid-20s for bulimia. What can be done?

7 PORTFOLIO WRITING

A Write an application (180-220 words) for a new school programme to be a mentor to a younger student. Mention all your positive qualities and any experience that will help inspire someone.

B Write a satirical article (220-260 words) about 'how to be a bad role model'. Give examples showing how points that are usually 'bad' are 'good' for this role model.

8 LITERATURE in English

A Work in pairs. Choose Maya Angelou or Jack Kerouac and give a formal presentation about the image of each author.

B Discuss the authors you presented. Are they cool? Do they make literature cool?

♦ Maya Angelou

I Know Why The Caged Bird Sings (1970): Autobiographical novel. Abandoned by her parents, Maya is raised in Arkansas by her grandmother, who becomes a powerful moral figure for her. Maya experiences racism many times.

On a visit to her mother, her mother's boyfriend rapes her and is later killed by underworld friends of Maya's family. Maya feels guilty about his death.

She goes to live in San Francisco with her mother and her mother's new husband, who becomes a positive father figure. At 15, Maya fights to become the first black street car conductor. At 16, she gets pregnant, hiding it until she graduates from high school. The book ends with her confident about becoming a mother.

Biography: *Born in St. Louis in 1928, Marguerite Johnson (her real name) became a poet, historian, author, dancer, actress, playwright, civil-rights activist and English professor. She has written ten books, and many plays.*

Maya Angelou

♦ Jack Kerouac

On the Road (1950): Semi-autobiographical novel, based on Kerouac and his friends. Just out of prison, Dean Moriarty (based on Neal Cassidy) meets Sal Paradise (Jack Kerouac), a writer and the novel's narrator, in New York city. Wild and carefree, Dean is fascinated with Sal's intellectual friends like the poet, Carlo Marx (Allen Ginsberg). For three years, Dean and Sal travel across the US. Dean teaches Sal how to be free and to live life to the full. Sal and his friends introduce Dean to intellectual thought. The novel ends with Sal finding a steady relationship in New York, while Dean travels on.

Biography: *Jean-Louis Lebris de Kerouac (1922-1969) was from Massachusetts. He left university to travel and become a writer; eventually becoming the Beat Generation's most famous writer. His work has a sense of urgency and an appreciation of all things in life. He wrote 11 more books.*

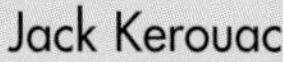

Jack Kerouac

9 FURTHER DISCUSSION

Discuss in pairs. Use the words and phrases from this unit and **Language Bank 14** to develop and justify your ideas and arguments.

A Are role models different for men and women? Is it acceptable to have a role model from the opposite sex?

B Can friends be good role models? What life lessons and values can we learn from them?

C Are people in some careers more likely to be positive role models? Give examples.

D Do role models change as we get older? Can children become role models for parents?

E How are role models affected by stereotypes?

10 *Your answer*: DO WE NEED SOMEONE TO LOOK UP TO?

Why do we want to find other people to model our lives on? Could we not learn these skills or values on our own?

Snowboard Nirvana

Luke Beuchat

This blog by an Australian snowboarder is informal in style and contains slang expressions. One of the meanings of 'crap'* is 'something useless, or rubbish'.

Ever heard of Laax Crap? Well neither had we! After all who names a resort Crap – it's a sure way to discourage snowboarders and skiers alike.

Myself and five friends, Bear, Juz, Dan, Trav and Doz, were currently in Verbier, Switzerland. We were being plagued by bad conditions. We were not surprised since Europe is gaining a reputation for poor winters and below average snowfall. This year appeared to be no different. It hadn't snowed for two weeks.

What do you do when there is no powder to be found? Simple answer: find a mountain with a good pipe and a rockin' park. But in Switzerland alone there are more resorts than there are sheep in New Zealand (well almost), so how do you find out which mountain has the best the pipe in Switzerland? Well you go to the local snowboard shop of course. This meant no limits board-riding, Verbier. So we casually strolled inside. Of course we are in Switzerland and they speak French here so to the snowboard shop guy we posed the stock question, "Parlez-vous anglais?", praying that the answer would be "Oui." He looked up from what he was doing, which was what every snowboard shop guy does – read a snowboard mag and look cool. He paused for a moment as if to tease us then quietly said, "Oui, un petit peu." (Yes, a little.) We almost cheered.

After about an hour of jibbering, much hand waving and broken English, he spurted out a name, "Laax Crap". You must be joking I thought, this guy is surely pulling our leg. But he was serious. He continued, "Laax Crap, best half pipe in Suisse." We had no other options but to take his word. We pulled out our beaten and battered road map and he pointed to Laax in the far south-east corner of Switzerland, near the Austrian border. It not only had a dodgy name, but the road there looked highly dodgy as well, with many mountain passes.

We all agreed that we were willing to give this place a go. To the tune of Tonic, Off Spring, Blink 182 and some Bon Jovi for good measure, we drove towards Laax Crap.

Before we knew it, we began seeing signs that said mountain passes closed ahead, along with signs that indicated that to cross over the mountain passes you would have to put your car on a train. This sounded like fun and it in fact turned out to be pretty cool. The Swiss, ingenious people that they are, had decided that it was simply too hard to drive over the mountain, so instead they drilled a huge hole right through the mountain. Now you simply drive onto a train, sit in your car and crack a few jokes, whilst the train takes you and your car to the other side.

Eight hours later we turned into the Laax car park and we were greeted by a huge fluorescent sign that read LAAX CRAP. At the time it was tempting to insert the word "is" on the sign. But as we had never ridden here before we all decided it was best not to judge a book by its cover, or a mountain by its entrance sign. As we drove around the car park we noticed the local bar, right opposite the main lift station. You can only guess what it was called. None other than the Crap Bar. We all made a mental note of checking it out at a later date.

1 READING

A Read through the extract and answer:

1. Why do the snowboarders decide to travel to Laax Crap?
2. What do they think of the mountain?
3. What difference does the writer see between Swiss Germans and Swiss French?

B

1. What is the appeal of snowboarding and its lifestyle?
2. Why do you think these young Australians would travel so much?

2 IDIOMS

A Match these meanings with the idioms underlined in the text:

1. to recover one's normal senses / state of mind
2. to become known for something
3. to decide to try something
4. to fool someone
5. to form an opinion about something / someone from its / his / her appearance
6. to remember something

B Complete the sentences using the idioms from 2A. Change the verb tense where necessary.

1. Why don't you .... surfing .... ? You'll like it.
2. Ron quickly .... for talking too much.
3. You're .... Nobody can hold their breath for six minutes.
4. I .... what she said in case she denied it later.
5. Hey! .... it! You almost stepped in front of that bus.
6. You can't .... He's not as mean as he looks.

* Note: The original meaning of the slang 'crap' is excrement. This very informal register should be used with care.

We stopped at the main lift station and gazed up at the nountain. We nearly fainted – the mountain was huge. At the eak, or what we thought was the peak which appeared to be million miles away, was a very distinctive restaurant and otel. We later discovered that it was called the Crap Sogn Gion and was the focal point of Laax.

We also discovered that the Crap Sogn Gion is only the alfway point of the mountain, located about 1,100 vertical netres above the base. From the Crap Sogn Gion the mountain ises another 800 metres to the mighty Vorab Glacier that ffers year-round snowboarding. Our legs felt the pain and gony of this discovery. Try riding 2,000 vertical metres in one it and you'll know what I mean when I say agony. In terms of he size of Laax – Mammoth Mountain in California is a nisnomer – it is over double the vertical of Mammoth.

Finally, as the sun began to set over this truly enormous nountain we snapped out of our disbelieving daze and realised hat we had to organise some accommodation quick smart inless we wanted to sleep in the car, which was not a comforting thought given that the outside temperature was 10 elow. After speaking to the Office of Tourism (this is always the first place to go for assistance in Europe) we realised we ad a few options. As it turned out with six Aussies the heapest option was to rent.

By this time we had discovered to our shock and horror that they don't speak French in this part of Switzerland. Rather, they speak Swiss German. A whole different culture came with the anguage change. We found that the Swiss Germans were riendlier than the Swiss French and also seemed to drink about ten times as much. We could no longer use our well-worn French phrase, "Parlez-vous anglais?" We now had to learn a German phrase "Sprechen Sie Englisch?" to which we would now pray for the answer "Ja!" rather than "Oui."

3 IN THE POWDER

Identify five snowboarding-related words or expressions in the extract.

4 PORTFOLIO WRITING

A Summarise the extract (180-200 words) from the viewpoint of one of Luke Beuchat's friends.

B Creative writing: Write about what happened (210-250 words) on the trip where you see AND THEN! and the photos in the snowboarder's blog.

5 INTERACTIVE TASK

Work in pairs. A chooses one of the comments below to start and B asks questions to find out more about the situation, then discusses it with A. You should both use all the Language Banks you have covered so far and eliciting reponses (Language Bank 20). Switch roles when you have talked about the first comment for four minutes.

> My brother is going to take a year off to go travelling before he goes to university. He doesn't have much money but he's optimistic that he can get work as he goes along.

> I've been offered a new job in another city. It's a great opportunity, a promotion in fact, but I'm not sure I want to go so far away from my family and friends.

AND THEN!

It was with great sadness that we drove past the Laax Crap sign on our way home. We had learnt many things about this awesome mountain but most importantly we had learnt the meaning of the word "crap". In German "crap" means boulder or rock. So now as we departed, instead of wanting to insert an "is" on the sign we wanted to change Crap to its English equivalent, rock, that is "Laax rocks!". We were all convinced that Laax was the best snowboard resort in all the universe.

Unit 15 Family matters

WHAT'S NEW?

Subject: Roles in the family
Function: Generalising
Language: Conditionals

The BIG question: WHAT'S A NORMAL FAMILY?

VIEWPOINT

Average number of children per family around the world

Country	Average number of children
Germany	1.3
Japan	1.4
Canada	1.6
France	1.7
South Korea	1.7
United Kingdom	1.7
India	3.1
Philippines	3.6
Paraguay	4.2
Somalia	7.3

Your basic extended family today includes your ex-husband or wife, your ex's new mate, your new mate, possibly your new mate's ex and any new mate that your new mate's ex has acquired.
Delia Ephron

? Would you like to be in a bigger or smaller family?

1 WORD POWER

A 1 Which of these terms could fit the people in the photos above ?

- single-parent family
- nuclear family
- cousin
- step-children
- extended family
- in-laws
- divorced / separated
- uncle / aunt
- adopted child
- newlyweds

2 Do any of these relationships apply to your family?

B How common are these relationships? Use the generalising phrases from **Language Bank 15** to help you.

C 1 Is there social pressure from people in your family to get married and have children?
2 Are families matriarchal, patriarchal or something else?
3 Are blood ties more important than marriage ties?

SEE WORKBOOK FOR MORE ACTIVITIES.

2 READING

A 1 Skim through the first article to find out how today's women try to balance education, work / career and family.
2 Describe how younger women might want to do things differently, and how their mothers might react to this. Use words or phrases from the article and conditionals from **Language Bank 15**.
Example: *If I have children, I will...*
If they had families and careers, they would...
If I was an older woman, I would...

B Compare the ways Australia's working mothers and Britain's divorced fathers try to solve their problems about spending more time with their children. Think about the effect of different gender roles, differences between generations and social values.

C 1 How different from their parents' lives do young people today expect their lives to be?
2 Is it fair to say that either mothers or fathers would generally make better single parents?

3 SPEAK YOUR MIND

A Who do you consider to be family? Are friends part of your family?

B If both parents work, how can they balance work, family and personal time?

C What are the childcare options? Why would women today want to stay at home with their children?

D Should fathers have the same rights as mothers concerning children? Should they get paternity leave?

'NEW WIVES' OPT FOR HOME

Dawn Gibson, The West Australian, Australia

Is the ideal of the superwoman dead? Since the 1960s, women have been told that they can have it all – high-powered career, husband and happy family. But after watching their mothers juggle these roles with varying degrees of success, Australian women at the top end of the job pool are deserting the corporate jungle and returning to the kitchen and nursery in droves.

Census data shows the number of university-educated women with partners and children who have dumped paid work more than doubled in Western Australia in the decade to 2001. The WA figures mirror a national trend, according to the Australian Bureau of Statistics. In 1991, just over 35,000 university-educated women with partners and children described themselves as outside the paid workforce. In 2001, that figure had skyrocketed to almost 70,000, reflecting a new social trend as well as the increasing number of women with degrees. And it is not just a case of women spending a few months at home after the baby is born – about half will not return to paid work until their children are at school, and a minority will become so comfortable in domestic bliss that they will never return.

According to social researcher Hugh Mackay, the trend is a reaction among young women who do not want to go down the same path as their own mothers. They had grown up with two working parents and realised they did not want to become the frazzled person their mother was.

While women in their 40s and 50s saw earning their own money as the key to independence, younger

women believed independence was all about having choice – whether that was working, staying home or a bit of both. Mr. Mackay said, "Their mothers saw themselves as revolutionaries and pioneers who made these choices possible for their daughters, but their daughters are not at all grateful. They are critical of their mothers for leading absurdly stressful lives and do not see that as liberation."

FIGHT FOR FATHERS' RIGHTS

Rana Foroohar, Newsweek, USA

A militant new movement is sweeping Britain, generating headlines and sparking protests. In one protest, a young man dressed as Spider-man dangled himself from a crane near London Bridge, holding up construction for six days. This July a handful of protesters dressed as vicars, nuns and monks stormed a Sunday service in York Minster. Not even Prime Minister Tony Blair has been able to avoid the onslaught: the P.M. was pelted with purple powder during a speech in the House of Commons. Is this a return of the poll-tax protesters? Rabid animal-rights activists? No – it's the Angry Dads.

British fathers are increasingly fed up with a system that they see as favoring mothers during custody battles. In 80 percent of the cases, children end up living with their mothers after divorce; British law frowns upon shared parenting, citing the confusion that dual residences can cause a child. And while most cases are settled out of court – allowing parents to arrange their own solutions – British courts have little leeway to penalize parents who do try to thwart visits in contentious cases. The reason is that a judge's only recourse in such circumstances is to fine the mother or throw her in jail, which is rarely if ever in the child's interest.

"We just want to see our kids," says Matthew O'Connor, founder of Fathers4Justice, a new lobbying group that boasts 10,000 members. Interest in the fathers' rights movement is catching on, too: Fathers4Justice now has offshoots in 33 countries, other activist groups are copying its tactics and high-profile divorced dads like rock impresario Bob Geldof are calling for the government to take more aggressive action. Until it does, expect to see more of Spider-Dad.

4 LISTEN 15

Teenage mother Courtney Cassidy and her three children

A Look at the photo and answer the questions.

1. What is the best age to have children?
2. What difficulties do teenage parents experience?
3. What effect would being young parents have on children?
4. What can be done to prevent teenage pregnancy?

B Listen to the audio clip about single mother Courtney Cassidy and complete the sentences.

> Courtney has been attracting a lot of attention from the (1) .... The reason is that she has had (2) ...... children from (3) .... different fathers. She (4) .... to have her first child at the age of 14. Courtney thought she could manage because her (5) .... had done this already. She believes that she can care for her children as well as (6) ...... women. She was (7) ...... when she had her third child with her current partner. About the future, she thinks that she will still be able to have a (8) .... when she is older.

C You decide: Should teenage pregnancy be seen as a problem? In the past, many girls were married and pregnant by 14. Why do we find it so shocking or unusual today?

5 TEAMWORK

Work in pairs. Read the **Teamwork Scenario**. Show your network diagram to your partner, give some information about the people on it and explain your relationship with them. Explain how you feel your generation is different from or like previous generations by using examples from your family, including values and attitudes to politics, work, family bonds, marriage, sex / sexuality, social issues and religion.

6 CONTROVERSY

Work in groups of four. Prepare a debate with another group. Use expressions from **Language Bank 15**.

In past decades, it has become common for childless couples in developed countries to adopt children from developing countries. A television channel has arranged a special debate on the issue.

Group A: You are politicians from developing countries.
Some points you may wish to mention:

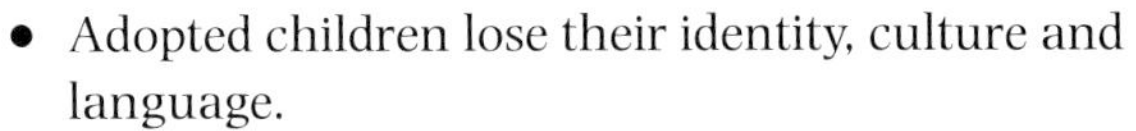

- Adopted children lose their identity, culture and language.
- How is this different from buying babies?
- Would British people approve of so many British children being adopted by foreign parents?
- Loss of adopted child's contribution to their home country

Group B: You are a British support group for adoptive parents. Some points you could mention:

- Higher standard of living in Britain
- Prospective parents checked by authorities in both countries
- Adoption waiting list too long in the UK
- These children may not be adopted otherwise.

7 PORTFOLIO WRITING

A Write a magazine article (220-260 words) about how families have changed over the last 30 years.

B Write a letter or email (180-220 words) to a friend describing the wedding of someone you both know.

8 HOME ECONOMICS *in English*

A Work in pairs. You both give a formal presentation comparing how this family and yours manage a household. Give examples of differences or similarities in planning schedules and allocating tasks and the time spent on them, as well as the balance of leisure time with the demands of household tasks, school and work.

B After the presentations, discuss the physical, emotional and financial demands of family life, and any differences between large and small families.

Reg and Catherine from Quebec are the proud parents of 10 children: Kristy (17), Sandy (16), Chloë (15), Margo (13), Phil (11), James (9), Rachel (7), Colin (4), Holly (2) and Cynthia (1). Five of the children have home schooling. Reg works in the evenings so he can help around the house during the day. Household jobs are on a rota that changes every week.

WHO DOES WHAT?

Parents
Childcare, cooking, washing, cleaning, home schooling, work outside house.

Children
Setting / clearing the table, loading the dishwasher, cleaning, home schooling, leisure activities.

LEISURE

Children have the afternoon and evening free for activities like playing the piano, sewing, drawing, playing basketball or video games. Parents have some free time in the evening.

FOOD

Food is homemade for freshness, flavour and economy.
Pizza for lunch: Ingredients: 1.4 kg flour, yeast, 600 gr cheese, 1 litre homemade tomato sauce, 500 gr pepperoni.
Evening meal: 2 loaves of homemade bread, 2.5 litres of homemade soup.

AN AVERAGE WEEKDAY

Morning
6.00 Sandy gets up and goes to school.
8.30 Reg and Catherine make breakfast – Reg feeds the youngest. The children do jobs like clearing the table.
9pm Home school starts. Reg and Catherine also look after the younger ones.
12.30 The family's main meal is at lunchtime. Same jobs as at breakfast.

Afternoon and evening
1.30 Reg goes to work.
4.30 Evening meal. Same jobs as for breakfast. Sandy clears up after the younger ones.
5pm The family watches a video; some of the older children chat online.
8.30 Children's bedtime. Catherine runs a chat group for large families on the internet.
10.40 Reg gets home from work.
11.30 Parents go to bed.

9 FURTHER DISCUSSION

Discuss in pairs. Use the words and phrases from this unit and **Language Bank 15**, taking turns to develop and justify your ideas and arguments.

A Who does the housework in your family? What are your jobs? Have they changed over the years?

B What role do grandparents and members of your extended family have in your family?

C How hard is it to be a parent today? Should parents be trained in parenting?

D In some countries, marriages are arranged by parents. What do you think of this?

10 *Your answer*: WHAT'S A NORMAL FAMILY?

Is any family ever normal? What makes your family special or unique? What does family mean to you?

Unit 16 Let's change the subject!

WHAT'S NEW?

Subject: School curriculum
Function: Asserting
Language: Signposting phrases: Sequencing

The BIG question: ARE STUDENTS LEARNING THE RIGHT THINGS?

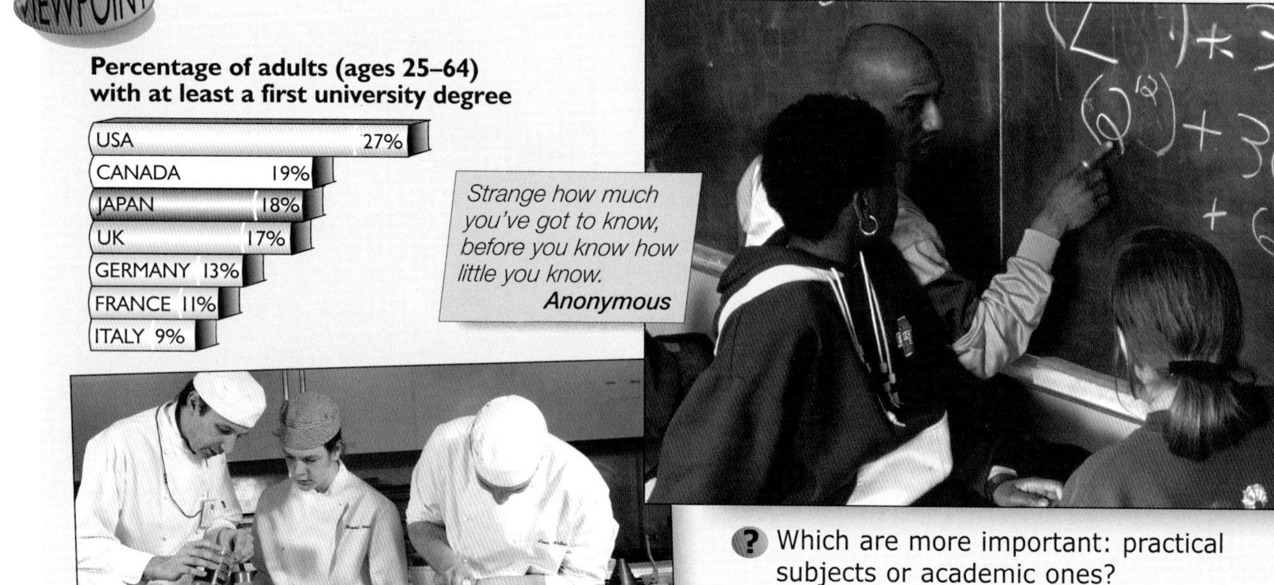

? Which are more important: practical subjects or academic ones?

1 WORD POWER

A When teachers are planning a curriculum they have to take many factors into account. Rank the factors below in order of importance, using the signposting phrases in **Language Bank 16**.

- adolescent psychology
- standardised testing
- subject matter
- student needs
- government policy
- allocating the budget
- books and equipment

B Explain how a school would need to adapt for these people and situations. Use the asserting expressions in **Language Bank 16** to help you.

1. A dyslexic student
2. A newly arrived immigrant student
3. A pregnant student
4. A new teacher
5. Budget cuts

C
1. Should the school year be longer? Why / Why not?
2. Should sex education be taught in schools?
3. Should students take subjects such as ancient Greek and Latin, or religious studies?

SEE WORKBOOK FOR MORE ACTIVITIES.

2 READING

A Find the words in the first article for these definitions:

1. radical change of appearance or nature *n.*
2. re-establishing friendly relations between people *n.*
3. accepting others into a group *adj.*
4. to influence or control in a negative way *v.*
5. not paying attention to *adj.*

B
1. In the first article which metaphor does the minister use to describe the past situation in South Africa? Why do you think it is used?
2. In the second article is the view of UK education positive or negative? Explain your answer.
3. Which factors from **Word Power** were taken into consideration in South Africa for planning a curriculum? Which were the factors for the UK??

C
1. Why does it matter who writes school textbooks?
2. Do you think your education system is better or worse than the UK's?

3 SPEAK YOUR MIND

A. What are your favourite school subjects? What are the best and worst things about school?

B. Is it a good idea that non-academic students have specialised training for jobs?

C. Do schools often have budget problems? If money is short, which courses are cut most often?

D. Why would someone want to change the way history is written in textbooks?

TEARFUL ASMAL HAILS NEW HISTORY OF SOUTH AFRICA

A'yesha Kassiem, Daily News, South Africa

The Department of Education celebrated 10 years of the transformation of education with the launch of a high school history book series aimed at creating an African view of the country's past.

The series, *Turning Points*, was initiated by the Institute for Justice and Reconciliation as part of its Reconciliation and Social Reconstruction Programme. High schools nationwide will each receive eight volumes, written by South African scholars.

At the launch in Cape Town, Education Minister Kader Asmal said: "We inherited an education system from apartheid that caused serious damage.

"The Bantu education system was a system that disabled our people, denying them the opportunity to be part of society. But we are starting to build a truly South African system that will enable us to teach the truth about our history. For so long, the facts were deviously manipulated and we need to look at the kind of memory we are building for our children. We need to build an inclusive memory where the heroes and heroines of the past belong not only to certain sectors, but to us all. Memory is identity and we cannot have a divided identity."

Asmal fought back tears as he spoke, saying he was proud of the country's youth — some of whom performed at the event — who were the "fruits of our freedom".

Extracts from the books by people who had lived under the Bantu education system were read out, recalling the inequalities of the apartheid regime.

"In the (African) past, the hunter or the victor has always written our history — a history that served the hunter's interest. But now we want to hear the lion's story. Let Africa write its own history, because our future is an African future. And then, from our own history we will work out our own understanding of what it means to be African," he said.

Nobel Laureate Nadine Gordimer, also present at the event, echoed Asmal's words and reiterated the importance of "unmasking the other side of history". "But we need a truly literate society. Literacy is a basic human right," she said.

Series co-ordinator Fanie du Toit said: "The books are about reclaiming our heritage and acknowledging the often neglected voices of our past. Keeping the memory alive will help us in shaping the future."

CALL FOR 'FAIRER' SCHOOLS SYSTEM

BBC News, UK

A "genuine comprehensive system" is needed to improve pupils' school performances, the leader of Britain's biggest teachers' union argues.

Doug McAvoy, general secretary of the National Union of Teachers, claimed specialist schools — favoured by the government in England — "work against the diversity of all our young people". He proposed Finland, which has reduced its level of pupil selection, as an example for the UK to follow.

Mr McAvoy's comments come after the international PISA study of educational achievement found Finnish children had the highest level of literacy in the world. In Britain, 25% of children leave primary school unable to read, write and count well. Half leaving secondary school in England have fewer than five good GCSEs.

Mr McAvoy told a London conference to discuss the PISA findings: "Finnish schools have a high degree of autonomy in teaching and in the curriculum. Finnish teachers have more say than their colleagues in other countries in determining course content, establishing student assessment policies, deciding which courses the school should offer and allocating budgets."

But the government is defending its push towards more specialist schools, which offer more teaching in specific subjects such as science or languages. The School Standards Minister, David Milliband, argued at the conference that specialism encouraged excellence and raised general standards. Mr Milliband accepted that PISA had shown England had one of the "most unequal education systems in the industrialised world".

"Far too many children who have the brains and skills and potential to succeed are not given the opportunities to fulfil that potential," he said. "What is more, they are not any old children, they are those least likely to have a home background that makes up for poor schooling. They are born into disadvantage and then condemned to it."

4 LISTEN

A Look at the pictures and answer:

1. How do students learn about different religions?
2. Many countries have laws that separate the church and the state. Why?
3. How were the world and people created?

B Listen to the audio clip and choose the best answer.

1. What is science teacher Julie Bias worried about?
   A The teaching of creationism in science class.
   B The lack of teaching time for different units.
   C The budget for the science program.
2. What does local resident Al Scott believe?
   A Evolution is a philosophy.
   B Humans are descended from primates.
   C Humans originate from inorganic matter.
3. What does the school superintendent think?
   A Evolution should be part of the curriculum.
   B Creationism should also be taught in class.
   C He wants to take evolution out of class.
4. What does Skip Evans suggest about creationists?
   A They are making reasonable arguments.
   B They want to end science teaching.
   C They are dishonest in their tactics.

C You decide: What role should religion have in state education? Should creationism be taught in science classes? Who should decide whether controversial subjects are taught: governments, communities, teachers, parents or someone else?

5 TEAMWORK

Work in pairs. Read the **Teamwork Scenario** and think about how the school subjects you study can be useful later in everyday life. Share your ideas with another pair.

6 CONTROVERSY

Work in groups of four. Prepare a debate with another group. Use expressions from **Language Bank 16**.

Girls-only and boys-only schools have become more popular again in the UK. At an international conference on education there is to be a debate about single-sex schools.

Group A

You are teachers and parents for single-sex schools. Some points you may wish to mention:

- Fewer distractions, more time for learning
- Less gender-stereotyping; girls take more science, boys take more arts subjects
- Co-educational curriculum is often gender-biased against girls
- Less chance of inappropriate behaviour between boys and girls

Group B

You are teachers and parent for co-educational schools. Some points you may wish to mention:

- School is also about learning to socialise.
- Some studies show school results / marks do not improve with the change to single-sex schools.
- No chance to find out about the other gender's views
- Both genders less prepared for dealing with the other

7 PORTFOLIO WRITING

A Write a letter (180-210 words) to your country's education minister about how the education system could be improved. Make general comments or focus on one area that you think needs to be changed.

B Creative writing: Imagine you are an exchange student going to study in another country, such as Canada, Australia or South Africa. Write a letter to a friend saying what you think it will be like (180-210 words).

8 PHYSICAL EDUCATION *in English*

A Work in pairs. Some educational activities give students a chance to learn through experience. Each student gives a formal presentation on one of these courses, explaining what you can learn from outdoor sports and activities. Use any information you know about these kind of courses and phrases from **Language Bank 16**.

B After the presentations, discuss how useful these courses would be for students.

OUTWARD BOUND COURSES

- Started 1941 in Wales by Kurt Hahn
- Now in over 30 countries
- Hands-on learning in the wilderness
- Adventure trips of 5 to 72 days
- Students age 11+

Teaches:

- Survival and outdoor skills
- Self-confidence, problem-solving, leadership, teamwork
- Sailing, kayaking, hill walking, climbing, mountain biking

TALL SHIP *DANMARK* – MARITIME SCHOOL

- 80 cadets (co-educational male and female)
- Five months at sea, hands-on apprenticeship
- Cadets must be 16+, physically fit, good swimmers, not afraid of heights, not colour blind
- Must have passed school-leaving exam

Teaches:

- Sailing skills (ropes, sails, maintenance)
- Navigation and weather conditions
- Physical fitness
- How to take and give orders
- Self-confidence, leadership and teamwork

9 FURTHER DISCUSSION

Discuss in pairs. Use words and phrases from this unit and **Language Bank 16**, taking turns to develop and justify your ideas and arguments.

A Is it important to learn about literature? How can knowing about it help you?

B If people plan to specialise in science, arts or another subject, why should they take other subjects?

C What are tests and exams for? Are they fair? What factors affect testing?

D Is education a life-long activity? Do you see yourself learning for the rest of your life?

10 *Your answer*: ARE STUDENTS LEARNING THE RIGHT THINGS?

Are you happy with what you've learned? Would you change anything?
Are there any courses really worth studying?

Adventures in science

WHAT'S NEW?

Subject: Scientific developments
Function: Developing an argument
Language: Expressions used to introduce assertions

The BIG question: IS SCIENCE MAKING LIFE BETTER?

VIEWPOINT

- History of the universe:
  Big Bang, 13-14 billion years ago
  Origin of the Earth, 4.55 billion years ago
  First humans, 100-120,000 years ago

If it squirms, it's biology;
if it stinks, it's chemistry;
if it doesn't work, it's physics
and if you can't understand it,
it's mathematics.
Magnus Pyke

? What do you think of these ideas about science?

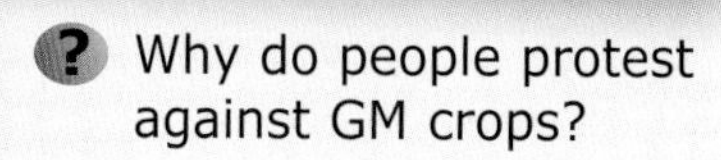

? Why do people protest against GM crops?

? What is molecule-sized nanotechnology? What could it be used for?

1 WORD POWER

A 1 Match the scientific field with the scientific development.

1 genetics	a machine that recognises human faces
2 superconductors	b magnetic levitation trains
3 alternative energy	c mapping the human genome (DNA)
4 AI / robotics	d artificial limbs for disabled people
5 bionics	e hydrogen fuel cells

2 Choose three developments. Use **Language Bank 17** to make assertions about why they are important.
3 How might these developments affect your life?

B Develop an argument about each of these using **Language Bank 17.**
1 People could grow new spinal nerves with stem cells.
2 The long-term health effects of eating genetically modified food are not known.
3 Applied science / engineering is more practical than pure science.
Example: *By extension, we can surmise that engineers are more important to our everyday lives. From here we can conclude that more government money should be spent on engineering.*

C 1 How can mapping the human genome (DNA) help us?
2 Which influences our development more – nature or nurture?

SEE WORKBOOK FOR MORE ACTIVITIES.

2 READING

A Which statements refer to HAL 3, spider-goats, to both or neither?
1 It was designed to mimic real organisms.
2 It was produced by a company.
3 It is a combination of machine and organism.
4 It will eventually help police.

B Imagine you are the inventor of HAL 3 giving a radio interview. Describe how it works while walking upstairs.

C 1 In what other ways might HAL be used?
2 Was it right to create spider-silk producing goats?

3 SPEAK YOUR MIND

A How does science help or harm us?

B In your opinion what have been the ten most important scientific discoveries?

C Who should decide ethical issues in science or medicine: the public, the government, experts or corporations? Why?

D Should companies be allowed to patent everything (new species like spider-goats, cures for diseases) for profit? How long should patents exist, a few years or forever?

BIONIC SUIT OFFERS WEARER SUPER STRENGTH

John Boyd, New Scientist, UK

A robot suit has been developed that could help older people or those with disabilities to walk or lift heavy objects. Dubbed HAL, or hybrid assistive limb, the latest versions of the suit were unveiled at the World Expo in Aichi, Japan. HAL is the result of 10 years' work by Yoshiyuki Sankai of the University of Tsukuba in Japan, and integrates mechanics, electronics, bionics and robotics in a new field known as cybernics. The most fully developed prototype, HAL 3, is a motor-driven metal 'exoskeleton' that you strap onto your legs to power-assist leg movements. A backpack holds a computer with a wireless network connection, and the batteries are on a belt.

Two control systems interact to help the wearer stand, walk and climb stairs. A 'bio-cybernic' system uses bioelectric sensors attached to the skin on the legs to monitor signals transmitted from the brain to the muscles. It can do this because when someone intends to stand or walk, the nerve signal to the muscles generates a detectable electric current on the skin's surface. These currents are picked up by the sensors and sent to the computer, which translates the nerve signals into signals of its own for controlling electric motors at the hips and knees of the exoskeleton. It takes a fraction of a second for the motors to respond accordingly, and in fact they respond fractionally faster to the original signal from the brain than the wearer's muscles do.

The HAL 4 and HAL 5 prototypes, don't just help a person to walk. They have an upper part to assist the arms, and will help a person lift up to 40 kilograms more than they can manage unaided. The new HALs will also eliminate the need for a backpack. Instead, the computer and wireless connection have been shrunk to fit in a pouch attached to the suit's belt. HAL 5 also has smaller motor housings, making the suit much less bulky around the hips and knees.

HAL 3 weighs 22 kilograms, but the help it gives the user is more than enough to compensate for this. "It's like riding on a robot, rather than wearing one," says Sankai. He adds that HAL 4 will weigh 17 kilograms, and he hopes HAL 5 may be lighter still.

'SPIDER-GOATS' START WORK ON WONDER WEB

Roger Highfield, The Daily Telegraph, UK

A herd of goats containing spider genes is about to be milked for the ingredients of spider silk to mass-produce one of nature's most sought-after materials. Scientists have for the first time spun synthetic spider silk fibres with properties approaching the real thing, paving the way for their use in artificial tendons, medical sutures, biodegradable fishing lines, soft body armour and a host of other applications.

Webster and Peter, genetically altered goats unveiled by the Canadian company Nexia, are the founders of a GM herd whose offspring will produce spider silk protein in their milk that can be collected, purified and spun into the fibres. Females will begin mass-producing spider milk for a variety of military and industrial uses.

A spider-goat

Spider silk has long been admired by material scientists for its unique combination of toughness, lightness and biodegradability. Dragline silk, which comprises the radiating spokes of a spider web, is stronger than the synthetic fibre Kevlar, stretches better than nylon and, weight for weight, is five times stronger than steel.

These incredible qualities are the product of 400 million years of evolution. Dr Jeffrey Turner, President of Nexia, said: "Mimicking spider silk properties has been the holy grail of material science and now we've been able to make useful fibres. It's incredible that a tiny animal found literally in your backyard can create such an amazing material by using only amino acids, the same building blocks used to make skin and hair."

4 WATCH AND LISTEN 

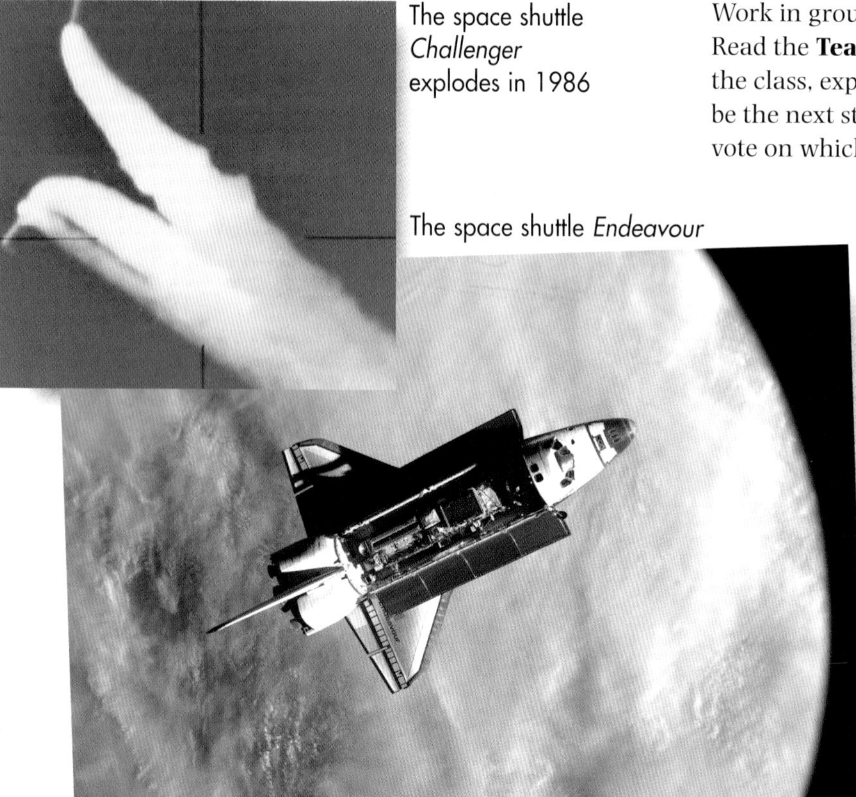

The space shuttle *Challenger* explodes in 1986

The space shuttle *Endeavour*

A Look at the photos and answer:
1 Why do humans want to explore space?
2 What can we learn from space exploration?
3 What successes and failures have there been so far?
4 How safe is space exploration?

B Before you watch, decide how the following relate to space debris:
- Satellites
- Fuel tanks
- Astronauts

Check your answers after watching.

C Watch the video clip and make notes to answer these questions.
1 How many large space objects (10 cm or larger) does ESA know of?
2 How many explosions have happened in space?
3 What happened to the solid aluminium block?

D At the end, Heiner Klinkrad discusses the consequences of space debris. Imagine he continues to discuss the effects on space programmes. What would he say?

E You decide: Space exploration is very expensive. Should we clean up the space debris before we explore space further? How would an end to space programmes affect life on Earth?

5 TEAMWORK

Work in groups of three. Imagine you are futurologists. Read the **Teamwork Scenario**. Share your ideas with the class, explaining why you think your devices might be the next state-of-the-art applications. The class can vote on which device will be the most successful.

6 CONTROVERSY

Work in groups of four. Prepare a debate with another group. Use expressions from **Language Bank 17**.

A company is trying to get approval to begin cloning human tissue and eventually even humans. Imagine the government has set up a public debate between the company and critics of human cloning.

Group A: You represent the company that wishes to begin cloning human tissue and eventually humans. Here are some questions you could ask.
- Cloned tissue could supply new organs for transplants. Don't you want to help patients in need?
- Couldn't cloning lead to cures for neural diseases and spinal cord injuries?
- Isn't cloning embryonic stem cells really about giving life, not taking it?

Group B: You are a group of scientists, politicians and religious leaders against cloning humans in any form. Some questions you could ask.
- Dolly the sheep was created after 276 failed attempts. Is this a way to treat a life?
- Don't clones have health problems? Dolly died young of a disease usually found in old sheep.
- Do clones have a soul? Are we playing God?

7 PORTFOLIO WRITING

A Write a report (220-260 words) for the government on the use of uranium (for example, in nuclear power), chlorine (water purification) or nitrogen (fertilisers). Discuss their main uses and drawbacks.

B Choose two scientific developments that you think will happen in your lifetime and write about them (220-260 words). Which aspect of life will they affect: everyday life, health, industry, or something else? Will it be something that would benefit a lot of people or a special group?

8 ENGINEERING *in English*

A Work in pairs. Each student gives a formal presentation on two engineering developments. Think about these points:

1. Are these developments at nano-, micro-, or macro-size?
2. Which area(s) of science (biology, chemistry, physics) are they in?
3. Why are these developments important now or in the future?

B After the presentations, ask questions about the presentation and discuss which scientific developments today would have seemed like science fiction fifty years ago?

Nanobots
Scientists have designed but not yet made a swimming robot 3 micrometres long that could in future deliver drugs in blood streams or unclog arteries. This model is still too big, and smaller ones need to be developed.

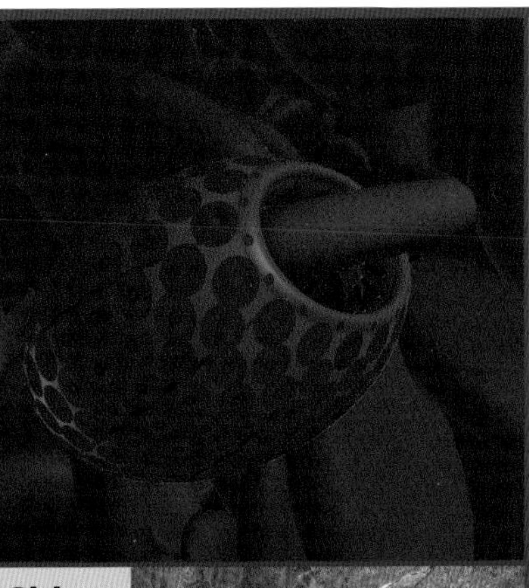

Biometric scanners
Iris, retina, fingerprint, voice or face recognition technology and DNA sampling can make individual identification absolutely certain. However, cloning of identical humans could also make biometrics useless.

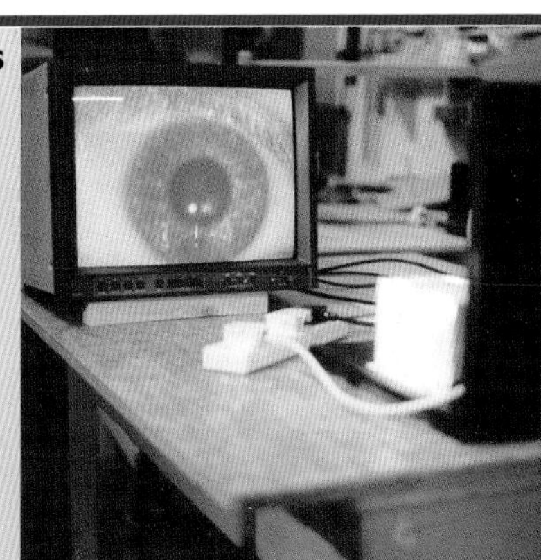

Three Gorges Dam, China
The world's largest hydroelectric dam is estimated to produce as much a ninth of China's power. The lake behind the dam displaced over a million people. The submerged, rotting vegetation in the lake produces large amounts of methane, a greenhouse gas twenty times as damaging as CO^2.

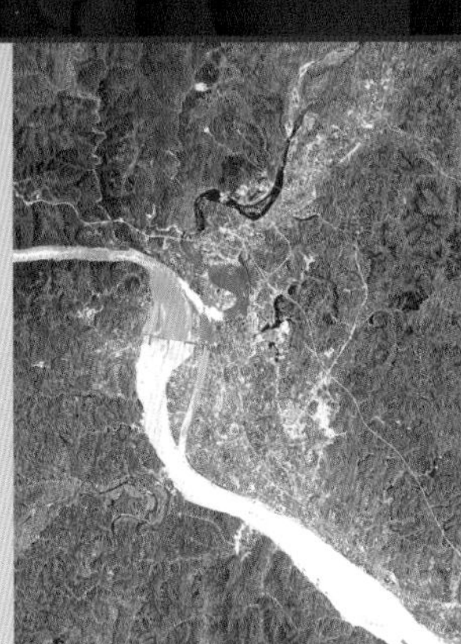

Microwave gun
Microwave guns can ignite fuel vapours, damage electronics and cause intense burning of skin for non-lethal crowd control. It's still uncertain whether these can be used safely on humans. Experts worry that these would make dangerous weapons in terrorist hands.

9 FURTHER DISCUSSION

Discuss in pairs. Use the words and phrases from this unit and **Language Bank 7**, taking turns to develop and justify your ideas and arguments.

A Name some different fields of engineering. What kinds of work do these engineers do? How is engineering similar to and different from science? Would you want to be an engineer?

B We know that primates can communicate and show empathy, so what separates humans from animals? What can studying animals tell us about ourselves?

C What is forensic science? How does it incorporate other fields of science? Give examples.

D How much do you know about how ordinary household things work? Name five products (for example, washing-up liquid, hairdryer). How are they made? Is it important to understand the science behind everyday things? Why / Why not?

10 *Your answer*: IS SCIENCE MAKING LIFE BETTER?

Are scientists working on the right areas? Why / Why not? If you could change anything about current research, what would it be?

The company we keep

WHAT'S NEW?

Subject: Social issues
Function: Summarising information, ideas and arguments
Language: Expressions used to contradict

The BIG question: ARE WE DOING ENOUGH TO HELP?

- In 2005 the UN helped over 19 million refugees and asylum seekers.
- In 2004-5 there were 10.8 million crimes in England and Wales.

Poverty is the parent of revolution and crime.
Aristotle

If I could get my membership fee back, I'd resign from the human race.
Fred Allen

? Who should help refugees?

? Should illegal immigrants be sent home?

1 WORD POWER

A Rank these social issues from 1 to 8 in order of importance. Are these social problems or individual problems?

- healthcare reform
- illegal immigration
- vandalism
- homelessness
- violent crime
- job creation
- substance abuse
- social integration

B How well does your country deal with these issues? Using **Language Bank 18**, summarise any approaches to these issues that you approve of and contradict other students who approve of approaches that you don't agree with.

C
1 Is two-tiered healthcare for those who can and can't afford to pay a good or bad idea? Why?
2 Should the government pay for drug rehabilitation centres? Why / Why not?
3 Is intolerance towards foreigners a problem in your country?

SEE WORKBOOK FOR MORE ACTIVITIES.

2 READING

A Match these headings to the paragraphs a-e in the first article.
1 Official rejection of estimates
2 Number-crunching
3 A house, but no home
4 The hidden masses
5 Solvable problems

B
1 In what sense are the homeless people in the first article hidden? In what sense are they homeless?
2 What do you think *rough sleepers* are?
3 What do the following verbs mean as used in the second article: *see, stem, face?*

C
1 You are a TV journalist. Use reported speech to tell the story of one of the hidden homeless.
2 Imagine a conversation between Graeme Martin and one of the hidden homeless.

D
1 What would life be like without a home?
2 How long should patients in pain have to wait for treatment?

3 SPEAK YOUR MIND

A Whose responsibility should it be to help solve social problems: individuals, charities, governments, big business?

B Are homeless people unfortunate, an annoyance, a part of life, or something else?

C Is healthcare a universal right? What do you think about the pay healthcare workers receive?

380,000 HOMELESS 'GOING UNRECORDED'

John Carvel, The Guardian, UK

a The housing shortage in Britain means that some 380,000 single people are effectively homeless without being officially classified as such, the charity Crisis said today. It said the 'hidden homeless' were sleeping on friends' floors, in squats or in hostels because they had no homes of their own. Unlike rough sleepers, the hidden homeless were not systematically counted by the authorities and rarely registered in the housing policy debate.

Family in bed-and-breakfast accommodation

b Crisis said: "Many are struggling with problems such as unemployment, family breakdown, mental ill-health and substance abuse. With the right support they could overcome these, but all too often they are left to cope alone. In an era of official audits on everything from health and poverty and recycling, it seems scandalous that there are no official figures for the number of hidden homeless people living in Britain today."

c Crisis said its estimate excluded families with dependents, as they had a statutory right to rehousing. It included about 75,000 single people in bed and breakfast accommodation or hostels; 10,000 squatters; up to 220,000 sharing overcrowded accommodation with family or friends, and up to 70,000 living on sufferance in a home where the head of the household would prefer them not to be there. Adding those at imminent risk of eviction brought the total to 380,000.

d The charity estimated the problem of hidden homelessness could cost Britain about £1.4bn. About half of this was due to the costs of housing benefit and charges for accommodation met by the state. The rest was due to lost income and taxes from people whose lack of a home made it harder to hold down a job. The charity called for an official census of hidden homelessness, using household surveys to establish its causes.

e The Office of the Deputy Prime Minister said the government did not accept the charity's figures. It had found that there were 97,290 homeless households living in temporary accommodation. "There may be wider groups of people who experience homelessness at some point in their lives but who do not turn to local authorities for help – possibly because they do not think of themselves as being homeless or inadequately housed," it said.

EX-SOLDIER TOLD OF 70-WEEK WAIT TO SEE NEUROLOGIST

The Scotsman, UK

A disabled former soldier has been told he faces waiting more than 70 weeks to see a consultant neurologist at Edinburgh's Western General Hospital. Graeme Martin thought there had been a typing error on the letter he received from the hospital in the summer of 2004, telling him he would be seen in October 2005.

Mr Martin, 43, from Duns, in the Borders, uses two types of morphine and diazepam to control chronic pain from a prolapsed lumbar disc and sciatica. He needs sticks to get around and his condition is worsening.

The former Royal Engineers corporal, with 16 years' military service, was forced to give up his job as a postman two years ago. He believes his medical problems stem from an accident during his time in the Army when he was crushed between two military vehicles.

Two years ago, patients being referred to the Western for neurosurgical treatment were having to wait up to 46 weeks for a first appointment. But now the gap between Mr Martin receiving notification of his appointment and the actual date he will be seen is 73 weeks.

Health minister Malcolm Chisholm said the wait faced by Mr Martin was 'utterly unacceptable'. But he said the Scottish Executive was taking action to cut outpatient waiting times.

Patients in a hospital waiting room

4 LISTEN 18

Life in the Favela by Massenzi

A Look at the picture and answer:
1. What causes ghettos / slums / shanty towns?
2. What is life like in these places?
3. Will these places always exist? Why / Why not?

B Before your listen, decide which of the following might be true about the people in Rio de Janeiro's *favelas*:
- They have lots of recreation areas.
- They have good employment opportunities.
- They have computer education programmes.
- They use the internet.

Check your answers after listening.

C Listen to the audio clip and complete these sentences (maximum three words).
1. ...... live in the *favelas*.
2. Eloise Fajeda makes a living by filming ....
3. The Committee to Democratise IT has trained approximately ....
4. The program is now also in .... and Chile.

D At the end of the audio clip, try to imagine what a former drug dealer might say after attending the programme.

E You decide: Will the computer training programme be enough to change life in the *favelas*? What else can be done? What can this example teach us about resolving social issues?

5 TEAMWORK

Work in groups of three. Read the **Teamwork Scenario**. Decide which would be the best suggestions for bringing new work opportunities to your community. The class discusses how effective each suggestion would be and votes on the three best solutions.

6 CONTROVERSY

In 2001 the Norwegian ship *Tampa* rescued 438 Afghan refugees when their boat sank. The Australian navy stopped them landing in Australia.

Work in groups of four. Prepare a debate with another group. Use expressions from **Language Bank 18**. Most countries now have very strict controls to limit legal and illegal immigration.

Group A: You are a group who favour repealing these strict laws. Some points you could mention:
- Birth rate – Western countries need immigration to maintain the population and economy.
- Immigrants are needed to fill jobs that local people can't or won't fill.
- Inherent racism limits the employment opportunities of many immigrants.
- Many immigrants are highly educated and eager to start a new life contributing to their new society.

Group B: You are a group who are against further immigration and want to keep the laws. Some points you may wish to mention:
- Many immigrants do not assimilate easily.
- Some immigrants abuse the welfare system.
- Immigrants could take jobs away from locals.
- Some immigrants' educational level does not meet the new country's standards.

7 PORTFOLIO WRITING

A Write a report (220-260 words) for the government on the level of crime in your community. Include information about common types of crime and suggestions for the police force on reducing crime.

B Write an email or letter (180-220 words) to a local politician to complain about your situation and the state of healthcare.

8 SOCIAL STUDIES *in English*

A Work in pairs. Each student gives a formal presentation on one of the cities. Use the information to explain how each city has developed. Use phrases from **Language Bank 18.**

B After the presentations, ask questions and discuss how community development is affected by ethnicity, poverty and environment. Are there geographical / class / ethnic divisions in your community?

	Chicago, USA	Stockholm, Sweden
Population	Chicago city: 2.9 million Greater Chicago: 9.2 million	Stockholm city: 760,000 Greater Stockholm: 1.8 million
Social history	1940-70: Immigration of blacks from South. Many whites moved out to expensive suburbs. Less integration since 1970s.	1950-1990: Immigration from Finland, ex-Yugoslavia and the Middle East to less expensive outer suburbs.
People per car	1.39	2.78
Public transport	1,472,000 passengers per day	650,000 passengers per day
Blue, green & grey	3% Water, 8% Parks, 89% Developed	13% Water, 34% Parks, 53% Developed
Affluent area	Highland Park (northern suburb)	Östermalm (near the centre)
Ethnicity ratios	Blacks 2%; whites 91%	Swedes 85%; 15% non-Swedes
Average income	$55,000	$43,290
Average house price	$380,000	$372,475
Population density	980 people/km^2	14,311 people/km^2
Violent crimes (2002)	19	969
Less affluent area	Englewood (central Chicago)	Fittja (southern suburb)
Ethnicity ratios	Blacks 98%; less than 1% whites	Swedes 34%; non-Swedes 66%
Average income	$6,000	$12,625
Average house price	$110,000	$228,462
Population density	4,743 people/km^2	372 people/km^2
Violent crimes	4,091	1,152

9 FURTHER DISCUSSION

Discuss in pairs. Use the words and phrases from this unit and **Language Bank 18** to summarise and contradict arguments.

A Which social issues are important politically in your country? Why are they important? What solutions do different political parties have for these problems?

B What are the major crime problems in your area? What are the causes of crime? Are crime and poverty connected? How should the governments tackle crime?

C How do you travel around your community? Is traffic ever a problem? How should city planners deal with transport?

D Are there many recent immigrants in the place you live? How do people react towards them? Do they benefit society? Do they integrate with the majority of society?

E Is affordable housing a right? What does your government do to help people get housing? Is there enough affordable housing in your community?

10 *Your answer*: ARE WE DOING ENOUGH TO HELP?

What more could we do? Can we fix all social problems? Can we solve social problems without doing something about poverty?

Stressed out!

WHAT'S NEW?

Subject: Stress management
Function: Calming
Language: Language of empathy and sympathy

The BIG question: ARE WE SERIOUSLY STRESSED?

VIEWPOINT

? Is stress good or bad?

- High-stress teens are twice as likely to smoke, drink, get drunk and use illegal drugs as low-stress teens.
- One in eight teenagers experience some form of depression. Girls are twice as likely to experience it.

Stress is an ignorant state. It believes everything is an emergency. Nothing is that important.
Natalie Goldberg

I have a new philosophy. I'm only going to dread one day at a time.
Charles Schulz

1 WORD POWER

A 1 What is happening in the cartoons in **Viewpoint**? Describe how someone would feel in each situation.
2 Role play in pairs. Try to help the person feeling stressed in each cartoon by using expressions for sympathy, empathy and calming in **Language Bank 19**.
3 What other situations might be stressful? Give at least three examples.

B Which of the following do you think would relieve stress? Do you know of any other ways of relieving stress?

- watching your diet
- drinking less coffee
- switching off from your job / studies
- lowering your ambitions
- reading aloud
- taking medication
- working out
- owning a pet
- talking to friends

C 1 Sufferers of post-traumatic stress disorder are often unable to function normally because they can't forget a terrifying event. What kind of events might lead to this condition?
2 Poor concentration is a symptom of both stress and depression. How might the two conditions be related?

SEE WORKBOOK FOR MORE ACTIVITIES.

2 READING

A Find the words with the following meanings in the two articles:
1 feeble
2 an operation
3 arbitrary
4 an attempt
5 established

B 1 How do you think the health problems of Tony Blair's parents have affected him?
2 Explain the fish tank experiment in your own words?

C 1 Tony Blair uses exercise to cope with stress. What less physically active methods would you recommend to someone in his job?
2 Is it fair to keep a pet for no other reason than to avoid stress? Could a pet cause stress?

3 SPEAK YOUR MIND

A To feel stress is a natural body function – how does it help us to survive or adapt to new situations?

B What factors in everyday life or work cause people stress? What stresses you?

C Only 20 per cent of highly stressed teenagers seek help. Is teenage stress taken seriously?

D Could a pet helping its owner deal with stress feel stress itself as a result?

BLAIR THE FITNESS FAN

BBC News, UK

Prime Minister Tony Blair is to undergo a heart procedure in hospital on Friday to correct a continuing 'flutter'. He was treated in October last year for supraventricular tachycardia (SVT), but the problem has returned.

Although he describes the condition as 'not particularly alarming', the news could be seen as at odds with Mr Blair's image as an action man prime minister. When he is not criss-crossing the world on red-eye flights attempting to solve diplomatic crises, he can be found pounding the treadmill or playing tennis in a bid to keep fit. Mr Blair, who turned 50 last year, says his stress-busting exercise regime ensures he feels 'great, physically'. In fact, weighing just under 13 stone, the prime minister reckons he does more exercise today than he has done since he was at school.

"I pay more attention to looking after myself – I watch my diet a bit. But really I find it's exercise that's fantastically helpful for coping with stress," he told Saga magazine last year.

Mr Blair often exercises early in the morning and works out several times a week using the gym running machine. While the youthful good looks he brought to office in 1997 have been worn by age and the pressures of seven years in the top job, he has kept in good health. The father-of-four has said in the past that he has no difficulty in switching off from the job, citing his family, tennis, swimming, football with the kids and playing his guitar as his pastimes.

The prime minister's elderly father was only 39 when he suffered a stroke, and took three years to recover his speech. While he returned to work and became an industrial tribunal chair, he was forced to leave behind his political ambitions. He was left frail by a second stroke two years ago. Tony Blair has spoken of how his own character was shaped by his father's setbacks.

His mother, Hazel, died in 1975 following a five-year fight against thyroid cancer. Asked once by Saga magazine if genetic factors had made him concerned about his own health, Mr Blair admitted: "Yes, I suppose so."

WATCHING FISH FOUND TO EASE HUMAN STRESS

www.disabilityuk.com, UK

Fish may be beneficial to your health. Not just eating them, but watching them. Three University of Pennsylvania researchers report that quietly watching fish swimming in a home aquarium eases stress, and may offer a means of treating high blood pressure. The fish are the key, the researchers say. People who watch fish tanks with bubbles, pebbles and plants – but no fish – don't benefit nearly as much.

"There is a sharp difference," says ecologist Alan Beck, director of the university's Center for the Interaction of Animals and Society. "Blood pressure drops with fishless fish tanks, but it doesn't drop as much and it creeps back up faster. With fish in the tanks, you truly get relaxation."

Petting a dog or cat is a known stress-reducer. One study showed that survivors of heart attacks tended to live longer if they owned a dog.

Beck, psychiatrist Aaron H. Katcher and biologist Erika Friedmann decided to see if interaction with other animals produced similar results.

The researchers divided 100 paid volunteers into two groups. One at a time, they were put in a room and asked to read aloud – a proven way to induce stress – for one minute. Then they were left alone with a fish tank for 20 minutes. Half the time there were fish in the aquarium; half the time there were none. A device automatically recorded the volunteers' blood pressure. Those who had fish to watch fared far better.

The random selection of volunteers resulted in the participation of some who suffered from high blood pressure. "For them, the fish were much better than for a normal person."

4 LISTEN

A Look at the photos and answer:

1. What makes you laugh? Can you make yourself laugh?
2. How do you feel after a good laugh?
3. Which is better: a funny joke, a funny book, or a funny film?
4. Why is humour contagious?

B Before you listen, decide which of the following probably happens at a Laughter Club:

- People's health improves.
- People tell jokes.
- People giggle.
- People talk to each other.

Check your answers after listening.

C Listen to the audio clip. When it pauses, decide how the New Delhi laughter guru, Umesh Sahgal, will answer the question.

D Listen and answer the questions.

1. How many Laughter Club members are there in Australia?
2. Why is it not hard to start laughing at the Laughter Club?
3. How did Doctor Madan Kataria start the Laughter Club?
4. What are Laughter Clubs also known as?

E You decide: Is laughter the best medicine? Does it help relieve stress? Would you ever join a Laughter Club? Why / Why not?

5 TEAMWORK

Work in pairs. Read the **Teamwork Scenario** and talk about phobias. What scares you? How does fear turn into a phobia?

6 CONTROVERSY

Work in groups of four. Prepare a debate with another group. Many people feel doctors turn too quickly to pharmaceutical solutions. Stress sufferers can often get better using alternative treatments like massage or acupuncture, with none of the drug side-effects.

Group A: You are doctors and alternative medicine practitioners who want to see more use of alternative treatments for stress and depression. Some issues you may wish to mention:

- Many anti-depressants work no better than placebos on children, but increase the risk of suicide.
- Children and teenagers represent five per cent of the anti-depressant market; increasing every year.
- Many high-stress individuals find alternative treatments to be highly effective.
- Many doctors receive incentives from drug companies to promote the use of drugs.

Group B: You are doctors and pharmaceutical industry representatives who want to see drugs used whenever and wherever needed. Some points you may wish to mention:

- Drugs have a proven record of treating depression and related illnesses.
- Drugs and therapy reduce symptoms of depression in 70 per cent of teenagers.
- Success of alternative treatments is largely anecdotal.
- Drugs work best in combination with counselling and therapy.

7 PORTFOLIO WRITING

A Write an article (220-260 words) for a company newsletter about ways of identifying and coping with stress in the workplace.

B Write a diary entry (220-260 words) about the most stressful day in your life.

8 BIOLOGY *in English*

A Work in pairs. You are running a workshop on stress management. Student A gives a formal presentation on how stress builds up. Student B talks about the effects of stress on the body and on behaviour.

B After the presentations, ask questions on the presentations and discuss whether modern life makes people more stressed than in past times.

PHASES OF STRESS	PHYSIOLOGICAL EFFECTS
Alarm:	
Detecting a perceived threat, the body increases stress hormones epinephrine and norepinephrine, causing the 'flight-or-fight' response. It usually lasts only a few minutes. 	This reaction increases heart and breathing rates, body temperature, sweating and production of stomach acid. Increased blood pressure damages blood vessels causing scar tissue and thickening of blood vessel walls.
Resistance:	
The body will usually return to its normal state. However, if the threat continues, the body will increase its production of stress hormones and release cortisol, a hormone which increases alertness. It can last for hours. 	This leads to emotional responses like anger, frustration, becoming upset and argumentative. It can influence behaviour and reactions in negative ways. Mental functions such as memory can be impaired.
Exhaustion:	
Eventually, the body runs out of hormones and proteins. Decreased cortisol leads to fatigue. If stress becomes chronic, the person usually remains in this state. It can also lead to the situation called 'burnout' where the person becomes incapable of dealing with even ordinary situations without feeling stress. 	Initially, this can lead to emotional responses like worry, guilt, depression and fatigue. Over time, this can lead to: – risk of heart attacks and strokes – digestive problems like ulcers – insomnia – lower immune system, more disease – migraines, headaches, backaches – possibly cancer

9 FURTHER DISCUSSION

Discuss in pairs. Use the words and phrases from this unit and **Language Bank 19** to develop and justify your ideas and arguments.

A How stressful is childhood? Adolescence? Adulthood? How does stress change as you get older?

B Are doing exams, writing essays or speaking in public stressful for you? Do you worry much about failure? Why / Why not?

C Why do you think 70 per cent of workers say stress in their job has increased?

D Do you get stressed about meeting deadlines and being on time for appointments? Do you manage your time effectively? If so, how? If not, why not?

10 *Your answer:* ARE WE SERIOUSLY STRESSED ?

Do we take stress seriously enough? What does your school, community or government do to help reduce stress? Is there sufficient education about stress?

Shock tactics

WHAT'S NEW!

Topic: Young people's behaviour
Function: Eliciting feedback
Language: Language of caution

The BIG question: ARE ALL TEENAGERS REBELS?

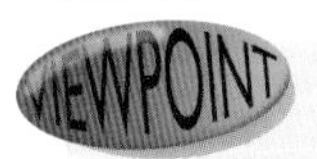

- British 15-year-old boys and girls who say they have drunk alcohol in the last seven days: 49% and 45%.
- 33% of males between 16 and 24 in the UK have used cannabis in the last year.

> *Cute teenagers exist only on television, I suspect. I know there are none in my neighbourhood.*
> ***Robert MacKenzie***

> *It's all the young can do for the old, to shock them and keep them up to date.*
> ***George Bernard Shaw***

? Do young people like to shock for the sake of it?

1 WORD POWER

A Youth behaviour only seems to be noticed when it's bad. Think about:

- tagging / graffiti
- loud music
- street gangs
- illegal drug use
- violent behaviour
- binge drinking
- body piercings
- vandalism
- promiscuity
- tattoos

1 How common is this kind of behaviour among young people?
2 How is this kind of thing reported on TV and radio or in the newspapers? Negatively or positively?
3 Do you see this behaviour as bad? Why? / Why not?

B Work in pairs using **Language Bank 20** to find out your partner's reaction to these statements. Your partner uses cautious answers.
1 "Straight-A students have problems too."
2 "There is a generation gap between parents and young people today."
3 "Something needs to be done about these yobs."
4 "Peer pressure pushes young people into risky behaviour."

C 1 Does everyone become more conventional as they get older? What do they do differently?
2 Give some examples of good youth behaviour.

SEE WORKBOOK FOR MORE ACTIVITIES.

2 READING

A Read the first article. Which of these statements refer to Straight Edgers?
1 Newspapers have been supportive of their movement.
2 They refuse to drink beer.
3 They were inspired by an anti-heroin song.
4 They are involved in gang activity.

B When you have read the second article, decide how each person might feel about the situation:
- A local farmer
- A student marijuana picker
- A police officer
- The parent of a student

C 1 Why would the Straight Edge culture appeal to young people?
2 Why would marijuana growers want to hire teenagers?

3 SPEAK YOUR MIND

A What is a typical young man or woman like – happy, sad, angry, frustrated, confused or something else? What do they like or not like doing?

B How much do young people care what others think of them? Are reputations based on fact or fiction?

C Why do people like joining a group? Can you be an individual when you are part of a group? How does the group mentality affect individual behaviour?

D Is youth crime different from adult crime? Why do young people commit criminal acts?

Walking the Straight Edge

Erica Dirksen, WireTap Magazine, USA

Straight Edge youth can be intimidating in a crowd with their 'XXX' tattoos, facial piercings and black attire. Because of this, they are repeatedly misrepresented and misunderstood – particularly by the mainstream media. A Canadian newspaper called Straight Edgers a 'vigilante do-gooder gang that targets those who sin', while others have called them 'suburban terrorists' and 'politically correct terrorists'. Their association with gangs is in many ways way off the mark – rather than dealing drugs and doing drive-by shootings, Straight Edgers adhere to a self-regulated lifestyle of no alcohol, no drugs and no promiscuous sex. The symbol 'XXX' is believed to represent a resistance to these three common vices. Many also claim to be vegetarians or vegans, and some don't drink caffeine.

So why the bad rep? A highly publicized incident that occurred in 1998, in which two Straight Edge teens were involved in the murder of a Latino youth in Salt Lake City, was a

key factor in shaping the public image of the Straight Edge movement. But even those unfamiliar with the incident point to loud, hard-core Straight Edge music and the wild thrashing mosh pits at Straight Edge shows as examples of violent behavior. Straight Edge came out of hard core punk music and remains tied to that genre. The music is loud and intense, and the dancing is more like a free-for-all karate-match than a style. And as with other extreme philosophies, those that adhere to being Straight Edge are often seen as being close-minded, rigid, and often hostile toward those who don't subscribe to their philosophy.

Many claim the Straight Edge movement was originally inspired by Ian MacKaye of Minor Threat, a hard core punk band, in the 1980s. MacKaye's song *Straight Edge* – written in memory of a friend who died of a heroin overdose – encouraged young people to abstain from drugs, alcohol and promiscuous sex.

While it is not a gang, a religion or a cult, those who consider themselves Straight Edge definitely feel as if they belong to a group – the support Straight Edgers get from one another helps them stay clean and keep their edge.

Marijuana growers hire rural Quebec students

Genevieve Beauchemin, CTV, Canada

Some high school students in rural Quebec are being recruited for work as part-time marijuana pickers. They are being lured to pick the illicit plants, often hidden in corn fields, by the growers who are often associated with organized crime.

It often consumes two to three days of their week – causing them to skip school in the process, said Claude Bernier, principal of a local high school in the region southeast of Montreal. If they aren't picking, they're on guard keeping locals away from the crop.

The mayor said the growers give 14-year-olds an all-terrain vehicle, a cellphone and pay them $25 per hour in cash. The high pay is creating a local labour shortage in traditional student jobs like washing dishes

Police seize cannabis plants.

"I know some guys who work for marijuana growers. I've been approached too, but I haven't done it," said one student – who has a more standard part-time job.

Police say growers take over patches of farmers' fields and then intimidate the landowners into silence. It's a big business in parts of Quebec. While police make constant seizures, they certainly aren't finding all of it. The Sûrété du Québec launched a major operation this week. Four hundred officers raided 250 fields and forests, arresting dozens of growers. "Last year we seized over 300,000 plants. So far we've seized 400,000 plants and the year isn't over yet," said François Doré, a police spokesman.

4 LISTEN

A
1. Compare and contrast the photos. How do you think the people are feeling?
2. How common is it for young people to binge drink in your country?
3. What are some problems associated with binge drinking?
4. Do young people act differently without older people around?

B Before you listen, decide what a trip out for young people in an Ibiza holiday resort would include:
- Swimming
- Responsible drinking
- Fun party games
- Sightseeing

Check your answers after listening.

C Listen to the audio clip and answer the questions.
1. What is the theme of the cruise?
2. What kind of music is going to be played?
3. Will food and drink be available on board?
4. What is the manager worried about?
5. Are the reps really worried about what happens to the people who drink too much?

D You decide: Why do people drink alcohol? How do alcohol and other drugs affect people's behaviour? Should we try to curb drinking among young people?
If so, how? If not, why not?

5 TEAMWORK

Work in groups of three. Imagine you are local politicians asked to create programmes to help young people in the community. Read the **Teamwork Scenario**. Discuss your programmes with another group and decide how successful you think these would be?

6 CONTROVERSY

Work in groups of four. Prepare a debate with another group. Use expressions from **Language Bank 20**.

Some parents want to ban all tattoo and body piercing parlours. A television station has arranged a debate about tattoos and body piercings.

Group A: You are parents concerned about tattoos and body piercings. Some questions you could ask.
- What happens when the tattoos and body piercings aren't trendy anymore?
- Won't it be harder for people to find work later on when they have tattoos and piercings?
- Don't people still associate tattoos with criminals?
- What about the possibility of catching HIV or hepatitis from dirty needles?

Group B: You are professional tattooists and body piercers. Some questions you could ask.
- Don't properly run tattoo parlours refuse to tattoo people under 18, or on the hands and face?
- Don't people of all ages and walks of life have tattoos and body piercings these days?
- Why can't we see tattoos as an expression of individuality and art?
- Doesn't the government regulate tattoo and body piercing parlours? Don't they ensure high levels of hygiene and proper sterilisation?

7 PORTFOLIO WRITING

A Write a report for the government (220-260 words) on youth behaviour today. Include suggestions on how the government should try to encourage good behaviour and discourage bad behaviour.

B Write an email or letter (180-220 words) to a teenage friend who needs advice about their boyfriend or girlfriend. Think about how sensitive people can feel about these relationships.

8 POETRY AND MUSIC in English

A Work in pairs. Each one reads a different verse, plus the chorus. Analyse the lyrics and present it to your partner. Some points to think about are: the speaker / narrator, the audience, the message(s), the situation, the types of emotion, any literal and figurative meanings.

B After the presentation, find out whether other people agree with your analysis or not. Discuss why people create and listen to music? Are music lyrics poetry?

Life for Rent

I haven't ever really found a place that I call home
I never stick around quite long enough to make it
I apologize that once again I'm not in love
But it's not as if I mind that your heart ain't exactly breaking
It's just a thought, only a thought

Chorus:
If my life is for rent and I don't learn to buy
Well I deserve nothing more than I get
Cos nothing I have is truly mine

Always thought that I would love to live by the sea
To travel the world alone and live more simply
I have no idea what's happened to that dream
Cos there's really nothing left here to stop me
It's just a thought, only a thought

Chorus (repeat twice)
While my heart is a shield and I won't let it down
While I am so afraid to fail so I won't even try
Well how can I say I'm alive

Chorus (repeat twice)
Nothing I have is truly mine
Nothing I have is truly mine
Nothing I have is truly mine

Words and music by Dido Armstrong and Rollo Armstrong

Dido

9 FURTHER DISCUSSION

Discuss in pairs. Use the words and phrases from this unit and **Language Bank 20** to develop and justify your argument.

A Do people behave differently at school, at work, at home or with friends? Is it possible to be all good or all bad in our behaviour?

B Young people often experiment with different ideas, alcohol, style and sex. Is it dangerous behaviour or just a part of growing up?

C What are the most important lessons in life young people need to learn? Should they learn by trial and error, from their friends, from TV or somewhere else?

D Does commercialising youth culture (for example, MTV) make young people more or less likely to rebel?

10 *Your answer*: ARE ALL TEENAGERS REBELS?

Why do young people often find themselves in conflict with their parents and the older generation? Do young people respect older people? Is there any point to youth rebellion?

NOT ALL NATIVES ARE CREATED EQUAL

B. H. Bates

This extract written by a Native American from Canada on a visit to the United States is very informal in style and contains many slang expressions.

As a fearless, naive Native of twenty-two, I strolled down the streets of a big, unfamiliar city in the United States. It being a warm and sunny day, I used that as an excuse to tip back a few cold ones. I walked straight into the first tavern I saw and sat down at the bar. As my eyes adjusted to the dimly light place, a cold chill came over my entire body. A realization set in – I wasn't as fearless as I thought I was!

The place went dead silent, as I looked at the reflection in the dirty mirror behind the bar. I could see that everyone in the place was staring at me with tight, mean frowns on their faces.

Big deal, you say, people staring at an unwelcome Injun, so what's new? What if I told you they were all 'black!' Just then a booming voice, that sounded like it was coming from the bottom of a hollow barrel, said: "That stinks!"

I turned to my left to see an extremely large black man with a scowl on his face, pointing at my cigarette. Again he pointed and again he said, "That stinks!" But this time his massive cheeks dimpled slightly, as he cracked a smile. It was only after seeing him smile, that I unclinch my own set of cheeks!

"Oh, this? Ah, ah, it's ah, um a Canadian brand." I stuttered, my voice cracking with uncertainty and a little fear. My uneasy feeling didn't go unnoticed by the big guy. Again he smiled, as he laughed, "Don't worry boy, I ain'a goin'a bite you!" As unsure as I was about the situation, I was still a smart ass at heart – I blurted out: "Bite me? Hell, I was worried about being eaten!"

Again his booming laugh filled the room and it seemed to put everyone at ease, about my presence. The chatter of voices in the room rose like someone had magically turned up the volume.

"Yo, cool! Where you from, boy? You'z sure in'a hell ain't from round here." He was right, I was a long way from my comfort zone. As I was walking around taking in the sights of the big city, I had unwittingly walked into a part of town, better known by the locals, as the 'hood!'

"You know it's funny that you should say that; Where you from?" I went on to explain that when two Natives meet for the first time, they too, always say the same thing: "Hi, where ya from?"

As we sat and drank, our differences and the time just seemed to melt away. All too soon, I had to excuse myself. Standing up to leave, my new friend Glenn, also stood up and shook my hand good-bye. I'll never forget him, for a number of reasons. First, his size was very impressive, his arm was as big as my leg and his leg was as big as I was!

Another thing that will last in my memory forever was the look of sincerity on his face, as he said, "It was nice meetin' ya. Y'all take care now!"

1 READING

A Read through the extract and answer:

1. Why was the writer scared?
2. Who did the writer talk to? How did it make him feel?
3. Why did the experience make the writer consider his own situation?

B

1. What stereotypes about different groups are you aware of?
2. Are stereotypes harmful or helpful? Why?

2 IDIOMS

A Match these meanings with the idioms underlined in the text:

1. expressing a lack of concern
2. the environment where someone feels secure
3. everyday existence, as opposed to an ideal state
4. to say something suddenly, usually without thinking
5. a person who makes sarcastic comments
6. to make people comfortable

B Complete the sentences using the idioms from 2A. Change the verb tense where necessary.

1. The police officer .... everyone .... with her warm smile.
2. That law was a good idea, but it will never work in ....
3. She is such a .... She is always making fun of everything.
4. When he started talking about religion, I felt a bit outside my ....
5. The man suddenly .... the answer.
6. What's the .... ? No one cares how you look when you go camping.

At that moment, it felt as if Glenn was the representative for the entire race of black people and we were all brothers under the same sun! I went away feeling happy. That is, until I stepped out of that tavern into the harsh light of the real world.

No more than ten steps from the front door, I encountered two other African-Americans brothers. Still feeling the glow of Glenn's friendship, I did nothing more than just nod my head in acknowledgment, as I was passing by. That's when one of them threw his arms back and jutted out his chin as he spat: "What the – – – – you lookin' at?"

It was back! That same cold feeling of fear engulfed me, followed closely by loathing and hatred! At that moment, that ignorant jerk was the representative of an entire race of people! I knew that what I was feeling wasn't true, but it was still a struggle not to hate.

'Hate' is one of the two strongest emotions we humans have. At that moment in time, if I could've willed it, not only him and his friend would've dropped dead right on the spot, so would've everyone he ever loved, and all of their dogs too!

It took me the rest of that day and most of the night to stop the hateful thoughts running through my mind. Every time I saw a person with dark skin I would curl my lip and scowl at them. It wasn't until I thought of big Glenn, and how nice he was, that I started to think more clearly.

It made me reflect on the way I'd been treated in the past and how I, as a Native, was looked upon. The way some people would take one look at me and think; "Alcoholic, Welfare, Reservation!"

Little did they know (and those are the 'key' words, when you're talking about prejudices), that I didn't live on a reservation or that I've owned my own business since I was eighteen and I no longer drink, smoke or even chew my fingernails!

Another thing it made me contemplate was: If you're an 'average, upper middle class, white person' – how would you know how it feels to be an object of bigotry and ignorance? Furthermore, that said, how could that person use those 'feelings' as a tool to understand, recognize and turn off prejudice?

I find it very worrisome, as a Native, to think that stereotypical profiling could be happening here in Canada. I'd hate to think, that just because of a few malcontent jerks, that some non-Native Canadians might look at Natives as objects of fear, loathing and with hatred!

Please remember – "Not all Natives are created equal!"

3 WHAZZUP?

English speakers around the world often make use of different grammar and spelling, which are referred to as non-standard English. 'Whazzup' is non-standard American English for 'What's happening?'.

A Identify five phrases with non-standard grammar. Give the standard English equivalent for each.

B Identify five words with non-standard spelling. Give the standard English equivalent for each.

C Why are these forms used these rather than standard grammar? What do you think of non-standard uses of your language?

4 PORTFOLIO WRITING

A Summarise the extract in your own words (180-200 words) without leaving out any important information.

B Creative writing: Imagine you were Big Glenn and had seen what happened outside the bar. Write a story (220-250 words) from Big Glenn's point of view about what happened next.

C Stereotypes and ethnic groups. Answer the questions (100 words for each):

1. How might stereotypes affect Native Americans and African-Americans?
2. What effect does misunderstanding or miscommunication have on the story?
3. How would this story change if the characters had been from different ethnic groups?

5 INTERACTIVE TASK

Work in pairs. A chooses one of the comments below to start talking and B asks questions to find out more about the situation, then discusses it with A. You should both use all the Language Banks you have covered so far and eliciting reponses (Language Bank 20). Switch roles when you have talked about the first comment for four minutes.

> "I went for an interview yesterday and they've offered me the job. The thing is that the other people in the office are years older than me, so I don't think it'll be much fun."

> "Did you see that horrible film on TV last night? It was full of Hollywood clichés about almost every nationality – the Arabs, the Mexicans, the French and so on. Why do they make films like that?"

WORKBOOK Buy now, think later

(SEE PAGES 8–11)

1 USE OF LANGUAGE: Prepositions

Complete the article with the right prepositions. See example (0).

In the last decade, the advertising world has moved far beyond the traditional ways (0) *of* attracting consumers (1) .... catchy radio jingles or sponsored TV programmes. The corporate logo has invaded areas previously considered off-limits to advertisers. One example has been (2) .... US universities. Once a sanctuary (3) .... commercialism, many universities and colleges have signed exclusive contracts with giant soft-drinks manufacturers to be the sole vendor (4) .... campus. Criticised (5) .... students and teaching staff alike, education administrators have emphasised the funds that accompany these deals. In some places, officially-approved marketing material has even begun appearing (6) .... the walls of public toilets.

City governments are not above making similar deals (7) .... make ends meet. A few daring American mayors have also entered (8) .... sponsorship contracts with US car manufacturers. The car companies can advertise where they want, and the city gets a new fleet of lorries and cars. While the issue of politicians making sponsorship deals (9) .... companies might make some uneasy, taxpayers seem to approve or, (10) .... least, to remain largely uninterested as long as it keeps taxes down.

2 WRITING

A Send a spam email (180-220 words) to persuade people to buy a trip to Antarctica.
B Choose a product you like. Write a product information sheet (220-260 words) for the company's website to make the product sound exciting.

3 SPEAKING STRATEGIES: Mapping the presentation

To lead the audience through your points logically, structure your presentation.
Use two of the structuring methods to map out a way to talk about these four points. Each method may provide more than one option.

Points for the presentation on food products

A (1688-1715) Benedictine monks produced first sparkling wines in France's Champagne region.
B (1970) Brazil begins large-scale planting of soybeans.
C (1565) Spaniards developed first orange groves in Florida.
D (4000 BC) First evidence of domesticated rice grown in Thailand's rice fields.

Some methods for structuring presentations

Categorical: *examples*: circles, triangles, squares; red, green, blue; commodities (grapes, oranges, soybeans, rice)
Chronological: *examples*: past, present, future; by date
Compare / contrast: *examples*: + vs. -; us vs. them; opposites
Confucius principle: *examples*: concentric circles; individual, family, town, etc.
Geographical: *examples*: north, south, east, west
Hierarchical: *examples*: top, middle, bottom; cost of items
Sequential: *examples*: first, secondly, thirdly / lastly / finally; historical dates; status of items; order first in your country

4 IDIOMS

Complete the sentences using the phrases in the box. What do these idioms mean?

a a blank cheque
b on the bandwagon
c an arm and a leg
d seen dead
e round the clock

1 Advertising counts on consumers *jumping* ....
2 Companies are happy *to give* advertising agencies .... if it will mean more sales.
3 That new car *costs* ....
4 Most teenagers *wouldn't be* .... wearing that!
5 We've been *working* .... to finish this new ad campaign.

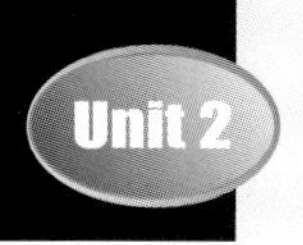

WORKBOOK Express yourself

(SEE PAGES 12–15)

1 WORD POWER

Rewrite these points as a presentation. Try to link the different art movements using the signposting phrases in **Language Bank 2**.

The **Renaissance** (15th–16th cent.): Important artistic and ideological revival; mixed elements of classical style, scientific inquiry and Christian themes.
Artists: Michelangelo, Da Vinci, Raphael.

The **Baroque** period (16th–17th cent.): Artists trying to capture emotions and drama and seeking more realism in their art.
Artists: Rubens, Rembrandt, Caravaggio.

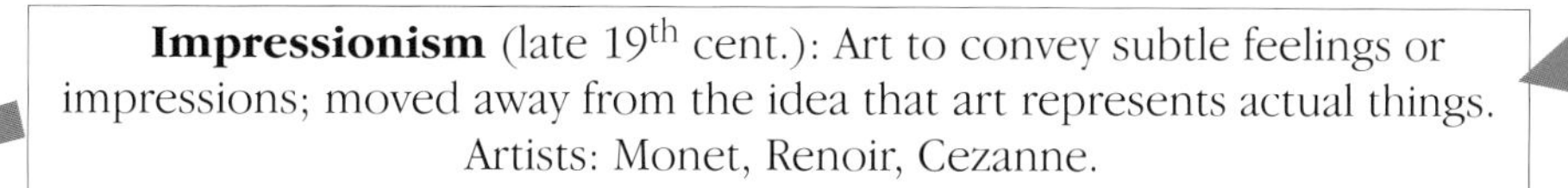

Impressionism (late 19th cent.): Art to convey subtle feelings or impressions; moved away from the idea that art represents actual things.
Artists: Monet, Renoir, Cezanne.

Expressionism (late 19th–early 20th cent.): Direct communication of feelings, especially anxiety and despair in their work.
Artists: Van Gogh, Munch, Grosz, Dix, Beckmann.

Surrealism (early 20th cent.): Influenced by psychological works of Freud and Jung; art sought to explore the subconscious.
Artists: Breton, Dali, Man Ray.

2 USE OF LANGUAGE: Word forms

Read the text and decide which form of the word (1-8) best fits each space.
An example is given: (0) think ⟶ *thought*

1 culture 2 mass 3 move 4 free 5 product 6 happy 7 sit 8 imagine

From 1900 to the start of World War II, Paris was a major focal point of artistic energy and (0) *thought*. The city had been a major (1) .... hub in Europe for centuries, but in these decades, it received a (2) .... flood of artists, writers, musicians and intellectuals from across Europe and the US. It was the age of '–isms'. Artistic and political (3) .... found a receptive audience here: Surrealism, Cubism, Dadaism, Symbolism, Communism, Existentialism. And it was the age of the Bohemian artist. Starving and poor, they shed the shackles of society for a life of (4) .... and self-expression.

As the American writer, Henry Miller, said of the (5) .... time that he spent in Paris: "I have no money, no resources, no hopes. I am the (6) .... man alive. A year ago, six months ago, I thought I was an artist. I no longer think about it, I am." At all hours, one could find artists and writers (7) .... in Montmartre cafés socialising, philosophising and debating the important issues of the day, although it may be difficult to (8) .... now.

3 WRITING

A Creative writing: Write a diary entry (250 words) for an artist living in 1930s Paris. Try to imagine a typical day for an artist back then.

B It took more than fifty years for jazz music to be thought of as high culture. Write a music review (250 words) for a song or a piece of music you think will be a classic in fifty years' time.

4 IDIOMS

Complete the sentence using the phrases in the box. Change the verb forms and possessive adjectives where necessary. What do these idioms mean?

a open mind
b be ahead of one's time
c budding artist
d king's ransom
e over one's head

1 She's a .... We expect big things from her in the future.
2 I found the whole conversation *went* .... What did he mean by Existentialism?
3 You often need to *keep an* .... when it comes to modern art.
4 I really think Picasso ....
5 You would have to *pay a* .... if you want to buy that Matisse.

WORKBOOK The sky's the limit!

(SEE PAGES 16–19)

1 USE OF LANGUAGE: Joining clauses

Read the text and find a word that best fits each space. An example (0) is given.

The story begins in 1990. (0) *While* on a train journey from Manchester to London, Joanne Rowling found a compelling idea taking shape in her mind. Most people now know (1) .... this story is about a young boy called Harry, (2) .... was a wizard without knowing it.

This spark of imagination would prove a life-changing event for Rowling, (3) .... had begun writing at the age of six. (4) .... the death of her mother, she moved to Portugal, (5) .... she taught English. During this time, she married a Portuguese man, with (6) .... she had her first child.

(7) .... the marriage didn't work out, she returned to Britain with a suitcase full of Harry Potter stories. To finish the manuscript, she went to cafés to write (8) .... her daughter slept. (9) .... five years of dedicated work and countless rewrites, she finally found a publisher for *Harry Potter and the Philosopher's Stone*. Since then, the Harry Potter titles have sold more than a quarter billion copies worldwide, (10) .... has lead to her appearance on the Forbes Billionaires list. Her life now seems almost as much a fantasy as the characters in her books – from struggling lone parent to queen of the publishing world.

2 WRITING

A Imagine you are J. K. Rowling. Write a letter or email (180-220 words) to a young person who would like to become a writer, explaining what it is like to be a writer including the satisfaction of being a writer and the sacrifices that have to be made.

B Imagine you are a motivational speaker. Write a short guide (220-260 words) to motivate people to succeed. Try to use phrases from **Language Bank 3**.

3 SPEAKING STRATEGIES: Get rhetorical

Rhetorical questions are questions that you ask and answer yourself to add weight to your argument. Complete the sentences using the correct response for each rhetorical question.

a I certainly hope not.
b I know I would.
c No, I don't think so,
d Some people can manage it
e To tell you the truth, it's the most important thing.
f Well, welfare has its problems.

1 Who wouldn't like to make a lot of money? .... The solution is to pick a good career early on.
2 So, just how important is charisma? .... if you want to be a politician, actor or business person.
3 Do you need to break the rules to succeed? .... , but in some cases, you might need to bend them a little.
4 Is it possible to have a successful career and a happy family life? .... , but I think it's very difficult for most of us.
5 So, what's the solution? .... , but taking away benefits will cause even more problems.
6 Is success all about luck? .... I think it's too fatalistic to think we can't change our own destiny.

4 IDIOMS

Complete the sentences using the phrases in the box. What do these idioms mean?

a control freak b movers and shakers c shark d stick-in-the-mud e down-to-earth f workaholic

1 For all his vast wealth, he is really .... He's very approachable.
2 She is a .... , putting in 70 hours a week. Her goal is to become a senior manager by 35.
3 He's a real .... He never lets his workers take any initiative on their own.
4 When she went into politics, she had the support of a lot of .... , so she had a lot of power.
5 Don't be such a .... You won't get anywhere with that kind of negative attitude.
6 Other barristers considered him a .... He was ruthless in the courtroom.

WORKBOOK Are you looking at me?

(SEE PAGES 20–23)

1 WORD POWER

Replace the words in italics with words from the unit. Then use the phrases in **Language Bank 4** to modify these statements.

1 The gang in Raul's neighborhood *scared* him when they walked past him in the street.
2 It is the role of parents to stop older children from *bullying* younger ones in the family.
3 The teacher seemed to *place the fault* on the victim rather than the bully.
4 Mitsuko's threatening behaviour became so bad that the head teacher wanted to *keep her out of* school.
5 Sophia felt she was weak and *couldn't do anything* because her father shouted at her all the time.

2 USE OF LANGUAGE: Word forms

Read the text and decide which form of the word (1–8) best fits each space. An example is given: (0) big ⟶ *bigger*.

(0) big	1 hide	3 call	5 act	7 psychology
2 secret	4 understand	6 relate	8 public	

Are girls (0) *bigger* bullies than boys? According to new research, girls might just be the great (1) .... tormentors. While boys tend to bully in open and physical ways, girls tend to participate in more (2) .... ways, which the researchers have taken to (3) .... 'relational aggression'. This goes beyond the tendency of girls to form cliques and gossip about others.

Although bullying can become physical abuse, it more often appears as mental abuse. Key to (4) .... this phenomenon is that girls have much stronger needs for social bonding. The (5) .... of these 'alpha' girls take the form of depriving targeted girls of these (6) .... Whether it's sending a text message to a group of girls so they all turn and laugh at the victim or spreading rumours that socially isolates the victim, the bullies act in ways which can easily be denied if they are confronted by grown-ups. The result is (7) .... stress that goes almost unchecked. This is believed to be behind a number of highly (8) .... teen suicides in Canada, the United States and other countries.

3 WRITING

A Imagine you have been bullied. Write a letter or email (180-220 words) to a friend about the experience.
B You are the head of a company. Write a report (220-260 words) to managers on how to prevent bullying and how to deal with cases of bullying in the workplace.

4 IDIOMS

Complete the sentences using the verbs in the box. Change the verb tense where necessary. What do these idioms mean?

a cross	b drive	c fight	d flog	e go	f play

1 Sandra .... *into* her bully's hands by mentioning her problems at home.
2 I wouldn't .... *swords* with him, if I were you.
3 Maybe I'm .... *a dead horse*, but you have to do something about bullying in this school.
4 She was nearly .... *over the edge* by students picking on her.
5 Alexander's parents .... *to great lengths* to get the bully excluded from school.
6 The bully was really surprised when his victim decided to .... *it out*.

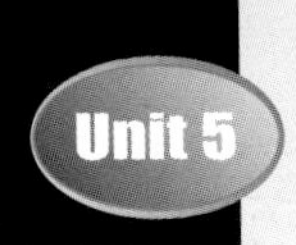

WORKBOOK Frills and thrills

(SEE PAGES 24–27)

1 WORD POWER

A Replace the adjectives in these sentences with more vivid adjectives from **Language Bank 5**.
B Write a sentence suggesting you'd like to buy or wouldn't like to buy the item. Use the **Language Bank 5** phrases for expressing ideas tentatively.

1 That Alvar Aalto glass vase is really nice. (You'd like to buy it.)
2 That car design is so unoriginal. .... (You don't want buy it.)
3 I think that designer dress is pretty good. .... (You'd like to buy it.)
4 Very small laptops are useless for everyday use. .... (You don't want buy it.)
5 I think this table design is very new and useful. .... (You'd like to buy it.)
6 This gold watch is too bright for me. .... (You don't want buy it.)

2 WRITING

A Imagine you work for a charity. Write a letter or email (180-220 words) to your favourite celebrity asking them if they would like to donate clothes, time or money to your cause.
B You work for a company that designs self-assembly furniture. Write an information sheet with instructions (180-220 words) for customers on how to put together a cupboard that has two doors and two shelves inside.
C You want to enter a contest to be the host of a new fashion or music TV program. Write a competition entry (180-220 words) as a letter to the judges to convince them to pick you.

3 SPEAKING STRATEGIES: De-emphasising

You can soften statements to make them seem less emphatic or strong by adding certain words and phrases. Complete the text with the words and phrases from the box. An example (0) is given.

Note: Three of the words and phrases are synonyms that can be used interchangeably.

a a little bit
b a bit
c actually
d all in all
e minor
f more or less
g pretty
h probably
i quite
j rather
k sometimes

Dave You're not (0) *actually* thinking about buying that, are you?
Rick Why? What's wrong with it? I thought it was (1) .... cool. Didn't David Beckham wear (2) .... the same thing on TV?
Dave But it's a leather kilt! You can't buy that!
Rick Oh sure. Coming from the guy who owns a pair of red trousers, that is (3) .... outrageous.
Dave Firstly, you're not even (4) .... Scottish.
Rick Not true. My uncle has a Scottish girlfriend.
Dave Secondly, it's made of leather. Won't your vegan girlfriend find that (5) .... tasteless?
Rick That's only a (6) .... problem. She hasn't found my leather Armani jacket yet.
Dave Thirdly, it (7) .... costs what you earn in a week.
Rick (8) .... , it still looks (9) .... good, don't you think?
Dave (10) .... , you're really hopeless.

4 IDIOMS

Complete the sentences using the verbs in the box. Change the verb tense where necessary.
What do these idioms mean?

a empty existence
b keeping up with the Joneses
c pay a pretty penny
d trendsetter
e upmarket

1 I couldn't care less about .... I am happy with what I have.
2 David Beckham has been a bit of a .... in men's fashion.
3 Many people try to find happiness through material possessions, but it's an ....
4 I bet he .... for those designer cufflinks.
5 Our boutique is for a more .... clientele. We sell only Italian designer goods.

(SEE PAGES 28-31)

1 WORD POWER

Replace the words in italics with words and phrases from the unit. Then use the phrases in **Language Bank 6** to express reservations about these statements.

1 I think the opposition party is heading for another *overwhelming win* in the polls.
2 The Russian team will *easily win* in this competition.
3 I don't think you can expect *fair play* between rivals.
4 The Australian swimmer was the *one expected to win*.
5 Any competition leads to a close *team feeling*.
6 The game show proved to be an *easy victory* for her.

2 USE OF LANGUAGE: The passive

Rewrite the underlined parts of the article using the passive voice. Change the subject and object as necessary.

Movie star now turned politician, Arnold Schwarzenegger told his parents at the age of 13, "I want to be the best-built man in the world". (1) They thought he was a little crazy, but the following year Arnold began his training with Kurt Marnul, a former Mr. Austria. By 17, Arnold had begun to compete actively. Like all Austrian men, (2) he had to do a year's military service in the Austrian army. Unfortunately, (3) his commanding officer would not give him permission to leave the base to compete in bodybuilding contests. (4) This did not deter Arnold however. He sneaked out of camp to compete in the Mr. Junior Western Europe. (5) Although he won the contest, he had to spend a week behind bars for his efforts. On leaving the army, (6) Arnold would enter and win Mr Europe, the Best Built Man in Europe and the International Powerlifting Championship. By this point, he was working out four to six hours a day. That same year, Arnold entered the Mr. Universe contest. Surprisingly, he lost to Chet Yorton (Mr. America), but it gave him the motivation to work harder for the following year. This time, (7) Arnold would dominate the event. Following his triumph, he went on to win Mr. Universe four more times. (8) He would cap this by winning the biggest event in bodybuilding, Mr. Olympia, a record seven times.

3 WRITING

A Creative writing: Imagine you are a drug-testing official for the International Olympic Committee. Write a press release (220-260 words) about an athlete who has tested positive for a banned substance.

B Creative writing: Imagine you are a sports reporter. Write a compelling account of a sports event (220-260 words), so the readers feel as if they are present at the event.

4 IDIOMS

Match the beginning of the sentences with the endings. What do these idioms mean?

1 Winning is...
2 If you want to win,...
3 I gave my kid brother...
4 We gave them...
5 With two players short, it was...
6 Losing badly,...

a *a run for their money*.
b *a sporting chance*, but he still lost.
c they *threw in the towel* and conceded the game.
d you have *to play the game*.
e *the name of the game*.
f *a whole new ballgame* now.

1 USE OF LANGUAGE: Transitive and Intransitive verbs

Read the text and choose a transitive or intransitive verb that best fits each space.
Use **Language Bank 7** to help you. An example (0) is given.

China is the new economic dynamo in the world. In 2005, the Asian giant averaged an official growth rate of 9.9% per year. *The Economist* believes that the figure should actually be (0) *increased* by at least 3%. So what has driven this amazing growth? Firstly, there is the demand for cheap labour by foreign multinationals. Foreign investment (1) .... steadily through the 1990s, totalling more than $270 billion to date. However, it seems to be (2) .... in recent years. Secondly, by promoting free enterprise and a revamp of Shanghai and other coastal cities, the Communist Party leaders have (3) .... construction in China dramatically. China's demand for raw materials is staggering. It caused the world consumption of steel to (4) .... by 90% in 2003 alone. This growth has helped other Asian countries as well. Between 1999 and 2003, Singapore's exports to China and Hong Kong (5) .... by $14.3 billion, while Thailand's exports (6) .... by $8 billion. Not all countries, however, welcome China's growth. In Mexico, the number of manufacturing plants has (7) .... by about three hundred, as many manufacturers have moved production to China. It's not clear whether China can continue to manage this rate of growth whie trying to (8) .... the predicted rise in inflation over the coming years.

2 WRITING

A Write an article (250 words) for a local newspaper on how to create more jobs for your community.
B Write a business email (180-220 words) to an investor. Explain that your business is making large profits but it now needs more investment to make it grow.

3 SPEAKING STRATEGIES: Discussing graphs

When using graphs, tables and charts for presentations, use specific phrases to point out important items. Complete the text using the verbs from the box. Change the verb form where necessary.

a draw b focus c show d look e see

As you can (1) .... here in the first graph, the rise in unemployment has meant people are saving more. When people are saving, they are not spending money. If you now (2) .... at graph number two, domestic sales have decreased dramatically during this period. And obviously, this has affected our profits. Going to the next graph, I'd like to (3) .... your attention to the third quarter of this year. As the graph (4) .... , we had decreased our production levels to match falling domestic sales. However, I'd like to (5) .... your attention on the forecast for next year. We expect some growth in sales and to be back into full production midway through the year.

4 IDIOMS

Complete the sentences using the phrases in the box. What do these idioms mean?

a cracks in the relationship
b the back of a lorry
c a windfall
d the driving force behind
e the poverty trap
f the red

1 The man trading in cut-price brand-name perfumes joked, "They *fell off* ...."
2 The EU *is* .... a new resolution to lower farm subsidies.
3 There are a number of .... between the EU and the US over trade.
4 Many of the world's poor *are caught in* .... They have no way out.
5 Most coffee farmers have *been in* .... since the coffee market collapsed.
6 She was lucky, she *had* .... when her shares went up in value.

1 WORD POWER

A Try to link the sentences using the signposting words in **Language Bank 8**.

The developing world presents a serious challenge for the environmental movement. (1) .... it may be easy to demand that developing countries follow the environmental line of developed countries, for many developing countries alleviating poverty comes first. (2) .... , industrial growth that leads to job creation may sometimes override issues such as pollution or loss of biodiversity.

Take Brazil, where the government is concerned about preserving the Amazon rainforest, but must balance this against the poverty that many landless Brazilians experience. (3) .... , in India, there are plans to build a giant dam across the Narmada River to aid industrial development, despite the protests of villagers and environmentalists. (4) .... the times are changing. Activists across the developing world are becoming more vocal about sustainable development — the idea that industry can co-exist with and even benefit the environment. (5) .... , we can see this increased awareness with the rise of Green parties in places like Bangladesh.

2 USE OF LANGUAGE: Verbs and prepositions

Complete the article about another possible threat to life on Earth, using the right preposition for each verb. Use only one word in each space. An example (0) is given.

GEOMAGNETIC REVERSAL

While most people are aware (0) *of* the Earth's strong magnetic field — ships, birds and whales use this field to navigate — fewer people seem (1) .... know why the field exists. The Earth's core consists (2) .... a solid metal core, surrounded (3) .... a molten liquid outer core. As the solid inner core rotates, it generates a powerful electric charge, which (4) .... turn creates our planet's magnetic field. Periodically, (5) .... a geomagnetic reversal, this inner core stops and changes direction — a process that can take (6) .... to 7,000 years to complete. Without this 'internal engine', the magnetic field will tail (7) ....

Scientists are concerned for two reasons. To begin (8) .... , the magnetic field prevents lethal solar radiation (9) .... flooding the planet's surface. Secondly, the Earth seems to be gearing (10) .... for another long overdue reversal. Scientists have calculated that the last reversal of the Earth's magnetic poles came (11) .... 600,000 years ago. The strength of the Earth's magnetic field appears to be decreasing (12) .... 5 per cent every hundred years.

3 WRITING

A Write an article for a popular science magazine (220-250 words) about what people can expect the world to be like in 2050.

B Creative writing: Write a fictional description (220-260 words) about a new space colony that is in perfect balance with its environment. Imagine you are a settler who has just arrived there.

4 IDIOMS

Match the beginning of the sentences with the endings. What do these idioms mean?

1 Freak weather patterns are just *the tip of...*
2 Some oil companies have *turned over...*
3 Genetically modifying viruses is *a recipe for...*
4 Bjorn Lomborg certainly *went against...*
5 So, El Niño makes it rain in Europe? Wow, *it's such...*
6 I think there is still at least *a ray of...*

a *a new leaf* by investing in renewable energy.
b *hope* for the environment.
c *the grain* by saying the Kyoto Protocol was not necessary.
d *disaster*, given how easily they might spread.
e *the iceberg* with global warming.
f *a small world!*

(SEE PAGES 42–45)

1 USE OF LANGUAGE: Word forms

Read the text and decide which form of the word (1-5) best fits each space. An example is given:
(0) dictate ⟶ *dictatorship.*

1 leave 2 nation 3 immune 4 democracy 5 assassin

Independence does not always immediately bring the benefits that people hope for. From 1934 to 1979, General Somoza and his sons ruled Nicaragua as a (0) *dictatorship*, amassing huge wealth, while (1) .... much of Nicaragua's population in poverty. When an uprising led by an opposition group, the Sandinistas, overthrew the regime, the Sandinistas quickly (2) .... the property of the Somozas and their supporters. With that money, they eliminated polio through an (3) .... programme, reduced infant mortality by 66 per cent, and lowered illiteracy rates from 50 per cent to 13 per cent. Despite being (4) .... elected in 1984, the Sandinistas were Marxist-Leninist, an ideology which the US could not accept. The US began secretly training and funding former Somoza security forces, the 'Contras'. These 'freedom fighters', as the US media called them, carried out terrorist acts like bombings and (5) .... With the Contra War and the United States trade embargo from 1985 to 1990, the Nicaraguan government could no longer fund its social projects. The Nicaraguans voted the Sandinistas out of office in 1990.

2 WRITING

A Write an article (220-250 words) about how people often take their independence for granted. Discuss how life would be different without mobility, or sight, hearing or other senses.

B Creative writing: write a story (220-250 words) about your town / city becoming an independent country. Discuss aspects like relationships with neighbouring countries, acceptance in the world community and the economy.

3 SPEAKING STRATEGIES: Using the active and passive voices

In presentations, we use the active voice to be more informal and direct, to convince people and build rapport. The passive voice is more formal and impersonal, and is often used to distance ourselves personally from issues or arguments. Give the missing active or passive voice for each of the following. You may need to add an appropriate subject. Check with **Language Bank 6**.

Active	Passive
Parents should not force their children to leave home.	1
2	Up till now responsibility for transport and road building has been taken by the central government.
Scottish Nationalists believe that Scotland would be better off as an independent country.	3
4	It is said that politicians demand independence only to gain more power.
We should promote environmentalism with development in the developing world.	5

4 IDIOMS

Complete the sentences using the phrases in the box. What do these idioms mean?

a a close-knit family
b an eye-opener
c a golden opportunity
d a turning point
e a red-letter day

1 1 He finally reached .... It was time to leave home.
2 It was .... , living on her own for the first time.
3 Canada had .... on 1 July, 1867; it officially became a country.
4 It was .... to settle the land dispute between the countries.
5 They were such .... , so it was hard having their daughter live so far away.

1 WORD POWER

A Using **Language Bank 10**, add intensifiers to each statement.
B Write a sentence challenging each statement.

1 Everyone I know agrees with me, we need to restrict immigration.

....

....

2 It goes against our country's beliefs to limit freedom of speech.

....

....

3 I think the police should have unlimited power to stop terrorists.

....

....

4 It's wrong that people have to pay inheritance tax. It's against the right to own property.

....

....

5 I disagree, criminals don't deserve any rights.

....

....

6 It is important to have people from a variety of backgrounds as candidates for political office.

....

....

2 USE OF LANGUAGE: Articles

Read the text and choose the article (*a, an, the* or -) that best fits each space. An example (0) is given.

The right to privacy has become (0) *an* increasingly important issue since the internet has become so widely used. In (1) .... past, it was often difficult to track (2) .... person's movements or contacts without some specialised knowledge in (3) .... private investigation. Now, when you visit many websites they automatically place (4) .... cookies on your computer. Cookies were originally intended to make surfing (5) .... internet easier for users and websites alike, since cookies are able to store small amounts of data, enough to show any web pages that were opened, passwords used or credit card information given.

(6) .... idea was that by storing this information, (7) .... user wouldn't have to re-type it every time they visited the same websites. And webservers could customise their online material for each user. Over time, however, online marketers caught on to the idea that by tracking where (8) .... individual user had gone on the internet, marketers could develop (9) .... detailed profile of that person. This profile could then be used to target the people interested in a certain company's products. While this seems largely harmless, security experts point to the fact that new versions of web browsers have often had bugs that could make this information available to someone accessing the computer illegally when it is (10) .... online.

3 WRITING

A Write a letter (180-210 words) to your local politician asking for the voting age to be lowered to 16.
B Creative writing: Write a brief summary (220-250 words) for a travel book about your country's government and individual rights.

4 IDIOMS

Complete the sentences using the phrases in the box. What do these idioms mean?

a	clock
b	cow
c	eye to eye
d	face to face
e	fence
f	kangaroo

1 Simon made the mistake of criticising free speech publicly! It's a *sacred* ....
2 She won't get a fair trial there. It's *a* .... *court*.
3 We're good friends, but we don't *see* .... on some issues.
4 Stop *sitting on the* .... ! You're either with us or against us.
5 Some conservative groups would like to *put the* .... *back* on women's rights.
6 It's hard to be against euthanasia when you come .... *with* patients in so much pain.

WORKBOOK Peace around the world

(SEE PAGES 50-53)

1 WORD POWER

Use the phrases for evaluating different standpoints in **Language Bank 11** to begin these statements. Then use the tentative expressions to respond to these different standpoints.

1 Regional conflicts have often been a threat to stability in the world.

....

....

2 I am optimistic that the world will always send money and help after natural disasters.

....

....

3 Peace comes from understanding others; globalisation will help increase both.

....

....

4 The UN needs forces for peace-making as well as for peace-keeping.

....

....

5 All elections should be monitored by international observers.

....

....

6 Civilians should never be caught up in wars.

....

....

7 Peaceful protest is the best way to change things.

....

....

8 Political corruption nearly always leads to a financial crisis.

....

....

2 WRITING

A Imagine you are a soldier on peace-keeping duty in another country.
Write an email (180-220 words) to your family about your experiences there.

B Summarise the *Chávez, Seeking Foreign Allies, Spends Billions* article from Unit 11, page 51 (220-260 words).

3 SPEAKING STRATEGIES: The power of three

You can create a lot of emphasis by grouping words or ideas together in threes. Match the beginnings of the sentences with the endings on the right. Practise saying these sentences aloud.

1 I am optimistic that we will see
2 Terrorism solves nothing. It's
3 The country was devastated
4 There are conflicts everywhere:
5 War is caused
6 The peace process got a boost

a by ignorance, by arrogance and by greed.
b by war, by famine and by disease.
c immoral, inhuman and unproductive.
d equality, peace and understanding in the world.
e from the EU, from the US and from Russia.
f in Asia, in Africa, in South America.

4 IDIOMS

Complete the sentences using the phrases in the box. What do these idioms mean?

a build   b explore   c pick   d reopen   e bury

1 The two countries have decided to .... *the hatchet*.
2 We hope to .... *bridges* between the warring factions.
3 The trade dispute .... *old wounds* between the former military rivals.
4 In the wake of the earthquake, the survivors tried to .... *up the pieces*.
5 The UN .... *every avenue* to resolve the crisis.

WORKBOOK Click here!

(SEE PAGES 54-57)

1 WORD POWER

Replace the words in italics with words or phrases from the unit. Use the expressions in **Language Bank 12** to deduce something about these sentences.

1 I *used the Google search engine* for all my research info.
2 Korean *high-speed internet* is so good, you can watch TV online.
3 A lot of people don't consider *using the internet to get* music without paying is a criminal activity.
4 Many companies produce special software to protect computer networks against *people who want to access these systems illegally*.
5 *Places where you talk online in real time* can be fun, but also a bit risky.
6 In my spare time I spend hours *looking at websites on* the internet.

2 USE OF LANGUAGE: Uncountable nouns

Fill in the missing blank spaces with the correct uncountable nouns from **Language Bank 12**. An example (0) has been given.

A growing amount of (0) *traffic* on the internet is now caused by spam. Some recent (1) .... suggests that spam accounts for over 40 per cent of all emails globally. If you consider that annually each employee receives about 2,100 junk emails and each takes about 6 seconds to delete, you can understand just how much (2) .... is lost. In the same way, if corporate servers need to hold that much extra email, this means companies are buying a lot of extra (3) .... just to store a lot of useless (4) .... There has been some (5) .... , with spam filters keeping out some spam. So what else can be done? Well, there was plenty of (6) .... about the news that a lot of (7) .... is on the way and spam will be soon be history. Although several solutions are being explored, a lot of (8) .... and hope is being placed on exploring the idea which gives each email an identifiable 'postage' stamp. If the email is returned as spam, the sender will have to pay a few cents for postage. A lot of returned (9) .... , say ten million, would indeed make spamming very expensive.

3 WRITING

A Write an email (180-220 words) to a friend about your first internet experience. What did you use it for – something you've done before or some completely new activity?
B Creative writing: Write a concept outline for a new video game (220-250 words). Include suggestions for the plot, characters and settings.
C Write an email as a competition entry (180-220 words) for a new contest: "My internet." Describe your own experience and discuss how the internet has changed your life.

4 IDIOMS

Fill in the missing word in the sentences. What do these idioms mean?

a sparks
b scratch
c unknown quantity
d haywire
e wolf
f standstill

1 When I opened the file with the virus in it, my computer *went* ....
2 The city-wide power cut *brought* all internet activity to a .... for two hours.
3 That hacker *was a lone* .... Police believe he acted alone.
4 .... *fly* when they start discussing the future of the internet.
5 All the course work I did on the computer was lost, so I had to *start from* ....
6 This new software *is a bit of an* ....

WORKBOOK What's in the news?

(SEE PAGES 58–61)

1 WORD POWER

Replace the words in italics with colloquialisms from **Language Bank 13**.
Then try to respond to each statement using the implying phrases.

1 All these reality shows on television are really *stupid.*

....

2 I read in the paper that train fares are going up by 10 per cent. They're going to be really *expensive.*

....

3 I heard there was more hooliganism at the *football* match last tonight.

....

4 Did you see that *television* programme about that bank manager who *stole* a million pounds?

....

5 Are you still *interested in* going to see that film tonight?

....

6 It's such a media stereotype! Not everyone from there is *rich.*

....

2 WRITING

A Write an article (220-250 words) for a political e-zine on an issue that everyone is talking about at the moment. Try to give it a strong right-wing or left-wing bias.
B Creative writing: Write a report (220-250 words) on the press in your country.

3 SPEAKING STRATEGIES: Use some quotes

You can make your presentation much livelier for your listeners by using a famous or interesting quote. Match the quotes with the correct transition phrases.

1 Prize-winning journalist Ellen Goodman notes, "In journalism, there has always been a tension between getting it first and getting it right."	a You might say that this is the basis of press freedom
2 "I may not agree with what you say, but I will defend to the death your right to say it."	b Let's look then at how one media owner could influence the way news is reported.
3 I would like to begin with a quote: 'Knowledge is power'.	c And it's true, journalists must not be afraid to ask those awkward questions.
4 Someone once said: "There aren't any embarrassing questions – only embarrassing answers."	d What she says is true, being the first to report a story is almost as important as getting the facts straight.
5 "Freedom of the press is guaranteed only to those who own one."	e This is a good starting point for discussing how informed people make informed decisions.

4 IDIOMS

Complete the sentences using the words in the box. Change the verb tense where needed. What do these idioms mean?

a mill
b skin
c story
d tongue
e box

1 You have to *have a thick* .... to be a politician.
2 Journalists Bob Woodward and Carl Bernstein were the first to *break the* .... on Watergate in 1972.
3 That TV presenter has a very *sharp* .... Don't get on his bad side!
4 We saw the story *on the* .... last night.
5 We heard *through the rumour* .... that those two are getting married.

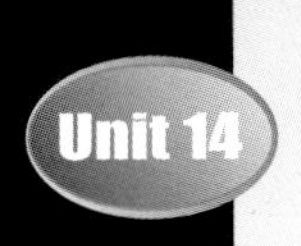

WORKBOOK Heroes and villains

(SEE PAGES 63–65)

1 WORD POWER

Use the expressions in **Language Bank 14** to soften these statements.
Then, try to respond to each using the idiomatic expressions.

1 I disagree with you about Eminem.

....

2 Parents expect celebrities to be unreasonably responsible.

....

3 I think a teenager's friends are their most important role models.

....

4 I have always looked up to my father.

....

5 We'll only play if she coaches the team.

....

6 When I was growing up my hero was Spider-man.

....

7 Most people were shocked by the arrest of the star.

....

8 She inspired me to become a doctor.

....

2 USE OF LANGUAGE: Joining clauses

Read the text and find the word that best fits each space. An example (0) is given.

In the world of sport, there is often a stark contrast between image and reality. Athletes are expected to be perfect role models to the young, (0) *but* at the same time they are still human. They make mistakes — a fact (1) .... is perhaps too readily exploited by the media. This naturally leads to the question of why we expect such high standards of behaviour from sports personalities.

Some might say (2) .... they should be paid well as an incentive to excel in their sport, and their private life is their own business; however, this is only part of the picture. It is important to examine (3) .... the role of sportspeople is in society. Many people (4) .... never have the chance to compete at such high levels place their hopes and expectations on the success of their idols. In a sense, the sports personalities become extensions of the fans' egos. (5) .... they win, their fans win and vice versa.

And yet, it is the pay cheque (6) .... holds the players accountable. Professional sport exists (7) .... loyal fans buy the tickets and merchandise. However, the fact remains (8) .... athletes who abuse their image and their fans' expectations do so at their own peril.

3 WRITING

A Write a personal letter (180-210 words) to a role model who inspired you as a child.

B Creative writing: Write an outline of a play (220-250 words) about your hero. Include suggestions for the plot, characters and settings.

4 IDIOMS

Match the beginning of the sentences with the endings. What do these idioms mean?

1 Some parents still see their teenage children as
2 Many young people *take...*
3 He *showed* a lot of...
4 Don't worry. They are *in...*
5 They want to stay *in their teacher's...*
6 She was kind enough to take me *under...*

a *guts* in saving the drowning woman.
b *good hands.*
c *her wing.*
d *good books.*
e *their cue* from famous sports personalities.
f *babes in arms.*

(SEE PAGES 68–71)

1 WORD POWER

Use **Language Bank 15** to answer these questions using the conditional tense.
Example: How do you like your coffee? *(zero conditional)*
If I drink coffee, I take milk and sugar.

1 Who do you go to for advice? (*zero*)
If I ....

2 Can you ask your mother to visit me? (*first*)
If I ....

3 What would your family do if you won the lottery? (*second*)
If I ....

4 If it had been you in that embarrassing situation, what would you have done? (*third*)
If I ....

5 How do your parents react if you arrive late? (*zero*)
If I ....

6 What's the secret of a happy family? (*first*)
If I ....

7 If you were a divorced father, what contact would you try to have with your kids? (*second*)
If I ....

8 If you had known ten years ago what you know now, how might you have changed your life? (*third*)
If I ....

2 WRITING

A Imagine a relative you haven't heard from for years has just sent you an email. Write back (180-210 words) giving news of what has been happening in your family.
B Creative writing: Write a description of a day in the life (220-250 words) of one of your descendants in the year 3000. Try to describe what families will be like then.

3 SPEAKING STRATEGIES: Emphasising a point

When you are speaking, you can emphasise a point by stressing modal verbs or negatives. Complete the text using the words in the box. An example (0) is given.

a **do** believe
b do **not**
c is **not**
d **should** matter
e **would** argue
f **do** function
g **do** place
h **never** expect
i should **not**

While I (0) ***do** believe* that families are changing, I (1) .... think it is necessarily a bad thing. It's funny that while we (2) .... people to be identical, we (3) .... these expectations on families. That (4) .... to say that there is anything wrong with aiming for the 'Mum, Dad and 2.1 kids' kind of family. It's just that families (5) .... be made to feel weird or different if they don't fit that pattern. Plenty of single-parent families (6) .... very well. In fact, I (7) .... that in some cases they may even work better than a number of two-parent families. Besides, the only thing that (8) .... is whether children are raised in a loving environment.

4 IDIOMS

Match the comments with the replies. What do the idioms mean?

Comments
1 Roger became a lawyer just like his father.
2 She will never give evidence against her brother.
3 Arthur's mother is always spoiling him.
4 He always puts his family before his work.
5 Monica just married a divorced man with three kids.
6 Stuart has had run-ins with the police.

Replies
a Yes, he's such *a family man.*
b So he's *the black sheep of the family?*
c He's a *real mummy's boy*, isn't he?
d Oh, so she's got herself a *ready-made family*.
e He's a *chip off the old block.*
f *Blood is thicker than water.*

WORKBOOK Let's change the subject!

(SEE PAGES 72–75)

1 WORD POWER

Put these steps for attending a university into a logical order, using the sequencing words in **Language Bank 16** to link them. Start with:

I'd put 'start saving money early for tuition fees and accommodation and living expenses' *first.*

- Register for classes
- Apply for accommodation if the university is away from where you live
- Visit or look at web pages of universities
- Apply for a loan and scholarships
- See an advisor to discuss which classes you should take
- Send a completed application form to the university
- Gather information about different universities

2 USE OF LANGUAGE: Gerund and infinitive

Complete the text with the correct gerund (example: *doing*) or infinitive (example: *to do*) using the verbs 1-10 in the box. Here is an example: (0) increase ⟶ *increasing*.

(0) increase	1 lead	3 pay	5 be excluded	7 end up	9 decide
2 continue	4 raise	6 learn	8 ensure	10 live	

The cost of going to university seems to be (0) *increasing* around the world. While the United States tends (1) .... the way with Ivy League colleges charging tuition fees close to $30,000 a year, other countries are following. British students interested in (2) .... onto higher education may expect (3) .... £3,000 or more a year. And it may just be a sign of things to come. Some top UK universities have talked about (4) .... tuition fees to three times this level. Many students are worried that this will create a two-level system, with poorer students (5) .... from the best universities. Only in a few places like Scandinavia is university education fully paid for by the government. Elsewhere, students who want (6) .... have to contribute towards tuition fees.

So are we likely (7) .... with universities being only for the few who can afford it? Not necessarily, many politicians are interested in (8) .... that access to education should be based on merit, not just ability to pay. The problem is how (9) .... where limited government funds go. With pensions and healthcare costing more and more, today's generation of students may have to learn (10) .... without state help for university education.

3 WRITING

A Creative writing: Write a diary entry (220-250 words) for a cadet on board the tall ship *Danmark*. Describe the daily life on the ship, including something about the people, the work and other aspects like weather conditions.

B Write an essay (220-250 words) about the importance of textbooks that reflect the different points of view of everyone in society. Use science and history textbooks as examples. Decide who should write the textbooks.

4 IDIOMS

Complete the sentences using the verbs in the box. Change the verb tense where needed. What do these idioms mean?

a	broaden
b	have
c	pass
d	pick
e	set
f	speak

1 Our teacher was great. She always let us .... *our minds.*
2 John felt that the exchange programme in Italy really .... *his mind.*
3 It was easy for Debbie to .... *up* another language.
4 Our teacher .... *the bar high.* We always felt we could do better.
5 Kim was always forgetting his lines in drama class. He .... *a memory like a sieve.*
6 Janet .... the test *with flying colours.*

(SEE PAGES 76-79)

1 WORD POWER

Join the sentences on the left with the sentences on the right using the phrases for developing an argument in **Language Bank 17**. An example (0) is given.

0 Thriving colonies of bacteria have been found in the freezing climate of Antarctica.		a ... they would be ideal to help rid landfill sites of toxic polyvinyl chloride.
1 Using stem cells, geneticists have grown miniature human kidneys inside mice.		b ...a manned mission to Mars could only succeed if water exists on the planet.
2 Belgian researchers have discovered a strain of bacteria that will eat chlorine.	*It follows logically then that...*	c ...in the future people might grow their own organs instead of waiting for a transplant.
3 It costs €20,000 to send just one litre of water into space.		d ...they would make an ideal pollution-free substitute for the internal combustion engine.
4 Hydrogen fuel cells produce electricity, pure water and heat.		e ...they could also survive in the cold, dry conditions of Mars.

2 WRITING

A Write an article (220-260 words) for a science magazine on the effects of one scientific development over the last 25 years.

B Write a report (220-260 words) to the editor of a local newspaper saying whether you support or reject the current developments in genetics and explaining why.

3 SPEAKING STRATEGIES: Key words

Good presenters speak to their audience; they don't read to them. This means memorising and practising the presentation. To help them remember, they use just a few key words or phrases (written on cards).

Summarise each of these sentences in a maximum of three key words. An example (0) is given.

0 *In 1989, highly respected chemists Fleischmann and Pons shocked the world with the claim that they had discovered cold fusion. – Cold fusion*
1 Fleischmann and Pons claimed electricity passing through a palladium electrode immersed in heavy water caused excess heat unexplainable by chemical reactions alone. It must therefore be a nuclear reaction.
2 The researchers announced their results to the media without first publishing their findings in a scientific journal. Later, duplicating the experiment proved difficult, and it was largely dismissed as a hoax.
3 Many think the idea merits further study. Numerous university laboratories and independent scientists are continuing the research.
4 Over 300 scientific papers have been written on the subject and there is even an annual conference on cold fusion.
5 Studies have found excess amounts of heat, tritium, helium and neutrons which researchers claim is consistent with nuclear reactions.
6 Although improvements to the process continue, it is still difficult to get consistent reactions.

4 IDIOMS

Fill in the blanks with the correct noun to complete the idiom.

a brains	1 He has *broken new* .... with his malaria research.
b cornerstone	2 Donna, can I *pick your* .... on these new quasar measurements?
c ground	3 I remember when the cloning of Dolly the sheep *hit the* .... in 1996.
d headlines	4 There are many challenging ethical questions *looming large on the* ....
e horizon	5 The ability to reproduce experiment results *is a* .... of the scientific method.

WORKBOOK The company we keep

(SEE PAGES 80–83)

1 WORD POWER

Replace the words in italics with words or phrases from the unit. Then, use the phrases in **Language Bank 18** to contradict these statements. Rewrite using the signposting phrases in **Language Bank 2**.

1 *Belief that members of other races are inferior* is the root cause of anti-immigration feelings.

....

2 *Different levels of medical care based on ability to pay* is the way of the future.

....

3 *Intentional damage to property* only occurs in deprived areas.

....

4 *Inappropriate use of drugs and alcohol* can lead to involvement with crime.

....

5 Young people move to large cities to find work, but many end up *sleeping out on the streets.*

....

6 The government isn't doing enough to stop *foreigners entering without legal permission.*

....

2 USE OF LANGUAGE: Word forms

Read the text and decide which form of the word (1–8) best fits each space.
Example: (0) moral ⟶ *morally*

(0) moral	2 immigrate	4 fall	6 nation	8 short
1 remain	3 employ	5 crash	7 danger	

While an anti-immigration policy is often difficult to justify (0) *morally*, it (1) .... a vote-getter in many countries. Australia, Denmark, Germany, the USA and others have recently reversed decades of moderate (2) .... restrictions, a policy that often plays well in areas where (3) .... is hard to find, although immigration is rarely a factor in this. In fact, immigration may become necessary because of (4) .... birth rates in Western countries. Fewer people will be working to support more and more senior citizens, and many of today's social structures could come (5) .... down as a result.

People move for work for many reasons. Large companies operating across the world want to recruit the best — regardless of (6) .... , and their employees may be asked to transfer between countries. At the other end of the scale are the jobs in cleaning or waste removal that ordinary citizens no longer want to do, but foreign labour often takes on. These jobs require no special skills and can be dirty and sometimes (7) ....

The general trend for most foreign workers is to earn money and return to their home country. As such, the visa system can allow for greater flexibility when there is a labour (8) .... , or oversupply.

3 WRITING

A Imagine you are an undercover reporter. Write a newspaper article (220-250 words) about sleeping rough on the streets of your town / city for a week.

B Imagine that you moved to another country a year ago. Write an email (180-220 words) to your friends at home telling them about your life since you moved.

4 IDIOMS

Match the sentence beginnings and endings. What do these idioms mean?

1 Since the government cut our child benefits...
2 I don't think all social programmes should be paid for...
3 Finding the murderer utterly remorseless,...
4 The government seems to be...
5 The city *took the drastic step of...*
6 The new drug rehab centre will help...

a *fighting a losing battle* against drugs.
b we've had to *tighten our belts.*
c many addicts to *kick the habit.*
d *out of the public purse.*
e the judge *threw the book at him.*
f imposing a 10pm curfew to stop violent crime.

WORKBOOK Stressed out!

(SEE PAGES 84–87)

1 WORD POWER

Replace the words in italics with words or phrases from the unit. Then, using **Language Bank 19** respond to the statements either using the language of sympathy and empathy or using the calming phrases.

1 I injured my back while I was *doing exercise to improve my body strength* at the gym.
....

2 I took the *overnight* flight to Lisbon and feel really tired and stressed today.
....

3 My doctor said I need to *be careful about the food I eat* if I want to improve my health.
....

4 I felt better after taking those *drugs to reduce depression*, but I didn't like the side-effects.
....

5 I'm worried about my husband — he finds it difficult to *stop thinking about his job* and gets stressed.
....
....

6 After serving in the army, my father developed severe *stress relating to a shocking experience.*
....
....

2 WRITING

A Write an e-mail (180-220 words) to a friend who is very stressed. Mention the cause of their stress and any suggestions you may have to help with their problem.

B Write an article (220-260 words) for a health and fitness magazine on the subject of stress and exercise.

3 SPEAKING STRATEGIES: Anticipating questions

After most presentations the audience can ask questions. The best way to prepare for this is to think of the questions that could be asked on the subject ahead of time and know how to answer them. You will be more confident in the presentation and answering these questions.

Match the subject with the question. How would you answer these questions? Think of another question someone could ask on each topic and how you would answer it.

Presentation subjects	Possible questions
1 Alternative treatments	a What can employers do to help lower employee stress?
2 Illnesses linked to stress	b How stressful would flying be for an aerophobe?
3 Nutrition and stress	c How is stress associated with depression?
4 Phobias	d How would caffeine increase stress in someone?
5 Stress at work	e What is the most stressful job in your opinion?
6 Stressful careers	f Why does laughter help with stress?

4 IDIOMS

Complete the sentences using the nouns in the box. What do these idioms mean?

a doctor
b plot
c notes
d price
e rollercoaster
f steam

1 I'm *losing the* .... Can you help me finish this report today?
2 Pat is beginning to *pay the* .... for studying so much.
3 At the medical conference, doctors *compared* .... on new treatments.
4 The weekend at the spa was *just what the* .... *ordered.*
5 She likes to play tennis to *let off* ....
6 Depression can be an *emotional* ....

WORKBOOK Shock tactics

(SEE PAGES 88–91)

1 WORD POWER

Use the phrases for expressing caution in **Language Bank 20** to respond to these statements.

1 Young people say they want to be individuals, but they just copy each other.
2 Young people should be allowed room to make mistakes.
3 Young women are never as bad as young men.
4 Television is responsible for making young people behave badly.
5 Teenagers can always get drugs or alcohol if they want. I don't think anything can stop that.
6 We can only hope having a good education will keep young people safe.

2 USE OF LANGUAGE: Verbs

Complete the text using synonyms for verbs 1 to 8 in the box. The first letter of the synonym is given. Change the verb tense as necessary. An example (0) is given.

0 began	2 transform	4 not be allowed	6 stay	8 demand
1 practise	3 grow	5 be afraid of	7 arrange	

Skateboarding (0) *originated* in the US in the 1950s as a way for surfers to (1) s............. their skills when the waves weren't breaking; they improvised the first skateboards from mini surfboards attached to roller skates. The skateboard's popularity first took off in the late 1970s when the Zephyr skateboarding team (2) r............. the sport by introducing exciting moves and jumps.

Today, while the sport continues to (3) i............. in popularity with championship events attracting corporate sponsorship, skateboarding has been (4) b.............. on the streets of many cities around the world. Skateboarding parks have been built to encourage skateboarders to stay off the street, but in countries where lawsuits are common owners of public spaces still (5) f............. liability claims from injured skateboarders.

In fact, the biggest reason for trying to keep skateboarding off the street is (6) r............. one of image and perception. Skateboarding is not a traditional team sport (7) o............. by parents, teachers or sports coaches. Young people do it for themselves out on the streets. Unfortunately, the public perception is that if teenagers are independent and out on the streets, they must be up to no good. There is also a fear that pedestrians walking in public spaces are in danger from reckless, out-of-control skateboarders. On the available evidence, pedestrians would be much better served by (8) r............. a ban on cars.

3 WRITING

A Write an email (180-210 words) to a local politician explaining why he / she should work to increase or lower the legal drinking age in your country.

B Creative writing: Imagine a school trip on a boat for a group of 17-year-old boys and girls. The boat sinks in a storm leaving the students stranded on a desert island. Write a story (220-250 words) about what their life would be like without any adults until they are rescued six months later.

4 IDIOMS

Complete the sentences using the verbs in the box. Change the verb tense where necessary. What do these idioms mean?

a nip
b open
c see
d scratch
e keep
f be

1 As far as David was concerned, he and his parents .... just *not on the same wavelength.*
2 She .... *everything in black and white.* For her, all young people are in gangs.
3 They worried that lowering the legal drinking age would .... *the floodgates* to widespread alcohol abuse.
4 Politicians hoped to .... house burglaries *in the bud* with a curfew on teenagers under 16.
5 He's a good kid. He has always .... *his nose clean.*
6 A lot of parents are left .... *their heads* over how to deal with difficult teenagers.

TEAMWORK SCENARIOS

(SEE PAGES 10, 14, 18)

UNIT 1

You work for a New York advertising agency competing to get an advertising contract for a very trendy clothing company called Area 51. Read Area 51's customer file. The **Idea Generator** may also help you. Create an outline for a television ad for your team to present to the class. Be creative: use pictures or diagrams, or act out the idea. Explain why you think your idea would work best. The class will be the Area 51 executives and will ask questions and vote on what is the best advertising idea. Use **Language Bank 1** before challenging, or to contradict points.

Customer File: Area 51

Product profile:
Designer denim jeans and cotton clothing

Slogan:
'Access all areas' (first used 1998)

Logo:
Grey alien with big black eyes

Market:
15–25 year olds, developed world

Marketshare:
Fifth largest with 7% of global market

Previous spokespeople:
Model Jennifer Diamonte, footballer / sportstar Jimmy Payton, DJ Johnny Zero

Budget:
$2.5 million including cost of TV commercials and airtime

Wants:
New TV commercial to update image and expand share of teen market

IDEA GENERATOR

Do you want a celebrity spokesperson?
■ actor ■ singer / musician ■ model
■ sportsperson ■ mythical creature
■ comedian ■ ordinary person

Style?
■ funny ■ romantic ■ sad ■ shocking
■ trendy ■ futuristic ■ abstract ■ fun

Setting?
■ home ■ restaurant ■ school ■ office
■ different cities, continents, seasons

Pop culture references?
■ TV shows ■ new movies ■ news events
■ famous people ■ new music trends

UNIT 2

Since the 1800s, artists have often written 'manifestos' to explain what their art is about. Imagine you are a group of artists, creating a manifesto for your art ideas. Use the example about the Futurists to help you. Be creative! Present your manifesto to the class.

Name: Futurists (1909, Italy)
Art form: Painting, sculpture, film / cinema
Politics: Absurdist, anti-historical
Aim: Stop talking about the past
For: Youth, science, war, danger
Against: 'Cult of the past', tradition, art critics, imitation
Idols: French sculptor Rodin, Spanish painter Goya
Quote: 'We are sickened by the foul laziness of artists, who ever since the sixteenth century have endlessly exploited the glories of the ancient Romans.'

UNIT 3

Choose a job: an astronaut, a Hollywood movie star or a politician. Brainstorm a list of the obstacles that someone would need to overcome to reach this goal.

Now, create a problem tree. Write the most difficult problems on the top branches down to the least difficult problems on the bottom branches. What solutions are there for the easy problems? How might someone overcome the more difficult problems?

Would you be willing to do what was needed for these jobs? Present your ideas to the class.

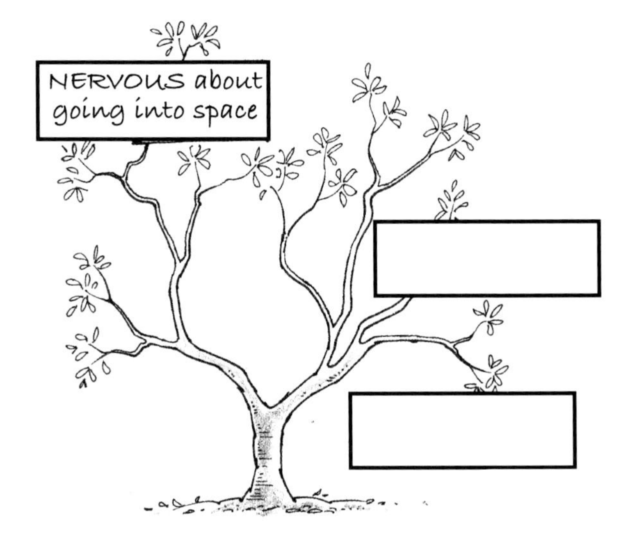

(SEE PAGES 22, 26, 30)

UNIT 4

In the picture, there is a bully and two victims. Decide who you think they are. Give reasons for your opinions. Present your ideas to another pair.

UNIT 5

Choose an ordinary object from home, school or work. Use **SCAMPER** to help you re-design or use the object differently.

		Example: Kitchen clock
S UBSTITUTE	Change the place, time, materials or process.	Made of recycled paper
C OMBINE	Put parts, features or products together.	Digital wall clock with a calendar screen
A DAPT	Change or alter some aspect or part.	Use solar cells for power.
M INIMISE or **M** AGNIFY	Make it smaller or bigger.	Wall-sized digital clock
P UT TO ANOTHER USE	Use it a different way.	Clock as a dartboard or a kitchen table
E LIMINATE	Take away something.	No hands, just two moving LCD dots
R EVERSE	Change around some aspect, part or the whole thing.	See-through mechanical clock

UNIT 6

You are TV producers and your TV channel has decided to produce a reality TV show featuring celebrity mud wrestling. In groups of three, create a line-up of celebrity wrestlers you think people in your country would like to see. Choose anyone inside or outside your country. Decide who you think would be likely to win and why?

	Celebrity Line-up			**Chances of winning: Most likely / Could be possible winners / Least likely**
Politicians	______________	vs.	______________	______________
Singers/Musicians	______________	vs.	______________	______________
Actors	______________	vs.	______________	______________
Sportspeople	______________	vs.	______________	______________
People in the news	______________	vs.	______________	______________

Present your line-up to the class. Why did you choose your contestants? Would you watch the show yourself? Why are reality TV shows so popular?

(SEE PAGES 34, 40, 44, 48)

UNIT 7

Is there a state pension system in your country? At what age do people retire? At what age would you like to retire? Pensions are set to become a big political issue in many countries, as people are living longer and retirement savings have been reduced. You have been asked by the government to reform the pension system. Here are some possible reform ideas:

- Make the retirement age higher, perhaps 70.
- Give tax incentives to people who invest privately for their retirement.
- Cut future pensions.
- Make younger workers pay larger pension contributions.
- Borrow money from financial institutions.
- Take money away from other areas like education, healthcare, defence.
- Make companies contribute more to their employees' pensions.
- No changes – leave it for the next generation to sort out.

Discuss the advantages and disadvantages of each idea. Which reform(s) do you think the politicians, companies and workers would prefer?

UNIT 8

One of the largest volcanoes in the world lies under Yellowstone National Park in the north-western United States. Scientists believe that it has erupted roughly every 600,000 years, with the last eruption about 640,000 years ago. If there was a large-scale eruption of the Yellowstone super-caldera, it could kill everything within a 1,000-mile (1,600-km) radius and send enough volcanic ash into the air to block out sunlight around the world for several years.

Imagine there has just been a television news report that Yellowstone has erupted. You are a group of European Union politicians. Decide what the effects of limited sunlight and pollution for several years would have on Europe and the world. What actions could the EU take to lessen the effects and save lives? What help would the EU send to the US? Make a five-point action plan to deal with this natural disaster.

UNIT 9

A friend of yours has decided to move out of his / her parent's home to have a place of his / her own for the first time. He / She is going to rent an unfurnished, one-bedroom flat but has no furniture except a bed. He / She owns clothes, some books, CDs and a small sound system.

1 Brainstorm a list of all the things that your friend would need and want to buy. Prioritise these from the most important to the least important.

2 Your friend's first job is full time and it pays 10 per cent more an hour than your country's minimum wage. Make up a moving-in budget for the first month. Be creative! Maybe you don't have to buy everything the first week. Try to include all the possible expenses, such as the cost of a reasonable rent in your area and the most important items needed from the list.

UNIT 10

People have decided to change your country's way of choosing a leader. They will not be voting but will choose a name at random in a lottery. Choose two imaginary people who might be your next leader to put into the lottery. To help you, create personal profiles for them. Think about their:

- age
- sex
- education
- job
- income
- ethnic background
- political beliefs
- religious beliefs
- sexuality
- where they are from

(SEE PAGES 52, 56, 60, 64)

UNIT 11

You are members of the newly-formed World Peace Institute. This think tank generates ideas for world peace. First, create a list of five reasons why countries go to war. Secondly, brainstorm two peaceful solutions for each of those five reasons. Thirdly, the first mission for the new Institute: try to use those ideas and others for resolving an international conflict that you are familiar with.

UNIT 12

You are web page designers. Make a rough outline for a new website on any subject that interests you. List the type of content you want:

- animation
- text
- images (still photos or artwork)
- video clips
- audio clips (speech or music)
- games
- chat rooms
- links to other pages on your website or to other websites.

Make a rough sketch of your home page to show the different parts of the website that people can access. Also think about how you might get web surfers to visit your website. Share your ideas with the class.

UNIT 13

World Weekly News often puts fictional stories next to real ones. Some past headlines have included 'Live mermaid found in tuna can' and 'Elvis is alive'. You are World Weekly News journalists who have to create four new headlines and rough story outlines. Use the **Idea Generator** to help you.

IDEA GENERATOR

■ 1000-kg ■ hairy ■ 3-metre tall ■ kung fu ■ baby
■ radioactive ■ singing ■ 100-year-old

■ Elvis Presley ■ Prince Charles ■ Marilyn Monroe
■ Santa Claus

■ mermaid ■ werewolf ■ alien ■ zombie ■ leprechaun
■ Batman ■ robot

■ battle ■ sue ■ predict ■ worship ■ gamble
■ discover ■ clone ■ picnic ■ marry

■ karaoke ■ on Mars ■ video games ■ toaster
■ Dead Sea scrolls ■ toothbrush ■ bowling

UNIT 14

For a parent group you are creating a rating of role models for teenagers. For each number on the rating scale, choose a female and a male role model. Write the names you choose in the boxes.

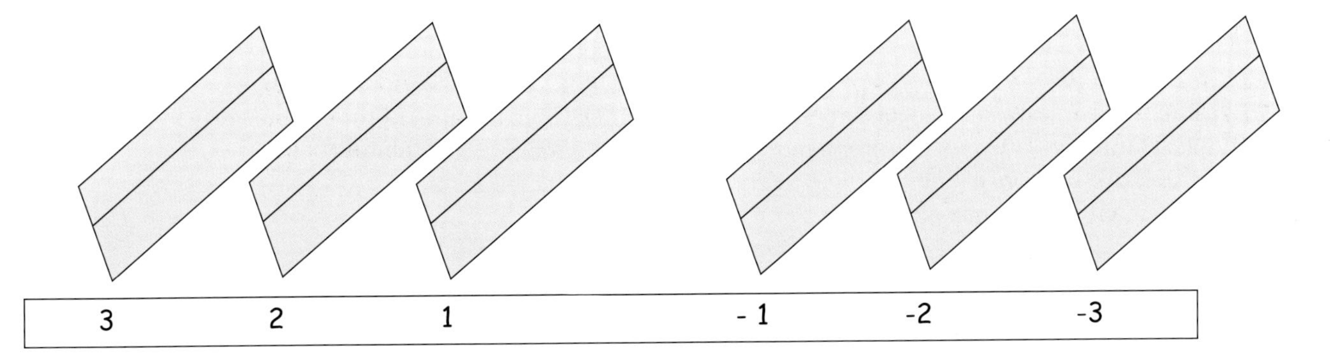

(SEE PAGES 70, 74, 78)

UNIT 15

1 Draw a diagram of your network of family and friends including full names and birthdates.

2 Show your network diagram to your partner. Give some very brief information about each person in the network and explain your relationship to each. **Example**: *This is my great-uncle Alfredo, he lives in Milan and was a carpenter before he retired. He's married to my great-aunt Sophia. This is my friend Jane, she lives in London and...*

3 Using examples from your family and your friends, explain how you think your generation is similar to or different from previous ones. Discuss values and attitudes to politics, work, family bonds, marriage, sex / sexuality, social issues and religion.

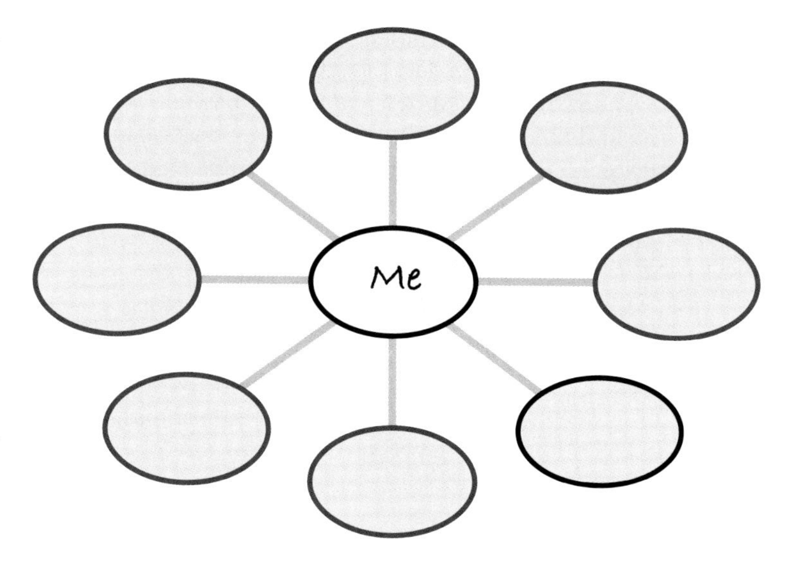

UNIT 16

Make a list of all the subjects students can take in your school. Think about the skills you learn when you study these subjects. Then choose three personal ads and decide how the person in each ad might use skills learned at school in their everyday lives. Which subject(s) would be useful for which person?

WOMEN SEEKING MEN

F, 28, divorced, marketing executive, likes yoga, travel, fine dining, theatre, art.

F, 23, single, carpenter, likes sports, reading, films, collecting Native American art.

F, 28, single, estate agent, loves sailing, shopping, jazz, café culture.

FOR OTHER FEMALE SOULMATES CALL OUR Hi LINE.

MEN SEEKING WOMEN

M, 35, psychology professor, likes running, crossword puzzles, collecting antiques.

M, 25, single, mechanic, likes gym, hanging out with friends, watching football.

M, 28, divorced, entrepreneur, crazy about golf, romance, wine, sushi, lively discussions.

FOR OTHER MALE SOULMATES CALL OUR Hi LINE.

UNIT 17

You will try to predict what will be the next big convergence of applications for consumer products.

1 Make a list of all the electronic gadgets, appliances or machines you can think of, for example: computers, TVs, refrigerators, mobile phones, automobiles, MP3 players.

2 Try combining two or more of these devices to create new products, for example:
- TV remote control + mobile phone
- computer + refrigerator.

3 Try to think about alternative ways of powering these devices (hydrogen fuel cells, solar energy, mechanical energy).

(SEE PAGES 82, 86, 90)

UNIT 18

You are members of the chamber of commerce in a small community where the only major employer has laid off its entire workforce and moved production to a country with much lower labour costs. Decide which would be the best suggestions for bringing new work opportunities to the community. Some areas you may wish to consider:

- Attract new enterprises (tax incentives, industrial parks, trained workforce)
- Bring in a government department (decentralise government offices to different communities)
- City redevelopment (city centre, historical sites, shopping centre)
- Tourism (adventure tourism, health spas, eco-tourism, culture tours)
- Organise special events (concerts, conventions, conferences)
- Shopping (factory outlet stores, big retailers)
- Waste management (use ex-industrial land for landfill; companies paying to incinerate waste)
- Unique new opportunities (university, military base, theme park, privatised prisons)
- Advertise the community (internet, international media, free trips for travel writers to visit)

Has this loss of industry happened in your country? If so, how well have these communities recovered?

UNIT 19

Choose three of these phobias. Try to imagine what life would be like for people who suffer from these phobias (what they can or cannot do). How would their life be different from yours? Share your ideas with another pair.

Aerophobia – fear of flying
Agoraphobia – fear of public spaces
Arachnophobia – fear of spiders
Acrophobia – fear of heights
Bacillophobia – fear of microbes
Bibliophobia – fear of books
Claustrophobia – fear of enclosed spaces
Latrophobia – fear of doctors
Logizomechanophobia – fear of computers
Lygophobia – fear of darkness

UNIT 20

Work in groups of three. Imagine you are local politicians in a city where youth crime, suicide and unemployment have begun to rise. Local residents have asked you to create five programmes to help young people in your community. These programmes should aim to achieve five results:

- To increase young people's self-confidence
- To help keep young people away from drugs or alcohol
- To increase youth career opportunities
- To improve physical fitness among young people
- To help stop youth violence

Some earlier ideas you could use or adapt: youth theatre, sports, peer counselling, internet chat rooms, youth magazines / e-zines, community youth centre, exchange programmes, career mentors, inviting speakers.

Share your ideas with another group. Explain how each programme will help achieve the five results you are aiming for. Discuss your programmes and decide how successful you think these programmes would be?

Glossary

Key:
Student's Book Page *18* Listening Unit *Au12*
Workbook Unit *Wb6* Scenario *S*

Unit 1 Buy now, think later See pages 8–11

big bucks (US)	a lot of money; (buck = dollar)	*9*
billboard	a large outdoor board with advertising posters	*8*
can, to	to fire	*9*
catchy	easily remembered	*Wb94*
celebrity endorsement	promotional advertising by a celebrity	*8*
classified ad	a small advert in a newspaper	*8*
con	a trick; deception	*8*
corporate image	the way a large business is seen by the public, or the picture it gives of itself	*11*
ditch, to	to drop	*9*
dump, to	to drop	*9*
fleet of lorries	a group of lorries that belong to the same company	*Wb94*
flyer	an advertising leaflet	8
going rate	the usual rate of pay for a particular job	*11*
heartland	the main area	*9*
hype	excessively positive advertising	*8*
jingle	a short tune, often with words, used in advertising	*Wb94*
junk mail	unwanted promotional material that comes by post	8
launch	when something is put on the market or is first shown	8
movie trailer	a short extract of a film used to advertise the film	8
network	a radio or TV company or group of companies	9
off-limits	an area into which you can't go	*Wb94*
overshadowed by	dominated by	9
pop-up ad	an internet advert that appears automatically on a computer screen	8
product placement	using a product in a TV programme or film	*8*
sanctuary	a safe place	*Wb94*
shy away from, to	to avoid	*9*
soybean (US)	soya bean	*Wb94*
spam	unwanted emails	*8*
spoof	something that appears serious but is really a joke in imitation of something else	*10*
spot	a short advertisement	*8*
surefire	guaranteed	*9*
sweatshop	a factory where the workers are badly paid and working conditions are very bad	*11*
tarnish, to	to spoil	*9*
under siege	under attack	*9*
up in the air	very uncertain	*9*

Unit 2 Express yourself See pages 12–15

Blackpool landlady	Blackpool is a popular, unsophisticated seaside resort in northwest England; a landlady is someone who runs a small hotel	*13*
credentials	general background and qualifications	*13*
culture vulture	a person who is very interested in high culture (art, music etc.)	*13*
forebears	ancestors	*13*
integration	a policy of including everyone in society	*15*
manifesto	a statement of aims and beliefs	*14*
mark someone / something out, to	to make someone / something seem obviously different	*13*
meniscus	a fine membrane	*Au2*
MTV	a TV station dedicated to popular music and culture	*12*
muddy, to	to make unclear	*13*
NAACP	National Association for the Advancement of Colored People	*15*
Proms, the	an annual series of classical music concerts at the Royal Albert Hall, London	*13*
prophylactic	preventing disease	*Au2*
reign	the length of time that someone is king or queen	*13*
rug weaving	making small carpets	*12*
segregation	separating people from different racial backgrounds, especially blacks and whites	*15*
shackles	things that prevent you from being free	*Wb99*
specimen	an example of something	*Au02*
umbrella organisation	an organisation that includes a lot of other organisations	*13*

Unit 3 The sky's the limit! See pages 16–19

adversity	difficulty	*16*
affluent	wealthy	*16*
Bollywood	the Indian film industry	*17*
burgeoning	growing and developing	*17*
Cannes	a town on the south coast of France famous for its film festival	*18*
celluloid elite	the richest or most talented film actors	*17*
charismatic	having a lot of charm	*16*
consign, to	to put someone in an unpleasant place or situation	*17*
consummate	complete and perfect	*17*
contingent	a large group	*17*
deadpan	apparently serious, with a blank expression	*17*
downplay, to	to treat something as though it is less important than it is	*16*
fatalistic	due to fate, outside our control	*Wb100*
flop	a failure	*17*
floundering	failing; struggling	*16*
grim	serious; bad or depressing	*16*
grinding	which never gets better and never ends	17
in the limelight	getting a lot of public attention	*17*
meteoric	extremely fast	*16*
motivational speaker	a person employed to speak at conferences to motivate those attending in their work	*Wb100*
no idle feat	a difficult thing to do	*17*
party animal	a person who enjoys going to lots of parties	17
persona	character; personality	17
piety	an insincere or conventional statement or act	17
put someone through their paces, to	to get someone to show how well they can do a particular thing	*17*
rat race	a competitive way of life	*18*
rigorous	disciplined	*17*
slapstick	unsophisticated comedy that uses a lot of non-verbal jokes	*17*

stunt work	performing dangerous and exciting actions for films	*17*
token	small or unimportant, and perhaps not sincere	*16*
wisecracking	joking	*17*

Unit 4 **Are you looking at me?** See pages 20–23

anecdotal	based on what people have observed, not on research and statistics	*21*
Antichrist, the	the opponent of Christ	*21*
bullying	using strength or words to frighten or hurt someone	*20*
cavort, to	to dance and jump around noisily	*21*
decapitate, to	to cut off someone's head	*21*
detention	at school, making a student stay behind after the end of classes as a punishment	*21*
GMTV	a popular breakfast TV station, featuring news, weather and chat shows	*21*
harassment	bullying or annoying someone	*22*
holler, to	to shout	*21*
informant	a person who gives people in authority information about others	*23*
intemperate	excessive and lacking self-control	*21*
irrefutable	which can't be denied	*21*
multifarious	many and varied	*21*
notorious	famous for negative reasons	*21*
passive-aggressive behaviour	behaviour which shows negative feelings in unassertive ways (not talking, being unhelpful etc.)	*22*
peremptorily	suddenly and without discussion	*21*
precipitous	done quickly and without thought	*21*
psychopath	a person with severe mental problems, who may be violent	*21*
push-up	an exercise in which you lie on the floor, face down, and push yourself up with your arms	*23*
reinstate, to	to restore	*21*
sadistic	taking pleasure from being cruel to others	*23*
sketchy	incomplete	*21*
smock	a loose-fitting piece of clothing	*24*
teasing	laughing at someone and making jokes about them	*20*
truancy	staying away from school without permission	*21*
unsubstantiated	not proved	*21*

Unit 5 **Frills and thrills** See pages 24–27

acknowledgement	recognition by others	*27*
bling	a style characterised by expensive jewellery, cars etc.	*27* *27*
brandstretching	a marketing technique in which a brand is associated with goods not connected with the main product	*24*
fulfilment	a sense of achievement and satisfaction	*27*
grooming products	products such as shampoos and skin creams	*24*
hulk	a big person	*25*
insurmountable	impossible to overcome	*25*
lust	strong desire	*25*
metrosexual man	a heterosexual man who is comfortable with traditionally female things (using grooming products, having his hair styled etc.)	*24*
pawnshop	people leave things at pawnshops in exchange for money; if they don't repay the money, the shop sells the goods	*25*
prestige	admiration and respect	*27*
retro	a word used to describe an old fashion which has become popular again	*24*
sarong	a large piece of cloth, worn wrapped round the lower body	*25*
shopping spree	time spent doing lots of shopping	*26*
straight	heterosexual; not gay	*24*
suave	sophisticated	*24*
surge	a large group, moving like a wave	*25*
vintage	a word used to describe an old fashion which has become popular again	*24*
way off the mark	very inaccurate	*25*

Unit 6 **Playing to win** See pages 28–31

back to back	immediately after each other	*31*
beauty pageant	a beauty competition	*30*
blister	a bubble in the skin caused, for example, by shoes that rub	*31*
blunder	a bad mistake	*29*
boast, to	to speak with arrogance	*28*
boorish	rude	*29*
cap, to	to do something even better	*Wb101*
capitalise on, to	to take advantage of	*29*
compelling	which really holds the attention	*Wb101*
draw	if a game ends in a draw, the competitors have exactly the same score	*29*
drop-out rate	the proportion of people who quit doing something	*30*
edge	an advantage	*29*
etiquette	politeness; an accepted form of behaviour	*29*
federal law	a law applying to the whole country, not just to an individual state within the country	*30*
flaunting	boasting	*29*
good sport, a	a person who accepts defeat with good grace	*28*
Labor Day	a public holiday in the US, on the first Monday in September, celebrating working people	*30*
landslide victory	a victory with a huge majority	*28*
ligament	tissue that connects bones	*31*
motto	a phrase expressing a belief or ideal	*28*
odds on	very likely	*28*
rawest	crudest; most obvious	*29*
relay team	a team who run relay races; in a relay race, each member of the team runs a set distance and has to hand a baton to the next runner	*29*
reservation	a doubt	*28*
rivalry	competition	*28*
ruthlessly	harshly; cruelly	*29*
sleep deprivation	lack of sleep	*31*
sportsmanship	respect for the rules of sport and for other competitors	*28*

Glossary

stakes: the stakes were high	there was a lot to lose	*29*
stem from, to	to be caused by	*29*
sunstroke	illness caused by too much exposure to the sun	*31*
tendon	tissue that connects bones to muscles	*31*
tie, to	to finish with the same score; to draw	*29*
triathlon	an athletics event involving three different sports	*31*
underdog	a person or team which isn't likely to win	*28*
walkover	a very easy victory	*28*
win hands down, to	to win very easily	*28*

Unit 7 **Profit and loss** **See pages 32–35**

across the board	applied in all circumstances	*33*
assets	things that you own which have value	*33*
black economy	buying, selling and producing goods and services without telling the government, so that no tax is paid on them	*35*
bunch	a group	*33*
close a deal, to	to finalise an agreement	*33*
commodities	goods that can be sold, e.g. minerals and agricultural produce	*32*
concession	a compromise	*33*
contend, to	to argue	*33*
dynamo	a source of energy	*Wb104*
Fairtrade products	goods produced and sold without exploiting people	*34*
free enterprise	an economic system in which businesses compete with each other without much government control	*Wb104*
free-market economy	an economy in which businesses decide prices and wages without being controlled by the government	*33*
gross domestic product (GDP)	the total value of all the goods that a country has produced and services that it has provided, excluding income made outside the country	*32*
jumpstart, to	to start a car engine by attaching its battery to the battery of another car	*34*
per capita	per head of population	*33*
quarter	a period of three months	*35*
recession	a period during which the economy does badly, when unemployment increases and business profits fall	*32*
revamp	restructuring and modernisation	*Wb104*
robust	strong and healthy	*33*
spawn, to	to generate; to create	*33*
staggering	astonishing	*Wb104*
subsidy	money paid by the government or other organisation to help an industry or business	*32*
watchdog	an organisation that monitors others to make sure that they behave legally and responsibly	*33*

Extended Reading 1 **See pages 36–37**

alacrity	speed	*37*
barrel, to	to move quickly	*37*
be a bust, to	to be bad; to be a failure	*36*
be clued into, to	to know about; to be aware of	*36*
cheese fondue	a dish of melted cheese	*36*
claw one's way out, to	to crawl out, on hands and knees	*37*
come to one's senses, to	to start acting normally again	*37*
countenance	a face	*37*
cremate, to	to burn	*37*
crooked	not straight	*37*
crumbling	falling down	*37*
dart, to	to move very fast and suddenly	*37*
denial syndrome	an attitude that shows you do not recognise the truth about something	*37*
depleted	diminished; used up	*37*
disintegrate, to	to break up; to be destroyed	*37*
exterminator	a killer of something	*36*
fang	a long, sharp tooth	*37*
feeding frenzy	eating a lot and fast	*36*
flank, to	to be on either side of something	*37*
flaw	a fault	*37*
fleeting	which only lasts a moment	*36*
flinch, to	to make a sudden, small, nervous movement	*37*
guarded truth, a	a statement that is not the entire truth	*36*
headstone	the stone on a person's grave, with their name and dates	*36*
husk	a shell	*36*
lethal	deadly	*37*
lumber, to	to move heavily	*37*
lunge, to	to make a sudden forwards movement	*37*
newbie	new	*37*
prowess	skill	*37*
regain one's footing, to	to become steady on one's feet again	*37*
resignation	acceptance	*36*
ridge	a raised line	*37*
run late, to	to be late; to be behind schedule	*37*
scowl, to	to make an angry or dissatisfied face	36
shortcut	a shorter way than usual of getting somewhere	*37*
silverware	knives, forks and spoons	*36*
skull and crossbones	a picture of a human skull (the bones of the head) and two other bones, used as a warning symbol and by pirates	*36*
slack, to	to lessen	*37*
slayer	a person who kills something	*37*
split second, a	a moment	*37*
stack, to	to pile	*36*
stagger, to	to walk very unsteadily	*37*
stake	a long piece of wood with a sharp end	*36*
stand one's ground, to	to face the situation; not to move	*37*
stranded	left without transport	*37*
stuffed	full of food	*36*
tattoo	a design on someone's skin, made using needles and colours	*36*
taut	tense	*37*
thrive, to	to do very well	*37*
tuned	sensitive	*37*
undertaker	a person who arranges funerals	*37*
vamp	a vampire	*37*
vampire	a legendary creature that come out of graves at night and sucks people's blood	*37*
wadded	folded until small and thick	*36*
woes	things that you are unhappy about	*36*
yank, to	to pull hard	*37*

Unit 8 — Into the future — See pages 38–41

Word	Definition	Page
abrupt	sudden	*39*
alleviate, to	to make something less serious	*Wb105*
asteroid	a rock that moves around the sun	38
at the mercy of …	in a situation in which you cannot avoid potentially being harmed by …	*39*
biodiversity	the total number of different plants and animals in a particular place	*38*
blaze	a fire	*39*
blueprint	a plan or model for how something would work	*39*
catastrophic	disastrous	*39*
climatologist	a person who studies the climate	*41*
collapse	a dramatic decline	*39*
debunk, to	to show that something is false or not as good as people thought	*Au8*
drastically	very much and in a negative way	*39*
eradicate, to	to eliminate; to get rid of completely	*39*
fleet	a group of ships	*40*
gear up, to	to prepare	*Wb105*
give a helping hand, to	to help	*39*
Gulf Stream, the	a warm current in the Atlantic Ocean, which moves northeast from the Gulf of Mexico towards northwestern Europe	*38*
halt, to	to stop	*39*
icecap	a large expanse of ice, as at the North and South Poles	*39*
landslide	the movement of earth and rock down mountainsides, caused by heavy rain	*41*
manipulate statistics, to	to use and interpret data dishonestly for one's own purposes	*40*
mass extinction	the complete disappearance of large numbers of different species	*38*
meteorology	the study of the weather	*41*
override, to	to be more important than	*Wb105*
ozone layer	the layer of the atmosphere which protects the Earth from ultraviolet rays	*38*
perpetrator	the person responsible for a crime or immoral act	*39*
police one's patch, to	to make sure that what happens in one's own area is legal and moral	*39*
quota	the number or amount of something that is allowed officially	*40*
rampage, to	to move violently	*39*
rogue	dishonest or criminal; causing damage	*39*
sanitation	the process of keeping places clean and healthy, especially by supplying water and processing sewage	*39*
sceptical	having doubts	*40*
stocks	the total amount of something that is available	*39*
strain	a genetic variety	*39*
swill	liquid food for pigs, made from waste food	*39*
switch allegiance, to	to change who or what you are loyal to	*39*
tipping point	the point at which something changes dramatically	*39*
trawler	a type of fishing boat that drags a large net behind it	*40*
ulterior motive	a hidden reason	*40*
unwittingly	unintentionally	*39*
virulent	very dangerous	*39*
weapons-grade anthrax	anthrax of a quality that could be used in weapons; anthrax is a serious bacterial infection	*39*
weird	very strange	*40*
wipe something out, to	to kill something off completely	*38*
with a vengeance	in an unexpectedly great and dramatic fashion	*39*

Unit 9 — Free to choose — See pages 42–45

Word	Definition	Page
autonomy	independence	*43*
barter, to	to exchange goods for other goods, not money	*44*
ceasefire	an agreement in a conflict to stop fighting	*43*
cold-blooded	without feelings	*43*
credibility	if you have credibility, people believe and trust you	*43*
deplore, to	to disapprove of strongly	*43*
devolution	transferring powers of government to a region	*45*
elated	very happy	*43*
ETA	a Basque guerrilla organisation that wants independence for the Basque Country	*43*
futile	pointless; destined not to work	*43*
grievance	something which you think is unfair	*43*
handiwork	work	*43*
handout	a gift of money	*43*
male chauvinist	a person who believes and acts as though men are superior to women	*43*
of my acquaintance	that I know	*42*
proclivity	a tendency	*43*
rebel	a person who is fighting the government	*43*
redress, to	to correct	*43*
reliable	that you can rely on; dependable	*43*
step up, to	to increase	*43*
sue, to	to take legal action against someone in order to get compensation for a wrong they have done to you	*43*
tempered	made less extreme	*43*
truce	an agreement to stop fighting	*43*
trustworthy	that can be trusted	*43*
upkeep	general living expenses	*43*
violate, to	to break	*43*
yearn, to	to want something very much	*43*

Unit 10 — Do I get a say? — See pages 46–49

Word	Definition	Page
abortion	the killing of an unborn baby for medical reasons or because it isn't wanted	*49*
against the odds	against a lot of difficulties, which make what you want to do unlikely to succeed	*47*
assembly	a group of people who have gathered together	*46*
asylum	if a foreigner is granted asylum, they are allowed to stay in the host country because it would be unsafe for them to return to their own country	*46*
candidate	a person who is standing for election	*46*
challenge, to	to question; to argue against	*49*

Glossary

charge, to — to accuse someone officially of a crime *46*
chore — a small job such as cleaning or doing the washing *47*
crack house — a house where people deal in and take drugs *47*
crackdown — a serious attempt to reduce something *47*
designate, to — to give something a particular name *47*
detain, to — to keep in prison *46*
disperse, to — to break up *47*
enforcement (of a law) — making sure that a law is obeyed *46*
euthanasia — the intentional killing of someone who is very ill so as to stop their suffering *48*
federal agencies — organisations of central government *49*
get a say, to — to be allowed to express one's opinion *46*
herder — a person who looks after sheep, goats or cattle *47*
host — if there is a host of something, there are a lot of them *47*
hotspot — a place where there is a particular problem *47*
inheritance tax — a tax that you have to pay if someone leaves you something when they die *Wb107*
law-abiding — respecting the law *47*
leftovers — food that is left after a meal *47*
locker — a kind of metal box that you can lock your things in to keep them safe *49*
nuisance neighbour — a neighbour who is anti-social, for example who makes a lot of noise at night *47*
paparazzo — a photographer who takes interesting or shocking photographs of celebrities to sell to newspapers *46*
picket, to — to stand outside a place in order to make a protest *46*
prevalence — how common something is *47*
restrict, to — to limit *46*
slippery slope — if you say that something is a slippery slope, you mean that you think it will get worse or increase in a bad way *48*
taboo subject — a subject that people won't talk about *46*
vandal — a person who damages property *47*
yob — an aggressive young person who behaves badly *46*

Unit 11 — Peace around the world — See pages 50–53

abduct, to — to kidnap *51*
be at odds, to — to disagree *52*
Bronx, the — a very poor area of New York City *51*
bulwark — a form of protection *51*
civilian — a person who isn't in the armed forces *53*
counterpoint — a contrast; a balance *51*
credit worthiness — if a country has credit worthiness, others would be willing to lend it money *51*
crude — crude oil; oil that hasn't yet been treated *51*
deride, to — to mock *51*
diaper (US) — a nappy (UK); cloth or soft paper clothing, like knickers or underpants, for babies 51
diplomacy — managing relations between different countries *50*
draft (mainly US) — the practice of compelling people to serve in the armed forces *53*
envoy — a person who represents a government; a diplomat *50*
extradition — being officially sent back to your own or to another country *51*
fivefold — five times *51*
foe — an enemy *51*
founding member — one of the people who created an organisation *51*
immunity — if you have immunity, you aren't subject to the law *51*
initiative — something that is intended to solve a problem *52*
intent on — determined to *51*
irritant — something annoying *51*
largesse — generosity *51*
leanings — beliefs and ideas *51*
mission — an important task *52*
nonaligned nations — countries which aren't allied with any of the world's major powers *51*
obliterate, to — to destroy completely *51*
pacifist — a person who doesn't believe in violence *50*
pet project — a favourite project *51*
profiteer — a person who makes a lot of money by charging very high prices for things that are in short supply *53*
recall, to — to call back *53*
reclaim, to — to get back *51*
repressive — which denies freedom *51*
resolve, to — to find a solution to something *50*
secular — not connected to religion *52*
surpass, to — to be more than *51*
suspend a law, to — if a law is suspended, it is no longer enforced *51*
trench — a long, narrow channel made in the ground *53* *53*
uprising — a rebellion against the people in power *50*
void — an empty space *51*
windfall — money that you receive unexpectedly *51*
withhold, to — to refuse to give *53*
witness — maintaining that something is true *51*

Unit 12 — Click here! — See pages 54–57

Anglocentric — centred or focused on English *56*
blossom, to — to flower; to grow and flourish *55*
broadband connection — a fast and powerful type of internet connection *54*
console — the control device used for playing computer games *55*
convict — a prisoner *55*
dot-com boom — a period of huge success for internet companies with names ending in ".com" *55*
dumpster (US) — a very large metal container for rubbish *57*
epaulette — a military-style decoration on the shoulders of a jacket *55*
face off, to — to compete *55*
gambling — betting money on a game or sport, for example on which horse will win a race *56*
gauge, to — to estimate 55
give up on, to — to stop using something because you no longer have any hope that it will work 56
google, to — to use the search engine Google to find something on the internet *54*
hacker — a person who breaks into other people's computers *54*

hairdo	a hairstyle	*55*
intervene, to	to become involved	*55*
landmark	something such as a building which is easily recognised	*55*
lose one's heart, to	to fall in love	*55*
lure, to	to attract	*55*
matchmaking	finding potential partners for people	*55*
mecca	a place to which lots of people go	*55*
netiquette	ways of communicating on the internet that are recognised as polite or acceptable	*54*
one, the	the only person	*55*
pro	a professional	*55*
profile	a description of someone	*55*
redundant	no longer useful	*55*
roll out, to	to introduce or extend the use of	*55*
script	a style of letters	*56*
search engine	a program used to search for things on the internet using keywords	*54*
server	part of a computer network that stores information centrally, for example emails	*Wb105*
take off, to	to become popular	*55*
tax-haven	a place where taxes are low	*56*
texting	sending messages by mobile phone	*54*

Unit 13 What's in the news? See pages 58–61

anomalous	different from what you might expect	*59*
applaud, to	to clap one's hands to show pleasure	*59*
biased	not neutral or impartial	*58*
bowling	a game in which the players try to hit a small target ball with larger balls	*59* *S117*
by a razor's edge	only just; by a very small margin indeed	
caste system	a society in which people are divided into strict social classes	*61*
clone	an animal or plant that has been produced artificially	*S117*
coalition	a government formed by members from different political parties	*59*
constrained	restricted	*59*
Dead Sea scrolls, the	a collection of manuscripts relating to the Bible	*S117*
de facto	a Latin phrase; if something happens de facto, it wasn't originally planned, but it is the case	*59*
disinformation	deliberately giving false or misleading information	*61*
distort, to	to represent something in a false way	*59*
drive, to	to influence; to decide	*59*
dumbing down	reducing the intellectual content; making more popular in appeal	*61*
dystopia	an imaginary place where everything is bad	*61*
elector	a person who votes in an election	*59*
fake	not true; invented	*61*
foreign correspondent	a journalist reporting from foreign countries	*58*
free press	press not controlled by the government	*58*
holding company	a company which controls other companies	*59*
holdings	shares	*59*
impact, to	to affect	*59*
install, to	to place someone in a job officially	*59*
integrity	honesty and strong moral values	*60*
karaoke	a form of entertainment in which people sing the words to a song being played on a machine	*S117*
legitimate	acceptable; understandable	*59*
leprechaun	in Irish folklore, a little man who knows where treasure is buried	*S117*
lowest common denominator	something designed to appeal to the majority of people	*59*
point the finger at, to	to blame; to say that something is responsible for a situation	*59*
ranking	how things rate in relation to each other	*58*
real time	the immediate present	*59*
satirical	critical but in a humorous way	*59*
sensationalistic	presented in a shocking way	*59*
stats	statistics	*59*
trail, to	to be behind	*59*
worship, to	to show respect to a god; to say prayers	*S117*

Unit 14 Heroes and villains See pages 62–65

advocate	if you are an advocate of something, you promote it	*63*
air play	being played on the radio	*63*
anti-establishment	against those in power	*62*
bigot	a person who has prejudices	*63*
bound	a leap	*63*
Brit award	an award for pop music	*63*
conglomeration	a mixture	*63*
conjure up, to	to imagine something; to make something appear	*63*
deep down	inside	*63*
embrace, to	to accept	*63*
feat	an impressive or difficult thing to do	*63*
foul-mouthed	using very bad language	*63*
gutter-dwelling	living in the gutter; a gutter is where the dirty water runs at the side of a street	*63*
idolised	revered; worshipped	*62*
implant	something that is put into a person's body	*63*
in your face	aggressive; which you can't fail to see or notice	*63*
incentive	an encouragement	*Wb 111*
invincible	which can't be beaten	*Au14*
mentor	a person who guides and advises	*62*
non-compromising	which doesn't hide the shocking nature of what it is about	*63*
outrage	a sense of scandal and anger	*63*
pressure wound	a sore on the body caused by not being able to change position	*63*
push-up bra	a bra that pushes up a woman's breasts and makes them look bigger and higher	*63*
quick-fire	very fast	*63*
rape, to	to force someone to have sex	*65*
slut	a woman who has had a lot of sexual partners and whom you disapprove of because of this behaviour (slang)	*63*
spark, to	to trigger	*63*
spinal cord	the nerves running together through the bones in the middle of your back	*63*

Glossary

stark contrast	a very sharp contrast	*Wb 111*
stem cell	a basic kind of cell from which specialised cells develop	*63*
stereotype	a simplified and standardised image	*65*
street car conductor (US)	the person in charge of a tram, who collects fares	*65*
underworld	the criminal part of society	*65*
up in arms	very angry	*63*

Extended Reading 2 **See pages 66–67**

agony	great pain	*67*
Aussie	an Australian	*67*
awesome	impressive; amazing	*67*
battered	in poor condition	*66*
broken English	hesitant, imperfect English	*66*
crack a joke, to	to tell a joke	66
daze	a state of surprise	*67*
dodgy	not very trustworthy	*66*
fluorescent	bright-coloured	*67*
focal point	the centre of attraction	*67*
footie	football	*66*
in one hit	without stopping	*67*
ingenious	clever	*66*
misnomer	a name that doesn't describe what a place is really like	*67*
oui	French for "yes"	*66*
Parlez-vous anglais?	French for "Do you speak English?"	*66*
pass	a route between mountains	*66*
pipe	a semi-circular slope on which snowboarders perform tricks	*66*
plagued by	troubled or annoyed by	*66*
quick smart	very fast	*66*
rock, to	to be cool, great	*67*
rockin'	= rocking, great	*66*
spurt out, to	to say very suddenly	*66*
stock question	a standard question	*66*
Suisse	the French name for Switzerland	*66*
take someone's word, to	to believe someone	*66*

Unit 15 **Family matters** **See pages 68–71**

adopted child	a child who has legally become part of someone's family	*68*
allocate, to	to distribute	*71*
bond	a strong link	*70*
census	an official population survey	*69*
contentious	likely to cause disagreement	*69*
custody battle	a serious disagreement between separated or divorced parents about which parent their child or children should live with	*69*
domestic bliss	being happy at home	*69*
fine, to	to make someone pay money as a punishment	*69*
frazzled	emotionally exhausted	*69*
frown upon, to	to disapprove of	*69*
home schooling	being taught at home	71
impresario	a person who produces or promotes entertainment	*69*
in droves	in large numbers	*69*
in-laws	the family of your husband or wife	*68*
job pool	all the available jobs	*69*
juggle, to	to do several things at the same time	*69*
leeway	room to do something differently	*69*
lobbying	campaigning on a particular political issue	*69*
matriarchal	in which women are in charge	*68*
militant	aggressively active	*69*
newlyweds	people who have just got married	*68*
offshoot	a related organisation	*69*
only recourse	the only thing that someone can do	*69*
onslaught	an attack	*69*
paternity leave	absence from work granted to a new father	*68*
patriarchal	in which men are in charge	*68*
pelt, to	to bombard; to hit	*69*
penalize, to	to punish	*69*
pioneer	the first person to do something	*69*
poll tax	a local tax in Britain in the 1980s; the tax was very unpopular and there were many demonstrations against it	*69*
prospective parents	people who are hoping to become parents	*70*
rabid	very angry	*69*
skyrocket, to	to increase dramatically	*69*
sweep, to	to move very quickly through a place	*69*
thwart, to	to try to stop	*69*
vicar	a priest in the Church of England	*69*

Unit 16 **Let's change the subject! See pages 72–75**

any old ...	it doesn't matter which ...	*73*
apartheid	the strict separation of white people from black people	*73*
be condemned, to	if you are condemned to something, you can't avoid it	*73*
brains	intelligence	*73*
budget	the money for a particular thing	*72*
co-educational	relating to schools in which girls and boys are taught together	*74*
colour blind	if a person is colour blind, they have difficulty seeing red and green	*75*
comprehensive system	a system of state schools in which students of all abilities are taught together	*73*
creationism	the belief that the story of the Creation in the Bible is true	*74*
deviously	in a dishonest and secretive manner	*73*
disable, to	to seriously restrict how well something functions	*73*
dyslexic	suffering from a minor disorder of the brain which prevents people from reading properly	*72*
GCSE	General Certificate of Secondary Education; GCSE exams are taken in British schools by students who are 15–16 years old	*73*
hands-on	actively involved	*75*
heritage	social and cultural background, inherited from previous generations	*73*
heroine	the feminine form of **hero**	*73*
inappropriate	unsuitable	*74*
initiate, to	to start	*73*
Ivy League (US)	a group of socially and academically prestigious universities in the northeastern United States	*Wb 10*[illegible]
kayaking	canoeing	*75*

literacy	the ability to read and write	*73*
literate	able to read and write	*73*
metaphor	an image used to describe something	*72*
push	a serious attempt to make something happen	*73*
reclaim, to	to take back something that was yours	*73*
reconciliation	when people who have been enemies become friends again, there is a reconciliation	*73*
reiterate, to	to repeat	*73*
scholar	an academic	*73*
sector	a part or an area of something larger	*73*
union	an organisation that defends the rights of workers	*73*
unmask, to	to uncover	*73*

Unit 17	**Adventures in science See pages 76–79**	
AI	artificial intelligence; the form of intelligence that advanced computers have	*76*
applied science	science used in practical ways; technology	*76*
assistive	which helps	*77*
bioelectric sensor	a small device that picks up the electrical energy given off by the human body	*77*
biometric scanner	a device which scans and measures parts of the body	*79*
bionics	combining robots with parts of the body	*76*
breakthrough	a major advance	*76*
bulky	big and awkward	*77*
detectable	which can be sensed	*77*
empathy	understanding of other people's feelings	*79*
ethical	moral	*76*
exoskeleton	hard tissue on the outside of an animal's body	*77*
forensic science	the science used to help solve crimes	*79*
fractionally	very slightly	*77*
holy grail, the	something that people would very much like to discover	*77*
housings	a case; a protective structure	*77*
human genome	the structure or human DNA	*76*
hydrogen fuel cell	a tank holding hydrogen to be used as a source of power	*76*
ignite, to	to set fire to	*79*
iris	the coloured part of the eye	*79*
levitation	rising above the ground and floating there	*76*
limb	an arm or leg	*77*
mechanics	the study of natural forces	*77*
mimic, to	to imitate	*76*
nanotechnology	technology that is very small indeed	*76*
neural disease	a disease of the nervous system	*78*
nurture	the way we are brought up	*76*
pave the way for, to	to create a situation in which something becomes possible	*77*
pouch	a small bag	*77*
prototype	a working model of something, before it is put on the market	*77*
retina	the area at the back of the eye	*79*
sought-after	in very great demand	*77*
spun	past participle of **spin**; to make a thread	*77*
squirm, to	to wriggle; to move from side to side, like a worm	*76*
state-of-the-art	best available and most up-to-date	*78*
stink, to	to smell bad	*76*
superconductor	a material that allows electricity to flow through it without any resistance and at low temperatures	*76*
suture	a stitch to join together tissues that have been cut or torn	*77*
unclog, to	to unblock	*79*
unveil, to	to reveal	*77*

Unit 18	**The company we keep See pages 80–83**	
assimilate, to	to become integrated	*82*
audit	an official assessment	*81*
birth rate	the number of babies being born	*82*
crush, to	to press something very hard and damage it	*81*
era	a period	*81*
eviction	officially forcing someone to leave their home	*81*
favela	a Brazilian word for a slum	*82*
ghetto	a poor area of a city or one where people of one particular race live	*82*
hold down a job, to	to keep a job	*81*
hostel	a large house used as temporary accommodation	*81*
inherent	if something is inherent in something, it is part of it	*82*
masses, the	lots of people	*80*
neurologist	a doctor who specialises in the nervous system	*81*
number-crunching	generating data and statistics	*80*
on sufferance	if you do something on sufferance, you are allowed to do it even though the person who gives their permission would rather you didn't	*81*
outpatient	a patient who goes to a hospital for a test or treatment but doesn't spend the night there	*81*
prolapsed lumbar disc	a medical condition in which one of the discs between the bones in the lower back has slipped	*81*
repeal a law, to	to abolish a law	*82*
rough sleeper	a person who sleeps on the streets	*80*
sciatica	a severe pain in your leg or lower back caused by pressure on the sciatic nerve	*81*
Scottish Executive, the	the government in Scotland	*81*
shanty town	an area of very poor huts where people live	*82*
slum	a very poor area of a city with bad houses and poor sanitation	*82*
squat	an abandoned building where people live illegally	*81*
statutory	legal	*81*
substance abuse	taking illegal drugs	*80*
two-tiered	with two levels	*80*

Unit 19	**Stressed out! See pages 84–87**	
blood vessel	any of the tubes in the body that carry blood	*87*
chair	a chairperson	*85*
contagious	spreads easily from person to person	*86*
creep back up, to	to increase again slowly	*85*
criss-cross, to	to go backwards and forwards over something	*85*

Glossary

fare better, to	to be more successful	*85*
flutter	an irregular heartbeat	*85*
frail	weak and ill	*85*
giggle, to	to laugh like a child	*86*
immune system	the body's system that fights disease and infection	*87*
impaired	damaged	*87*
incentive	financial encouragement or reward	*86*
induce, to	to cause	*85*
insomnia	an inability to sleep	*87*
migraine	a severe headache that affects half the head	*87*
pet, to	to stroke	*85*
phase	a stage	*87*
phobia	an irrational fear	*86*
physiological	relating to the body and its functions	*87*
placebo	in trials of new drugs, a harmless substance given instead of the drug	*86*
pound the treadmill, to	to run hard on a treadmill; in a gym, a treadmill is a running machine	*85*
red-eye flight	an overnight flight	*85*
scar tissue	hard or damaged tissue left behind after an injury	*87*
setback	something that delays or reverses progress	*85*
stress-busting	stress-beating 85	
stroke	if someone has a stroke, a blood vessel in their brain bursts, which may cause paralysis and problems with speech	*85*
supraventricular tachycardia (SVT)	an irregular heartbeat	*85*
thyroid	a gland in the neck that produces hormones which control growth and other functions	*85*
workshop	a short, practical, training session xx	

Unit 20 Shock tactics

See pages 88–91

all-terrain vehicle	a type of large car that can be used on rough ground	*89*
attire	clothing	*89*
binge drinking	drinking a lot of alcohol in a short space of time	*88*
body piercings	metal studs and rings in different parts of the body	*88*
by trial and error	through experience and experiment	*91*
close-minded	not open to new ideas	*89*
cult	a fairly small religious group, considered strange or secretive	*89*
curb, to	to control	*90*
do-gooder	a person who does things with the intention of helping others, but whom you think is interfering	*89*
free-for-all	a disorderly fight in which a lot of people take part	*89*
hard-core	a hard, extreme form of music	*89*
hepatitis	a serious disease of the liver	*90*
intimidating	which makes you feel anxious	*89*
Latino	a person of Latin American origin living in the US	*89*
liability	legal responsibility	*Wb113*
mainstream	normal and conventional	*89*
mosh pit	a place where people do an extreme form of dance that involves bashing into each other	*89*
patch	a small area	*89*
promiscuity	having a lot of casual sex	*88*
raid, to	to carry out a sudden invasion of a place	*89*
rep	a reputation	*89*
rep	a holiday rep (= representative), whose job it is to look after holidaymakers and organise entertainment	*90*
rigid	severe	*89*
seizure	the act of seizing something, such as drugs	*89*
skip school, to	to miss school deliberately	*89*
stick around, to	to stay in a place	*91*
straight-A student	a student who always gets top grades	*88*
subscribe to, to	to believe in	*89*
Sûreté du Québec	the provincial police force of Quebec	*89*
tagging	graffiti sign or name used in particular by gangs	*88*
thrashing	violent movement	*89*
vice	a criminal or immoral activity	*89*
vigilante	vigilantes are people who organise themselves into unofficial groups to protect others from crime	*89*

Extended Reading 3

See pages 92–93

bee in the bonnet	something that you are enthusiastic or very anxious about and that you think and talk about all the time	*92*
booming	very loud	*92*
cold one	a cold beer	*92*
crack, to	if your voice cracks, your tone changes because of strong emotion	*92*
dimple, to	if your cheeks dimple, little hollows appear in them	*92*
engulf, to	to overcome; to drown	*93*
excuse oneself, to	to say politely that you have to leave	*92*
jerk	an insulting term for someone you think is stupid	*93*
jut out, to	to stick out	*93*
loathing	hatred	*93*
malcontent	discontented	*93*
mean	bad-tempered or aggressive	*92*
profiling	a description of what someone is like	*93*
reservation	an area of land set aside for Native Americans to live	*93*
stutter, to	to say something with difficulty	*92*
tavern	a pub	*92*
tip back, to	to drink fast	*92*
unclinch, to	to open, unsqueeze	92
welfare (US)	money paid by the government to poor, unemployed or sick people	*93*
worrisome	worrying	*93*